lonely planet

JAPAN

Ray Bartlett, Tom Fay, Samantha Low, Craig McLachlan, Simon Richmond,
Lucy Dayman, Todd Fong, Rebecca Milner, Winnie Tan, Ted Taylor

Meet Our Writers

Ray Bartlett

@kaisoradotcom

A novelist and travel writer, Ray has worked on over 100 Lonely Planet titles, covering destinations as diverse as Mexico, Tanzania, Indonesia, Japan, the Philippines and Guatemala.

Tom Fay

@tomfay.jp X *@T_in_Japan*

Tom is a British travel and outdoors writer based in Japan since 2007. He is the lead author of a guidebook to hiking in the Japan Alps and Mt Fuji, and is working on a guidebook to Hokkaido. See www.thomasfay.com

Samantha Low

@rinoaskyes

Having lived in Kuala Lumpur, Sydney and Stockholm, Samantha now resides in Tokyo as a freelance writer, PR & marketing consultant and avid manga reader. She is passionate about martial arts, travel and video games.

Craig McLachlan

@yuricraig

Craig has walked the length of Japan, climbed its 100 Famous Mountains, hiked the 88 Sacred Temples of Shikoku Pilgrimage and more – he has been writing LP Japan guidebooks for 25 years.

Simon Richmond

@simonrichmond

A journalist, editor and photographer, Simon is a Japan expert and author of a guide to the best anime.

LMSPENCER/SHUTTERSTOCK ©

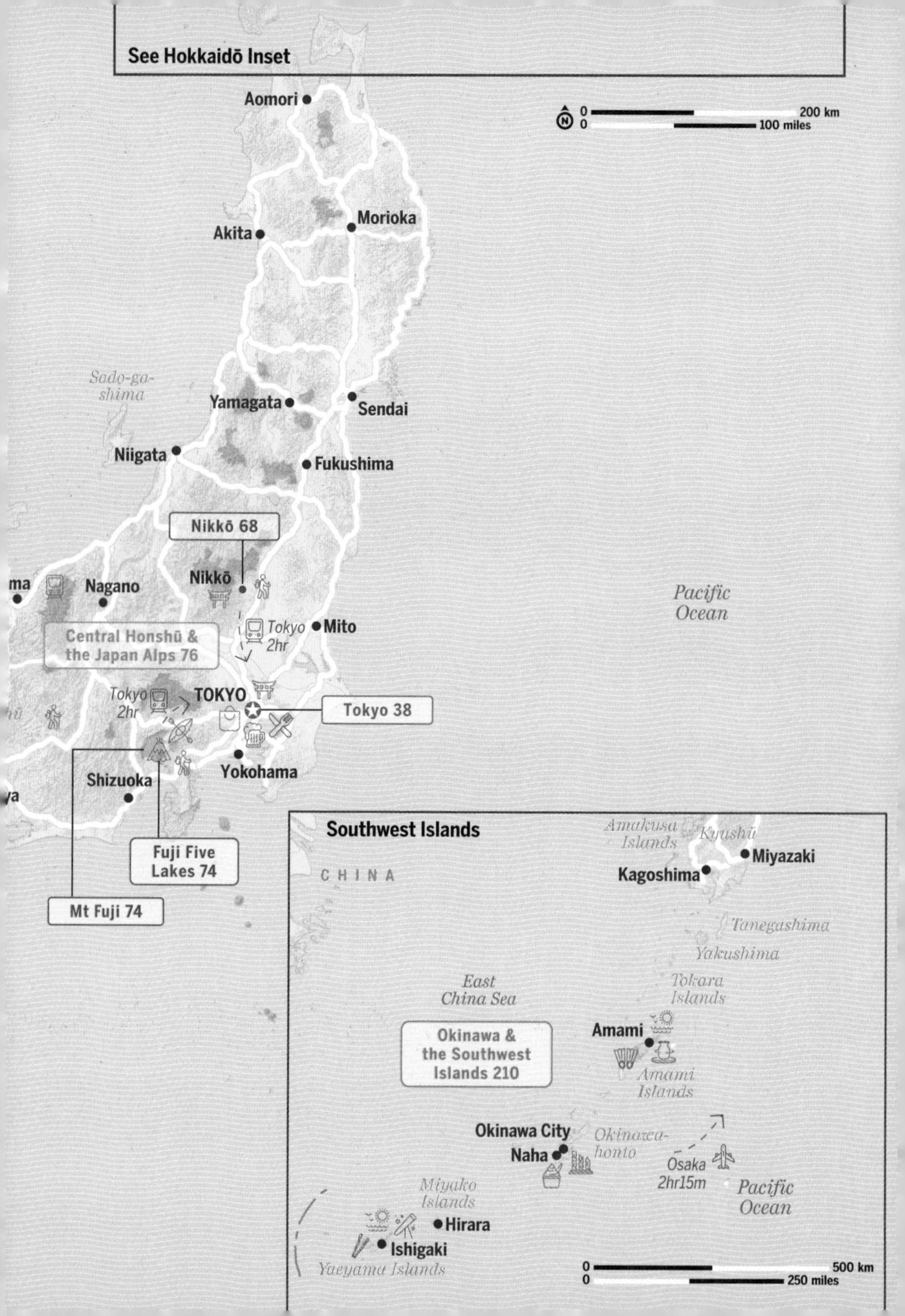

See Hokkaidō Inset

Aomori

0 200 km
0 100 miles

Morioka
Akita

Sado-ga-shima
Yamagata
Sendai
Niigata
Fukushima

Nikkō 68
Nikkō
Nagano
Central Honshū & the Japan Alps 76
Tokyo 2hr
Mito
Pacific Ocean
Tokyo 2hr
TOKYO
Tokyo 38
Yokohama
Shizuoka
Fuji Five Lakes 74
Mt Fuji 74

Southwest Islands

Amakusa Islands
Kyushu
Miyazaki
Kagoshima
CHINA
Tanegashima
Yakushima
East China Sea
Tokara Islands
Okinawa & the Southwest Islands 210
Amami
Amami Islands
Okinawa City
Okinawa-honto
Naha
Osaka 2hr15m
Pacific Ocean
Miyako Islands
Hirara
Ishigaki
Yaeyama Islands

0 500 km
0 250 miles

Hokkaidō
Rebun-to
Rishiri-to
Sea of Okhotsk
Shiretoko National Park
RUSSIA
Hokkaidō 192
Abashiri
Asahikawa
Akan-Mashu National Park
Daisetsuzan National Park
Kushiro-shitsugen National Park
Sea of Japan
Sapporo
Kushiro
Obihiro
Niseko
Tomakomai
Tokyo 1hr30m
Okushiri-to
Hakodate
0 200 km
0 100 miles
Honshū
Kanazawa
SOUTH KOREA
Fukui
Oki Islands
Kyoto 100
Tottori
Matsue
Gifu
Kyoto
Hiroshima & Western Honshū 150
Tokyo 4hr
Himeji
Osaka
Nara
Okayama
Hiroshima
Tsu-shima
Miyajima
Osaka 4hr
Kitakyushu
Tokushima
Matsuyama
Shikoku
Fukuoka
Nagasaki 2hr
Kochi
Kansai 128
Goto-retto
Oita
Kyūshū 174
Nagasaki
Kumamoto
See Southwest Islands Inset
Miyazaki
Kagoshima

Marvel at dazzlingly decorated temples and austere shrines. Taste the finest sake and go on a journey of culinary delights. Walk the roads of samurai and shoguns to stand in the shadow of magnificent castles. Let the hot springs wash your worries away. Glide down winter slopes and dive into glistening seas. Attend a tea ceremony and meet your favourite pop-culture icons. See the sunrise at the peak of the mountain you just conquered.

This is Japan.

TURN THE PAGE AND START PLANNING YOUR NEXT BEST TRIP →

Osaka-jō (p134), Osaka

Contributing Writers

Lucy Dayman
@lucy.dayman

Australian-born Lucy was a music journalist before moving to Tokyo on a whim and never leaving.

Todd Fong
@toddfong_travel

Born in California, Todd is based in the Tokyo area and travels Japan on writing and photography assignments.

Rebecca Milner
@tokyorebecca

Rebecca writes and edits from her sunny apartment in Tokyo, where she has lived since 2002.

Winnie Tan
@weeniemon

Winnie moved from Kuala Lumpur to Tokyo almost a decade ago and now writes about the city as well as presenting a podcast, *Monogatari: Tales from Japan*.

Ted Taylor

Ted followed his interests in Zen and the martial arts to Japan in 1994. See www.notesfromthenog.blogspot.com.

Contents

TAGU/SHUTTERSTOCK ©

Shimanami Kaidō route (p166)

VISUAL GUIDES

ESSAYS

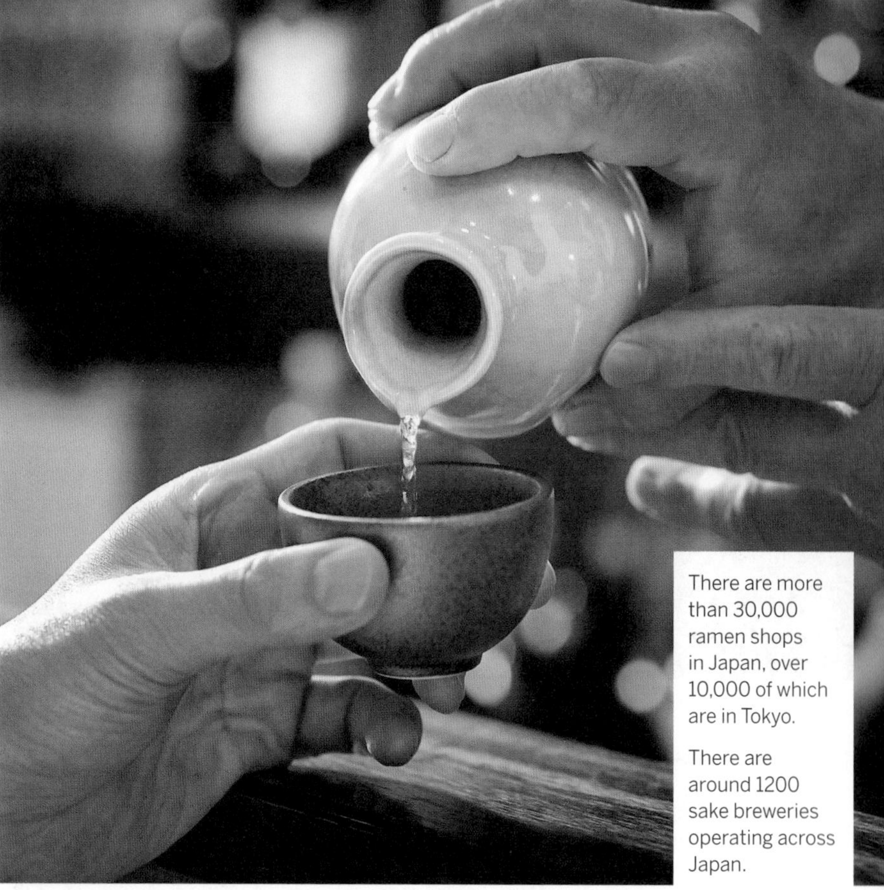

There are more than 30,000 ramen shops in Japan, over 10,000 of which are in Tokyo.

There are around 1200 sake breweries operating across Japan.

HEARTY RAMEN, **SMOOTH SAKE**

It's no exaggeration to say that Japan takes food seriously. For centuries, everything from growing rice and making miso (fermented soya bean paste) to concocting the perfect ramen broth has been elevated into an art form. There's something delicious to eat no matter where you go, and, with the best locally sourced ingredients available, you can taste the seas, the pastures and even the mountains of Japan right at the dinner table.

→ SIDE-ALLEY DINING

Tokyoites love their *yokochō*. The bar- and restaurant-filled alleyways are where they unwind on a Friday night, with *yakitori* (skewers) and cold beer.

▸ Learn more about *yokochō* on p52

URAIWONS/SHUTTERSTOCK ©

Left Serving sake from a flask
Right Omoide-yokochō (p52), Tokyo
Below Bowl of ramen

BIIRU!

Drop into any *izakaya* (pub-eatery) and you'll hear locals say *'Biiru, kudasai!'* (Beer, please!). Some prefectures even have their own signature brew and there is an increasing number of micro-breweries for craft ales.

RIGHT: ALPHA_7D/SHUTTERSTOCK ©
LEFT: YOSHIYOSHI HIROKAWA/GETTY IMAGES ©

↑ SLURP & BURP

Forget all you know about table manners at a ramen joint or soba restaurant: loud slurping isn't just allowed but encouraged. Join the locals in a noodle-sucking symphony.

▸ **Visit every foodie's mecca, Osaka – home of ramen, *tako-yaki* and conveyor-belt sushi.** (p136)

▸ **Discover the secrets of Okinawa's long-living residents: salty 'sea grapes', fresh sea-food and *awamori* liquor.** (p217)

▸ **Stuff your stomach with the soul food of Hiroshima, *okonomiyaki*, expertly prepared before you by *okonomiyaki* masters.** (p157)

▸ **Try traditional Japanese cooking at its finest in Kyoto, the nation's capital of *kaiseki*.** (p118)

▸ **Sample street food and some of Japan's finest sake in Takayama's old town.** (p82)

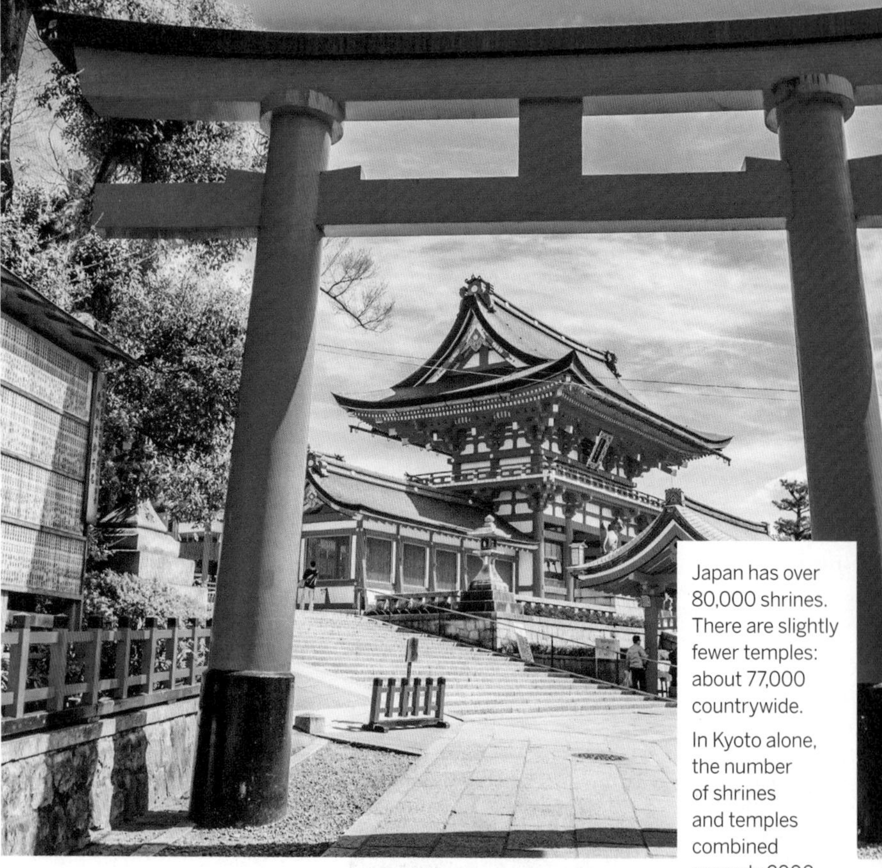

Japan has over 80,000 shrines. There are slightly fewer temples: about 77,000 countrywide.

In Kyoto alone, the number of shrines and temples combined exceeds 2000.

JOURNEY TO **ENLIGHTENMENT**

Discover the world of Japanese religion and spirituality: join the ranks of ancient pilgrims as you embark on a holy trek through the mountains, or take a crash course in Shintō and Buddhism as you visit shrines and temples across the country. Step through the *torii* (red entrance gate) into the world of the sacred, and journey one step further to finding inner peace.

Left Fushimi Inari-Taisha shrine, Kyoto (p126)
Right Kokūzō Bosatsū statue, Tōdai-ji (p140), Nara
Below Wooden *ema* at Meiji-jingū (p44), Tokyo

→ TEMPLE OR SHRINE?

If there's a *torii*, it's a shrine. On the other hand, Buddhist temples house statues of deities, while shrines do not.

COWARDLION/SHUTTERSTOCK ©

ETHICAL FOOD

Buddhist monks eat a vegetarian cuisine called *shōjin-ryōri*. Some temples serve it to guests too.

RIGHT: PABKOV/SHUTTERSTOCK ©, LEFT: TAKASHI IMAGES/SHUTTERSTOCK ©

↑ LUCKY TALISMANS

Write your wishes on an *ema* or buy an *omamori* for protection – you'll find good luck and blessings at Japan's many holy sites.

▶ Learn more about *ema* (p120) and *omamori* (p121)

▶ **Take a guided tour covering the culture and history of Kōya-san, a mountain monastery on the Kii Peninsula.** (p125)

▶ **Bask in the grandeur of Shimane Prefecture's Izumo Taisha, one of Japan's most important shrines.** (p161)

▶ **Visit Meiji-jingū shrine and its gardens, a green oasis in the bustling heart of Tokyo.** (p44)

▶ **See Kyoto's iconic 'Golden Pavilion' (Kinkaku-ji), or find respite at smaller, serene shrines like Shōden-ji.** (p114)

▶ **Pay respects to the bronze Daibutsu (Great Buddha) of Tōdai-ji in Nara.** (p140)

IN AN ANCIENT **LAND**

Scattered across the country are relics of a bygone era of shoguns and samurai. Explore the grand castles and noble quarters, but journey deep into the mountains and you'll also find remnants of an old, simpler way of life in rural villages and along winding, historical roads.

LEFT: SEAN PAVONE/SHUTTERSTOCK ©, BELOW: PIXHOUND/SHUTTERSTOCK ©

→ HOKKAIDŌ'S INDIGENOUS PEOPLE

Hokkaidō is home to an indigenous group called the Ainu. Today, there are at least 25,000 Ainu living in the prefecture.

▶ Learn more about the Ainu on p200

▶ **Admire Japan's grandest castle, Himeji-jō.** (p142)

▶ **Find a quiet escape at Shirakawa-gō, in remote villages unchanged for centuries.** (p90)

▶ **Walk Shiomi Nawate a road lined with the homes of former feudal retainers and samurai.** (p161)

▶ **Hike a section of the Nakasendō between Magome and Tsumago.** (p84)

▶ **Sail to Kudaka-jima in Okinawa, the birthplace of the Ryūkyū kingdom.** (p217)

← AGE OF SHOGUNS

Many of the old castles and villages seen today are remnants of the Edo period (1603–1868), built during the rule of the Tokugawa shogunate.

Above Himeji-jō. (p142)
Left Man in traditional Ainu dress (p200)
Right Kurokawa onsen (p181), Kyūshū

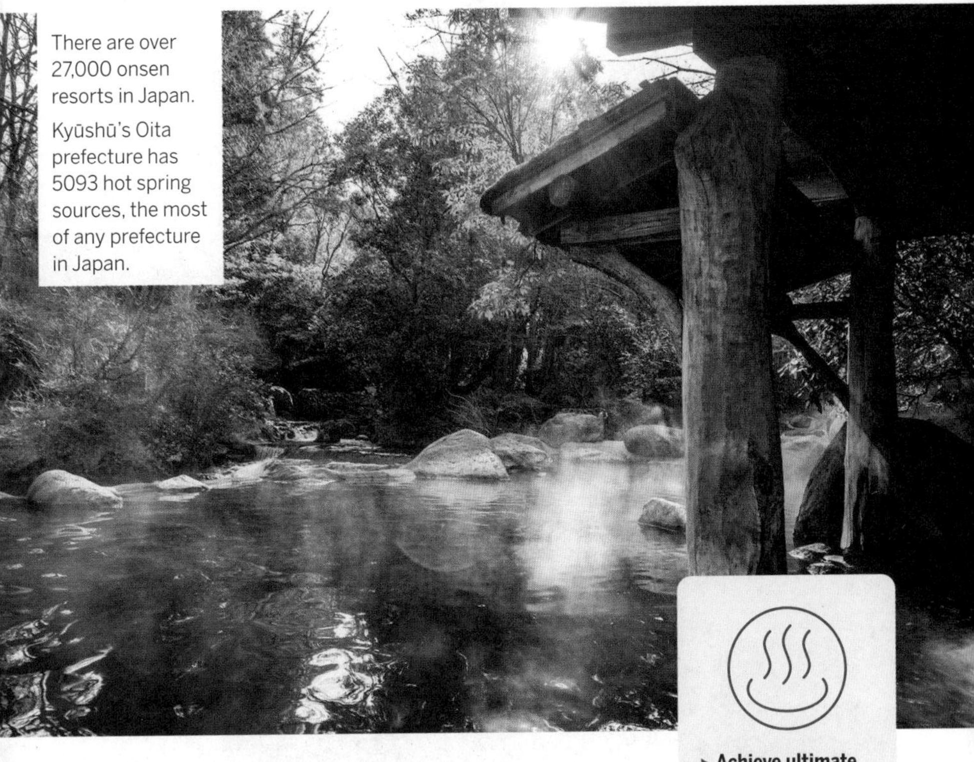

There are over 27,000 onsen resorts in Japan.

Kyūshū's Oita prefecture has 5093 hot spring sources, the most of any prefecture in Japan.

VOLCANIC **BATHS**

Japan's favourite way to relax is having a soak in an onsen (hot spring), followed by a cold glass of coffee-flavoured milk. However, onsen is more than just relaxation. Many believe in the waters' healing and beautifying powers, so it's no wonder the locals take a dip every chance they get.

▶ **Achieve ultimate relaxation by going onsen-hopping at Kurokawa Onsen.** (p181)

▶ **See Jigoku-dani, the steaming 'hell valley' of Hokkaidō, then visit Noboribetsu Onsen for a soak.** (p207)

▶ **Relax after a day of sightseeing around Nikkō at Kinugawa Onsen.** (p68)

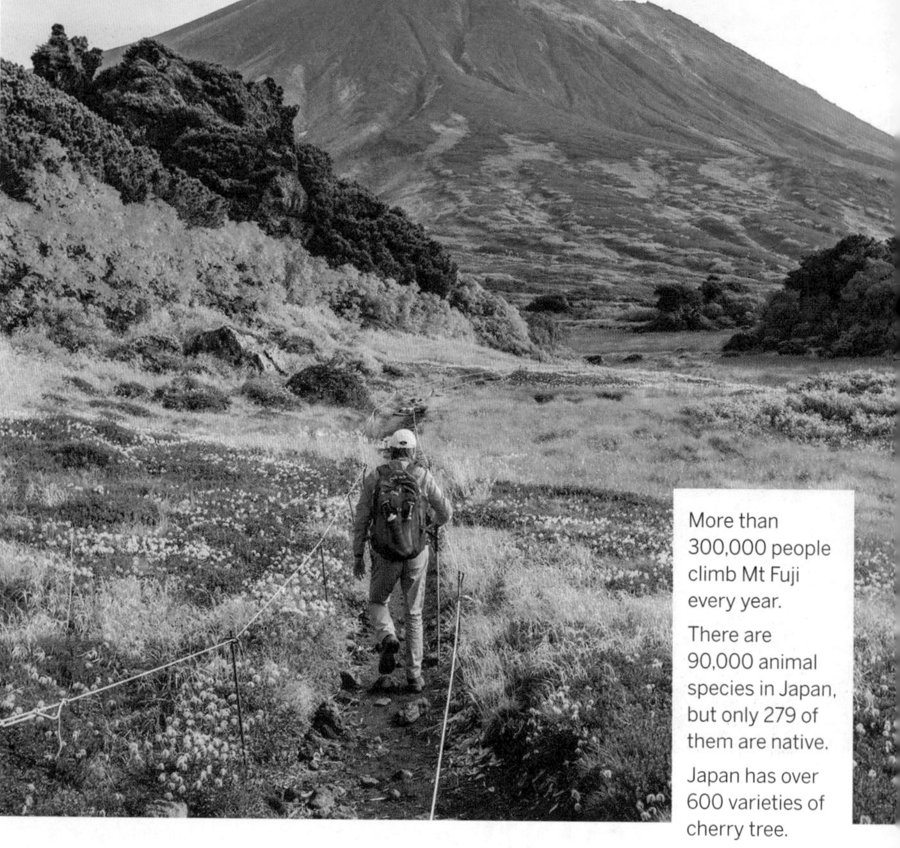

More than 300,000 people climb Mt Fuji every year.

There are 90,000 animal species in Japan, but only 279 of them are native.

Japan has over 600 varieties of cherry tree.

BEAUTIFUL **LANDSCAPES**

Trails through national parks, clear blue seas, a snow-capped Mt Fuji framed by *sakura* (cherry blossoms) – those are just some of the things you may encounter when you take a trip through the Japanese countryside. Whether you hike, sail, swim or climb, the views awaiting you along the way will be well worth the journey.

Left Hiking Daisetsuzan (p205), Hokkaidō
Right Climbing the Yoshida Trail (p71), Mt Fuji
Below *Hanami* parties (p25), Ueno-kōen, Tokyo

→ FAITH & MT FUJI

Mt Fuji has long held significance in Japanese religions like Shintō and Shugendō. Pilgrims have been climbing Mt Fuji as early as the Heian period (794–1185).

▶ Learn more about climbing Mt Fuji on p70

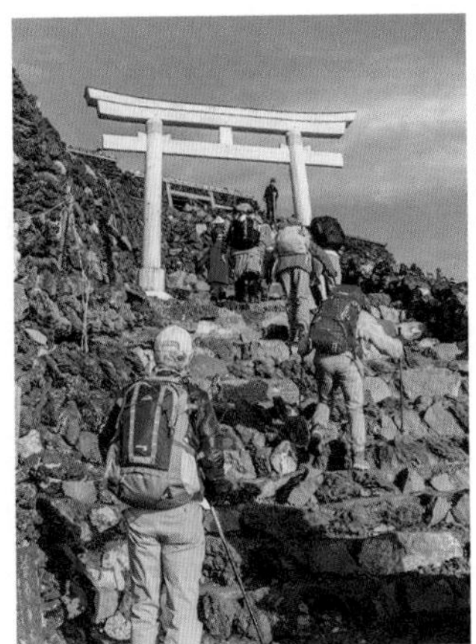

HOLY JOURNEY

Followers of the Japanese religion Shugendō practise by making pilgrimages through mountains and forests on foot.

▶ Learn more about Shugendō on p146

↑ SAKURA, SAKURA

The blooming of cherry blossoms signifies new beginnings, and the pink petals are ushered in with outdoor picnics called *hanami*.

▶ Read more about *sakura* on p110

- ▶ **Hike to the summits of the Japan Alps and see the reflective lakes of Kamikōchi.** (p86)
- ▶ **Swim and snorkel in the crystal-clear waters of the Yaeyama Islands.** (p222)
- ▶ **Spot brown bears and whales while cruising along the coast of Shiretoko National Park.** (p205)
- ▶ **Hike the Nakahechi Trail and make your way across the Kii Peninsula.** (p146)
- ▶ **Cruise or kayak along Urauchi-gawa, Okinawa's largest river.** (p223)

ADVENTURE INCOMING

The best way to experience Japan is to dive right in – climb mountains, try out a new sport or sing in front of complete strangers. Japan has plenty of surprises in store for the traveller who isn't afraid to stray from convention; all you need is a sense of adventure.

Nakasendō Trail

Journeyman's road

The 9km forest trail that connects two Edo-period post towns is tranquil and beginner-friendly. Reward yourself afterwards with some tea and Japanese sweets in Tsumago or Magome, depending on where you start.

2hr from Nagoya

▶ p84

Shimanami Kaidō

Island-hopping on two wheels

Rent a bicycle and begin your journey through a cluster of islands, enjoying the salty sea breeze and expansive coastal views. Visit temples and parks along the way, and when you're hungry, drop by some of the local shops for a snack.

1hr from Hiroshima

▶ p166

RUSSIA

NORTH KOREA

Sea of Japan

SOUTH KOREA

Oki-shotō

Kanazawa

Matsue

Nagoya

Kyoto

Okayama

Kōbe

Osaka

Tsushima

Hiroshima

Takamatsu

Fukuoka

Matsuyama

Kōchi

Gotō-rettō

Shikoku

Nagasaki

Kumamoto

Kyūshū

Pacific Ocean

Miyazaki

Kagoshima

See Southwest Islands Inset

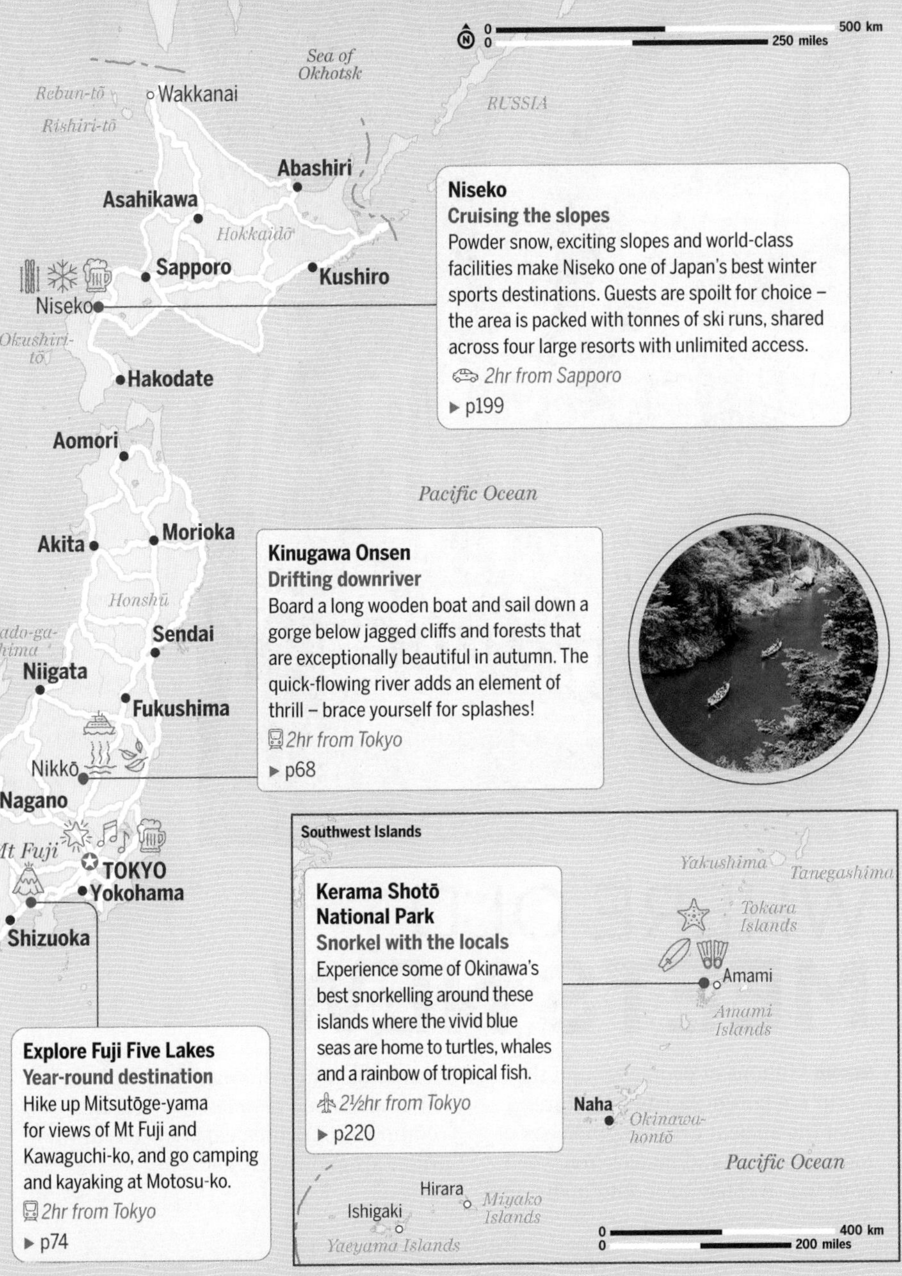

0 500 km
0 250 miles
Sea of Okhotsk
RUSSIA
Rebun-tō
Wakkanai
Rishiri-tō
Abashiri
Asahikawa
Hokkaidō
Sapporo
Kushiro
Niseko
Okushiri-tō
Hakodate
Niseko
Cruising the slopes
Powder snow, exciting slopes and world-class facilities make Niseko one of Japan's best winter sports destinations. Guests are spoilt for choice – the area is packed with tonnes of ski runs, shared across four large resorts with unlimited access.
2hr from Sapporo
▶ p199
Aomori
Pacific Ocean
Akita
Morioka
Honshū
Sado-ga-shima
Sendai
Niigata
Fukushima
Nikkō
Nagano
Kinugawa Onsen
Drifting downriver
Board a long wooden boat and sail down a gorge below jagged cliffs and forests that are exceptionally beautiful in autumn. The quick-flowing river adds an element of thrill – brace yourself for splashes!
2hr from Tokyo
▶ p68
Mt Fuji
TOKYO
Yokohama
Shizuoka
Explore Fuji Five Lakes
Year-round destination
Hike up Mitsutōge-yama for views of Mt Fuji and Kawaguchi-ko, and go camping and kayaking at Motosu-ko.
2hr from Tokyo
▶ p74
Southwest Islands
Yakushima
Tanegashima
Tokara Islands
Amami
Amami Islands
Kerama Shotō National Park
Snorkel with the locals
Experience some of Okinawa's best snorkelling around these islands where the vivid blue seas are home to turtles, whales and a rainbow of tropical fish.
2½hr from Tokyo
▶ p220
Naha
Okinawa-hontō
Pacific Ocean
Hirara
Miyako Islands
Ishigaki
Yaeyama Islands
0 400 km
0 200 miles

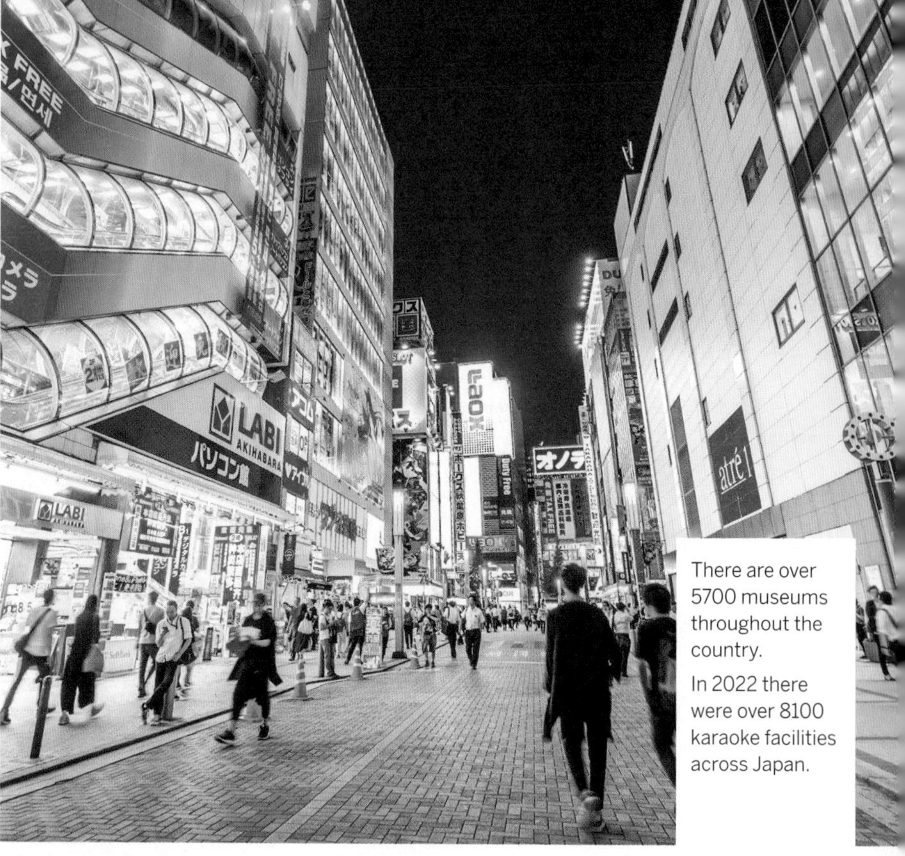

There are over 5700 museums throughout the country.

In 2022 there were over 8100 karaoke facilities across Japan.

WHERE OLD **MEETS NEW**

Millions of people around the world are fans of Japanese culture, from the ancient art of tea to lovers of modern anime and manga. You won't have to travel too far to find it all – in a country where heritage both old and new blend seamlessly together, a culturally enriching experience is always right around the corner.

Left Akihabara (p48), Tokyo
Right *Maiko* performance (p108), Kyoto
Below *Yurukyara*, Hokkaidō

→ ULTIMATE ENTERTAINERS

Aspiring geisha spend about six years learning their craft while being trained in music, dance, etiquette and tea ceremony.

▶ Learn more about geisha on p108

OSAZE CUOMO/SHUTTERSTOCK ©

TRADITIONAL SPOOKS

Yōkai (fictional monsters and ghosts) are alive in both traditional and pop culture of Japan. Spot them on everything from wood-block prints to anime.

▶ Read more about *yōkai* on p94

RIGHT: AJISAI13/SHUTTERSTOCK ©, LEFT: BYJENG/SHUTTERSTOCK ©

↑ MASCOT OBSESSION

Japan has a mascot for just about everything – companies, stations and even prefectures. They're called *yurukyara*, a combination of the words *yuru* (soft, fluffy) and *kyara* (character).

▶ **Experience the quiet meditativeness and Zen spirit of a traditional tea ceremony in Kyoto.** (p106)

▶ **Immerse yourself in Japanese pop culture at the Ghibli Park near Nagoya.** (p96)

▶ **Reflect on the horrors of war in Hiroshima's Peace Memorial Park and Museum.** (p157)

▶ **Spend a night with the locals at a traditional *gassho-zukuri* house in Shirakawa-gō.** (p90)

▶ **Enjoy the cream of Japanese contemporary art and architecture on the beautiful Inland Sea island of Naoshima.** (p162)

Japanese schoolchildren are on summer break from mid-July to the end of August. Marine Day (third Monday in July) creates a long weekend and Mountain Day on 11 August is also a public holiday.

↙ Island Escape

Okinawa is a summer hot spot. Try the Kerama Islands for some of the best snorkelling in Japan.

Kerama Shotō National Park, p220

▸ env.go.jp/park/kerama

Demand for accommodation peaks during Obon week (mid-August). Book tours and overnight adventures in advance.

▸ lonelyplanet.com/japan

Buy a folding fan or handheld motor fan to cool down during Japan's notoriously humid summers.

JUNE

Average daytime max: 27°C

JULY

Japan in SUMMER

↘ Walk on the Wild Side

Go hiking in Japan's largest national park in summer, when trails are largely snow-free.

Daisetsuzan, p205

▸ env.go.jp/park/daisetsu/

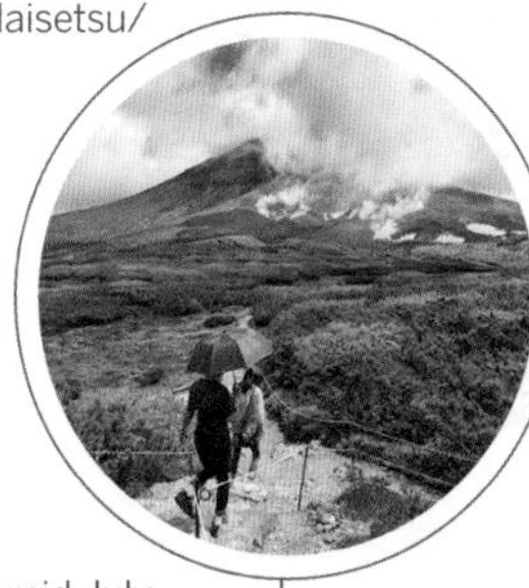

From early June to mid-July, spot hydrangeas blooming everywhere from large parks to residential areas.

↑ Alpine Adventures

Escape the ruthless city heat and go camping and hiking at Kamikōchi in the Japan Alps.

Kamikōchi, p86

▸ kamikochi.org

Days of rainfall: 13

AUGUST

Average daytime max: 30°C
Days of rainfall: 12

← Lighting Up the Sky

Fireworks festivals are popular in summer. Locals go in *yukata*, a summer kimono-like attire.

Packing Notes

Bring a hat, plenty of sun-screen and a face towel to help keep the sweat off.

Typhoon season starts in summer but can continue through October. Pay close attention to weather warnings.

← Sink your teeth into Japan's sweet persimmons, in season from October. Nara is especially famous for these.

Nara, p140

Demand for accommodation peaks during autum-foliage week, from late October through November. Book tours and overnight adventures in advance.

▶ lonelyplanet.com/japan

Japan's quintessential autumn leaf is the *momiji* (Japanese maple), found in abundance around temples and parks.

SEPTEMBER

Average daytime max: 28°C

OCTOBER

Japan in AUTUMN

CLOCKWISE FROM BOTTOM LEFT: OL_DMI/SHUTTERSTOCK ©, KAI KEISUKE/SHUTTERSTOCK ©, ONEINCHPUNCH/SHUTTERSTOCK ©, KITTICHAI/SHUTTERSTOCK ©

↘ Island Retreat

Ride the ropeway (cable car) up Misen, Miyajima's tallest mountain, for fabulous displays of autumnal colours. Peak viewing time is early November.

Miyajima, p158

▶ miyajima-ropeway.info/english

↖ Drive the mountain roads around Nikkō

The hairpin bends of the route up to the waterfall Kegon-no-taki are surrounded by magnificent autumn folliage between the end of October and mid November.

Nikkō, p68

▶ kegon.jp

Days of rainfall: 13

NOVEMBER

Average daytime max: 21°C
Days of rainfall: 13

Throwback: Edo Culture

While city folk flock to rural areas to see the autumn foliage, experience Japan's national sport at the Ryōgoku Kokugikan.

▶ Ryōgoku Kokugikan, p56

▶ sumo.or.jp

Packing Notes

Keep a jacket or your favourite clothing layers on hand for chillier nights.

The period after Christmas and the first week of January is the Japanese New Year holidays. Many shops and restaurants are closed nationwide.

↖ Snowy Villages

The winter light-up event at Ogimachi village in Shirakawa-gō is a storybook cottage scene come to life. Expect crowds.

Ogimachi, p93

▶ vill.shirakawa.lg.jp/en

Demand for accommodation peaks during Christmas and the Lunar New Year (late January to early February). Book tours and overnight adventures in advance.

▶ lonelyplanet.com/japan

Japanese strawberries are the sweetest in January but are available from December through to May.

DECEMBER

Average daytime max: 12°C

JANUARY

Japan in WINTER

↘ Sapporo Snow Festival

See giant snow sculptures and join in the fun at the Sapporo Snow Festival, over a week in early February.

Sapporo, p199

▸ snowfes.com

↓ Eat Your Way Through the Islands

Instead of a holiday in the snow, head south and take a culinary trip through subtropical Okinawa.

Okinawa-hontō, p214

▸ visitokinawajapan.com

For those long days out in the cold, disposable pocket warmers called *kairo* are cheaply available at convenience stores.

Days of rainfall: 9

FEBRUARY

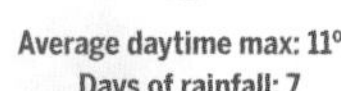

Average daytime max: 11°C
Days of rainfall: 7

← Relax in an Onsen

One of the best winter experiences is having a bath in a *rotemburo* (outdoor bath) surrounded by snow. Available at some ryokan.

Packing Notes

Bring thermal underclothes and a down jacket, plus sturdy boots or ice cleats for rural areas with heavy snow.

Golden Week is packed with public holidays, from late April to the beginning of May. Large crowds are everywhere.

↙ Takayama Spring Matsuri

On 14 and 15 April Takayama hosts the Sannō Matsuri, the Spring edition of its most famous festival with a parade of spectacular floats lit with lanterns.

Takayama, p82

▸ hida.jp/english

Demand for accommodation peaks during cherry-blossom season (late March to early April). Book tours and overnight adventures in advance.

▸ lonelyplanet.com/japan

See the magenta plum blossom from late February to early March, with cherry blossoms soon after.

MARCH

Average daytime max: 16°C

APRIL

Japan in SPRING

↘ Pedalling the Petals

Cycle around Kyoto to chase down the cherry blossoms, riding along old paths and rivers as you go.

Kyoto, p100

▸ kctp.net

↖ Hanami Heaven

During *sakura* season, many convenience stores sell tarp sheets for impromptu cherry-blossom-viewing parties.

Days of rainfall: 14

MAY

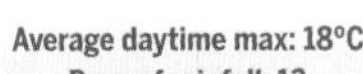

Average daytime max: 18°C
Days of rainfall: 13

↙ Peonies at Yūshien

Marvel at a sea of vibrant blooming peonies at Yūshien, a Japanese-style garden on an island in the middle of Lake Nakaumi.

Yūshien, p169

▸ yuushien.com

Packing Notes

Bring a thick jacket for cold nights, and a small umbrella for spring showers.

TOKYO
Trip Builder

TAKE YOUR PICK OF MUST-SEES AND HIDDEN GEMS

The region around Tokyo (known as Kantō) is the perfect sampler of everything Japan has to offer – vibrant city life, fascinating culture and gorgeous nature. Tokyo itself provides endless experiences, but ultra-convenient public transport means taking short trips out of the city is easy-peasy.

Trip Notes

Hub town Tokyo

How long Allow 10 days

Getting around Train and subway will get you anywhere within Tokyo and to neighbouring prefectures. For more flexibility on the outskirts, rent a car.

Tips Avoid taking the train in Tokyo during the morning rush hour between 7.30am and 9am. Highways in and out of the city can get congested in the evening from 5pm to 7.30pm.

Nikko National Park
Nikko
Imaichi
Nikkō
See beautiful autumn foliage and the extravagant shrine of Tōshō-gū, a World Heritage Site just two hours by train from the city.
2 days
Utsunomiya
Mashiko
Ueno
Spend an afternoon immersed in art and history at some of Tokyo's largest museums.
1 day
Maebashi
Takasaki
Oyama
Shimodate
Mito
Kumagaya
Mitaka
Take a breather in this quieter part of town, home to the Ghibli Museum and Mitaka.
½ day
Chichibu
Kasukabe
Kashiwa
Ryōgoku
Book tickets to see sumo wrestling at Japan's largest sumo stadium.
½ day
Ome
TOKYO
Hachioji
Sagamihara
Chiba
Odaiba
Browse malls and other fun attractions on an artificial island in Tokyo Bay – a place to unleash your inner child.
1 day
Tokyo Bay
Ichihara
Kawasaki
Shibuya
Experience peak city life in Tokyo – there are plenty of places to eat and shop, and *yokochō* (alleyways) to explore.
½ day
Kisarazu
Odawara
Boso Peninsula
Katsuura

JAPAN ALPS AND CHŪBU
Trip Builder

TAKE YOUR PICK OF MUST-SEES AND HIDDEN GEMS

Japan's middle region, Chūbu, is defined by the Japan Alps, dense pine forests and remote villages. It's the ultimate destination for outdoor lovers, or someone looking to escape the metropolis for a while. Pack your hiking boots.

Trip Notes

Hub town Nagoya

How long Allow 10 to 12 days

Getting around Travel between prefectures by limited-express trains or shinkansen (bullet trains). For rural destinations, take buses. Families can consider renting a car for easier travel.

Tips This region experiences heavy snow and strong winds. Be extra cautious if you're driving, and ask for a rental car with snow tyres.

Shirakawa-gō
Wake up surrounded by mountains in the quiet villages of Shirakawa-gō, and experience the slow, serene pace of life for a while.
3–4 days

Takayama
A gateway to the Japan Alps, Takayama is a small characterful town that's also famous for its excellent sake and succulent beef.
1–2 days

Nagoya
Feast on lots of tasty food options here in Chūbu's largest city. A favourite local speciality is *tebasaki* (chicken wings).
½ day

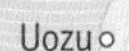

Hakuba

Tateyama

Nagano

Shinano-
omachi

*Chubu-
Sangaku
National Park*

Kamikōchi

Open between late April and mid November, this stunning Japan Alps resort is the base station for everything from easy river side hikes to assaults on some of Japan's highest mountains.

3–4 days

Karuizawa

Azumino

Kamikochi

Matsumoto

Shiojiri

Suwa

Aidara

Narai

Nakasendō

Head to the Kiso Valley to hike along this original Edo-period highway through the forest from Magome to Tsumago.

1–2 days

*Chichibu-Tama
National Park*

*Minami Alps
National
Park*

Iida

Fuji-
yoshida

*Fuji-Hakone-
Izu National
Park*

Mt Fuji

Gotemba

Ghibli Park

Book ahead for tickets to this theme park that brings to life the animated worlds from some of Studio Ghibli's most famous movies.

1 day

Fuji

Numazu

Shizuoka

KANSAI
Trip Builder

TAKE YOUR PICK OF MUST-SEES AND HIDDEN GEMS

A visit to Kansai, the centre of old Japanese traditions and culture, will most certainly be an enriching one. Not only will you deepen your understanding of Japanese history, but you'll also get to treat yourself to some of the nation's best dishes.

Trip Notes

Hub towns Osaka, Kyoto

How long Allow 9 to 12 days

Getting around Most spots in this region are accessible by train or shinkansen from Osaka. Cycling is a great way to see Kyoto. Use either the public bus or a rental car around the Kii Peninsula.

Tips Discover some real gems by walking around the cities of Osaka and Kyoto, but be warned that they are among the hottest places in Japan in summer.

FROM LEFT: MIRKO KUZMANOVIC/SHUTTERSTOCK ©, PATRICK FOTO/SHUTTERSTOCK ©, SUPERJOSEPH/SHUTTERSTOCK ©

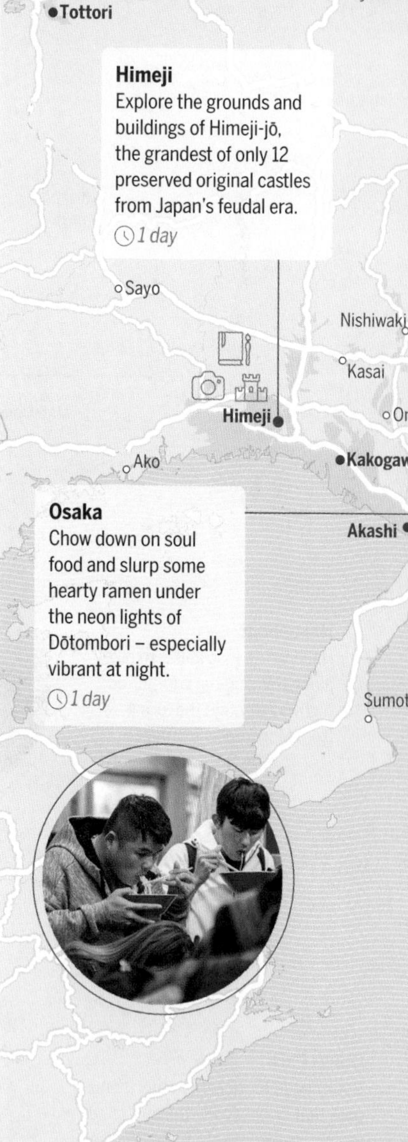

Miyazu
Kyoto
Experience Japan's old traditions of geisha, tea ceremony, shrines, temples and more in its former capital city.
3 days
Nagoya
Kuwana
Kyoto
Otsu
Kusatsu
Yokkaichi
Sanda
Kawanishi
Mino
Uji
Nara
Make friends with the wild deer that roam freely around Nara-kōen, a verdant park in this historical city.
1 day
Kobe
Osaka
Nara
Sakai
Haibara
Osaka-wan
Kishiwada
Sennan
Hashimoto
Gojō
Iwade
Wakayama
Koya-san
Kii-nagashima
Arida
Owase
Gobō
Kumano
Kii Peninsula
Go on a spiritual journey through forests and mountains following the ancient Kumano Kodō network of roads.
2–4 days
Hongū
Takijiri-ōji
Tanabe
Shingū
Nachi-Katsuura
Kii-Katsuura
0
50 km
0
25 miles
Kushimoto

HIROSHIMA, KYŪSHŪ & OKINAWA Trip Builder

TAKE YOUR PICK OF MUST-SEES AND HIDDEN GEMS

The southern region of Japan can be overlooked by travellers, but it's where you'll have experiences unlike anywhere else in the country. Visit some of the most significant cities in modern Japanese history, or sink your toes into white beaches of pristine islands.

Trip Notes

Hub towns Fukuoka, Hiroshima, Naha

How long Allow 12 to 14 days

Getting around Trains, buses and cars are all options around Kyūshū. Take short flights to the islands, then get around by car.

Tips Heavy traffic jams and difficulty finding parking are common issues in Okinawa. Leave early, and stay clear of the bus-only lanes on the left side.

See Southern Islands Inset

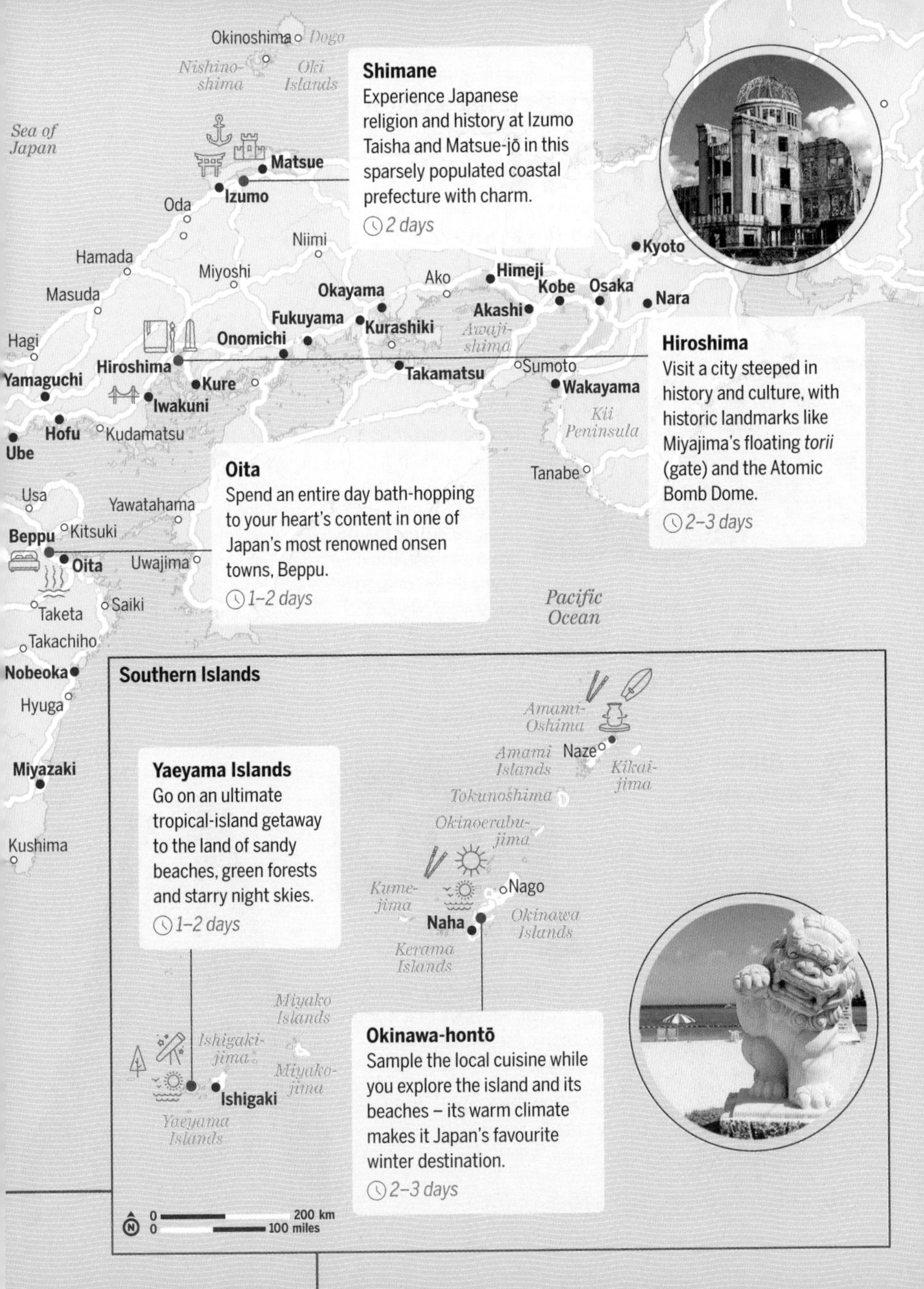
Okinoshima
Dogo
Nishinoshima
Oki Islands
Sea of Japan
Shimane
Experience Japanese religion and history at Izumo Taisha and Matsue-jō in this sparsely populated coastal prefecture with charm.
2 days
Matsue
Izumo
Oda
Niimi
Hamada
Miyoshi
Masuda
Hagi
Yamaguchi
Hofu
Ube
Hiroshima
Kure
Iwakuni
Kudamatsu
Onomichi
Fukuyama
Okayama
Kurashiki
Ako
Himeji
Kobe
Osaka
Kyoto
Nara
Akashi
Awaji-shima
Takamatsu
Sumoto
Wakayama
Kii Peninsula
Tanabe
Hiroshima
Visit a city steeped in history and culture, with historic landmarks like Miyajima's floating *torii* (gate) and the Atomic Bomb Dome.
2–3 days
Oita
Spend an entire day bath-hopping to your heart's content in one of Japan's most renowned onsen towns, Beppu.
1–2 days
Usa
Yawatahama
Beppu
Kitsuki
Oita
Uwajima
Taketa
Saiki
Takachiho
Nobeoka
Hyuga
Miyazaki
Kushima
Pacific Ocean
Southern Islands
Amami-Oshima
Naze
Amami Islands
Kikai-jima
Tokunoshima
Okinoerabu-jima
Kume-jima
Nago
Naha
Okinawa Islands
Kerama Islands
Yaeyama Islands
Go on an ultimate tropical-island getaway to the land of sandy beaches, green forests and starry night skies.
1–2 days
Miyako Islands
Ishigaki-jima
Miyako-jima
Ishigaki
Yaeyama Islands
Okinawa-hontō
Sample the local cuisine while you explore the island and its beaches – its warm climate makes it Japan's favourite winter destination.
2–3 days
0
200 km
0
100 miles

Things to Know About JAPAN

INSIDER TIPS TO HIT THE GROUND RUNNING

1 Crazy Commute

For Tokyoites, the morning commute is a contact sport. On weekdays from 7.30am to 9am, millions squeeze into trains across the city, sometimes helped along by station staff who make sure everyone's packed in. Shinjuku Station, the busiest in the world, sees an average of 3.6 million commuters a day; there are more than 200 exits leading in and out of the complex.

▶See more about travelling around Tokyo on p42

2 Public Etiquette

Avoid speaking loudly, eating, drinking or blowing your nose on public transport. Always ride on one side of the escalator – left in Kantō, right in Kansai. All food waste, wrappings and paper go with burnable rubbish, while clean plastic, metal cans and glass are non-burnable rubbish.

▶See more about travel essentials on p238

3 Edible Souvenirs

They are called *omiyage* – food meant for gifting. Locals buy them for family, friends or co-workers, but you can enjoy them yourself!

▶See classic *omiyage* on p129

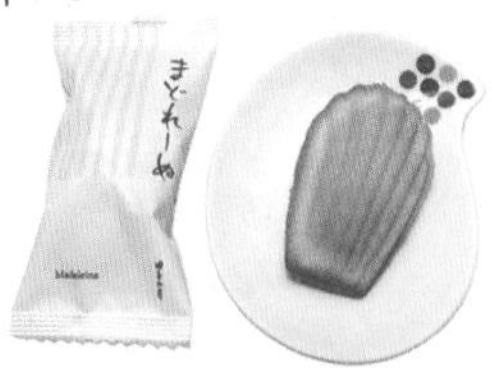

4 The Proper Way to Pay

Don't hand money to the cashier – always place your cash or credit card on the tray in front of you.

▶See more about managing money on p233

1. ROB ZS/SHUTTERSTOCK ©, 2. VOVA_31/SHUTTERSTOCK ©; SOFIJA DJUKIC/SHUTTERSTOCK ©, 3. SERGIO YONED/SHUTTERSTOCK ©, 4. NAZARII M/SHUTTERSTOCK ©; DEAWSS/SHUTTERSTOCK ©, 5. DJENT/SHUTTERSTOCK ©, 7. YUKIMCO/SHUTTERSTOCK ©.

5 Getting Around After Hours

There's no 24-hour public transport in Japan. The trains in Tokyo run until 1am at the latest, and you'll want to be at the station well before the last train. If you miss it, the alternative is to catch a taxi, but they can be expensive.

▶See more about getting around on p230

6 Local Lingo

Here are some Japanese words that will come in handy when dining out:

ōmori – large portion (often free at ramen stalls)

namimori – regular portion

okawari – refill

mochikaeri – takeaway

tennai de – eat-in

Foreigners usually get a free pass, but politeness is imperative in Japanese culture and language. Here's how to be respectful to a local.

onegai shimasu – Follow up any of your orders or requests with this. For example, if you want tea, say *'Ocha onegai shimasu.'*

arigatō gozaimasu – Because it's a bit of a mouthful, some may be tempted to shorten it to simply *arigatō*. This is fine when said among friends, but take the time to thank a helpful local the right way.

▶See the Language chapter on p240

7 Braving the Elements

Japan experiences sweltering summers and chilly winters. You'll be doing a lot of walking too, especially if you're in the city. Be sure to carry these items with you:

Folding umbrella with UV blocking For sudden showers and shade from the sun.

Cooling wipes Buy these at convenience stores to wipe away the sweat.

Pocket warmer Effectively warms cold hands; adhesive ones stick to the inside of your coat.

▶See more about the seasons on p18

Read, Listen, Watch & Follow

READ

Convenience Store Woman (Sayaka Murata; 2016) A woman figures out how she fits into society's standards.

The Bells of Old Tokyo (Anna Sherman, 2019) Part memoir, part evocative cultural history of a transient city.

Norwegian Wood (Haruki Murakami; 1987) Coming-of-age tale of Tokyo college students amid the protests of the 1960s.

Rashomon and Seventeen Other Stories (Ryunosuke Akutagawa; 2009) Tales by Japan's most prominent short-story writer.

LISTEN

Pop Virus (Hoshino Gen; 2018) Funky tunes to dance to, with cheerful, catchy hooks that stay in your head.

The Book 3 (YOASOBI, 2023) Includes the electro-pop duo's single *Idol*, the longest-running number one in the Japan Hot 100 chart history.

Your Name (Radwimps; 2016) Everything from energetic anthems to moving ballads by one of Japan's most popular bands (pictured right).

Singles 2000 (Miyuki Nakajima; 2002) A compilation of timeless melodies from Japan's most recognisable singer-songwriter.

Abroad in Japan (abroadinjapan.com) Podcast discussing culture, current events and all things weird and wacky happening in Japan.

WATCH

Shoplifters (2018) A self-made family of grifters navigates a life of poverty on Tokyo's outskirts.

Your Name (2016) Hit romance anime about body-swapping teens trying to avert a natural disaster.

Drive My Car (2021) Internationally award winning drama of about a grieving theatre director and his chauffer.

Midnight Diner: Tokyo Stories (2009–19) TV drama about people from different walks of life who wind up at a late-night diner.

Tampopo (1985) Itami Jûzô's comedy shines a light the Japanese obsession with food.

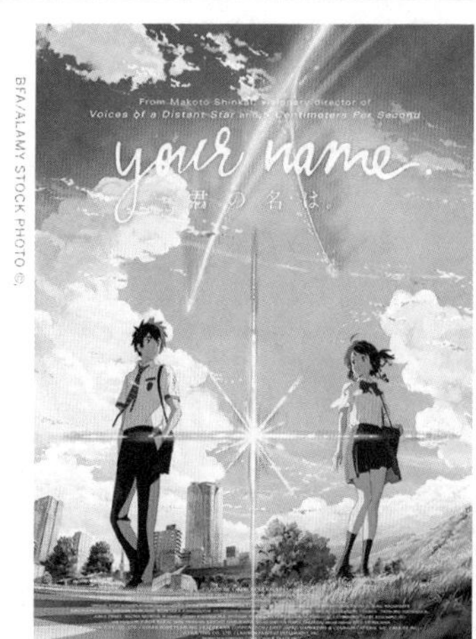

BFA/ALAMY STOCK PHOTO ©

FOLLOW

Metropolis Japan (metropolisjapan.com) Culture, events, travel and more.

Tokyo Weekender (tokyoweekender.com) Japan's oldest English-language magazine.

Storied (storiedmag.com) Stunning images and amazing stories from all over Japan.

Tokyo Cheapo (tokyocheapo.com) Comprehensive Japan travel and living advice.

@visitjapanjp Official account of Japan National Tourism Organisation.

Sate your Japan dreaming with a virtual trip at lonelyplanet.com/japan

TOKYO

CITY LIFE | CULTURE | ART

Akihabara (p48)

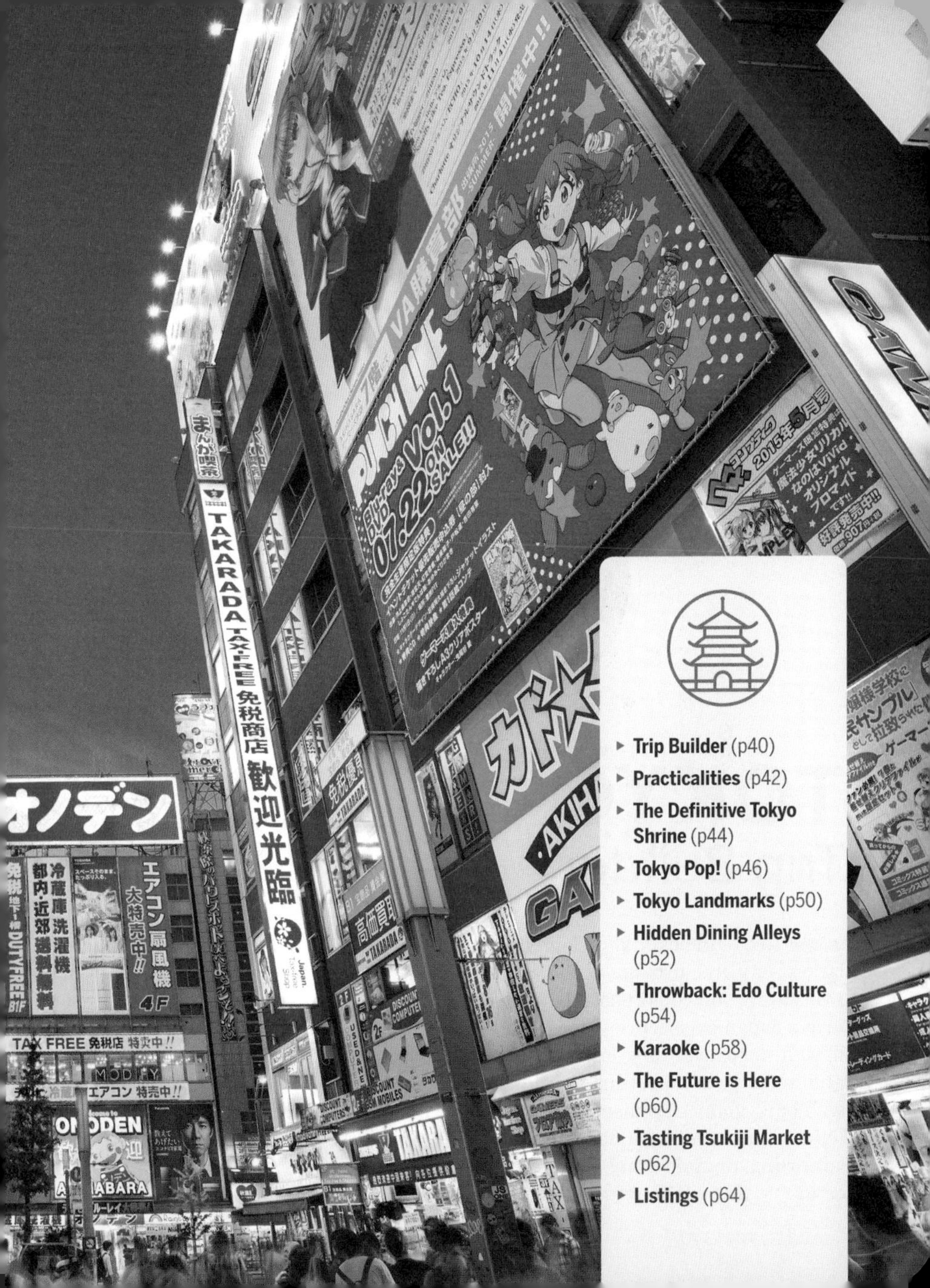
まんが喫茶
TAKARADA TAX-FREE 免税商店
歓迎光臨
オノデン
エアコン 扇風機 大特売中!!
冷蔵庫 洗濯機
TAX FREE 免税店 特売中!!
ONODEN
AKIHABARA
VA購買部
Vol.1
07.22 ON SALE!!
2015年5月号
DISCOUNT COMPUTER
TAKARADA

Visit the enchanting **Ghibli Museum, Mitaka** (p47)
30min walk from Mitaka city

Inokashira-kōen

New York Bar

Enjoy a laid-back weekend picnic in Tokyo's favourite park, **Yoyogi-kōen** (p64)
12min walk from Harajuku

TOKYO
Trip Builder

Tokyo, the capital of Japan, is the country's largest city and also one of the world's largest. Everything you could possibly want in terms of the urban Japan experience you can have here, and have it in spades: superlative restaurants, statement architecture, trend-setting boutiques, hole-in-the-wall bars, giant LED displays and flashing neon lights. More than any one sight, it's the city itself – a sprawling, organic thing, stretching as far as the eye can see – that enchants visitors.

Explore Shibuya, starting with its famous intersection, **Shibuya Crossing** (p51)
At the main entrance of Shibuya Station

0 4 km
0 2 miles

Ueno-kōen

Experience Tokyo's traditional side at Shintō shrine **Meiji-jingū** (p44)
2min walk from Harajuku Station

Enter the sub-culture in the anime district of **Akihabara** (p48)
4min train ride from Tokyo Station to Akihabara Station

Spectate a kabuki performance at the **Kabuki-za theatre** (p55)
Connected to Higashi-ginza Station

Shinjuku-gyoen

Fukiage Imperial Gardens

Meiji-jingū-gyoen

Shop around **Takeshita street**, in Harajuku, for independent boutiques and fun fashion (p49)
2min walk from Harajuku Station

Taste your way through Japanese seafood at **Tsukiji Market** (p62)
5min walk from Tsukiji Station

Step into the future at the newly constructed **Azabudai Hills** (p60)
11min walk from Kamiyachō Station

Go for a meal in one of Tokyo's atmospheric dining alleyways, like **Ebisu-yokochō** (p53)
4min walk from Ebisu Station

Tokyo Bay

Practicalities

WINDS/SHUTTERSTOCK ©

ARRIVING

Narita Airport Tokyo's primary gateway (pictured) most budget flights end up here. It's around ¥3000 (and 60 to 90 minutes) for an express train or bus to the city centre; buy tickets at the kiosks in the arrivals terminal. Discount buses (¥1000) run to Tokyo Station; purchase tickets on board. Fixed-fare taxis start at ¥23,000.

Haneda Airport Tokyo's smaller, closer airport has train and monorail access (15 minutes; ¥300 to ¥500) to the city centre. Fixed-fare taxis cost around ¥7000.

HOW MUCH FOR A

Bowl of noodles ¥800

Karaoke session ¥2000

Craft beer ¥1000

WHEN TO GO

JAN–MAR
Brisk but sunny days, perfect for winter sports.

APR–JUN
Warm days – a popular time to visit.

JUL–SEP
Rainy season; hot and humid days with typhoons.

OCT–DEC
The tail end of hiking season, with cooler weather.

GETTING AROUND

Subway and train The subway is the quickest and easiest way to get around central Tokyo. The overground Yamanote (loop) and Chuo-Sobu (central) train lines, both operated by East Japan Railway Company (JR East), also service major stations. Both run from 5am to midnight. Rides cost ¥170 to ¥320. Purchase prepaid fare cards (Suica or Pasmo) from one of the ticket vending machines.

Taxi Fares start at ¥420 for the first 1km, then rise by ¥80 for every 233m you travel. There's a surcharge of 20% between 10pm and 5am. Credit cards accepted.

Walking Subway stations are close in the city centre; save yen and see more by walking if you only need to go one stop.

EATING & DRINKING

Tokyo's dining scene careens nonchalantly between highs and lows, with top-class sushi restaurants and oil-spattered noodle joints earning similar accolades. There's very little you can't get here, but the one truly Tokyo dish is *nigiri-zushi* (hand-pressed sushi; pictured). Every neighbourhood has at least one sushi shop, with set meals from ¥2500. Tokyo's trendiest restaurants take the neo-bistro format, blending Japanese and international influences; look for them in Harajuku, Aoyama, Tomigaya, Ebisu and Meguro. Reservations are recommended for mid- to high-end restaurants.

Best craft cocktails
SG Club (p66)

Must-try ramen
Mensho (p65)

CONNECT & FIND YOUR WAY

Wi-fi There are plenty of free hot spots, though connection can be spotty. The best way to stay connected is to rent a pocket wi-fi device (at the airport) or buy a SIM card (data-only; at the airport or electronics shops).

Navigation Tokyo's address system is challenging, even for locals. All the more reason to have stable wi-fi, so you can rely on navigation apps.

DISCOUNT TRAVEL CARD

Tokyo Subway Ticket Gives unlimited rides on all subway lines (24/48/72hr ¥800/1200/1500; half-price for children), but not JR lines. (tokyometro.jp)

WHERE TO STAY

Tokyo is pricey, but there are plenty of attractive budget and midrange options. Pick somewhere near where you plan to spend the most time.

Neighbourhood	Pros/Cons
Shinjuku	Major transit hub. Widest range of options at all price points. Major crowds.
Shibuya	Nightlife at your door and big-city buzz (also a downside). Good transit links.
Roppongi	Art museums and nightlife. Noisy with less convenient outer areas.
Ginza	Central with great shopping and dining. Congested and pricey.
Ueno & Yanaka	Easy airport access and good value. Yanaka has a local feel and is quiet at night.
Asakusa	Best budget options. Quiet at night, with a long commute to west-side sights.

MONEY

Carry a few thousand yen in cash as some shops and restaurants don't take cards. **Tokyo Cheapo** (tokyocheapo.com) has budget tips.

01 The Definitive TOKYO SHRINE

CULTURE | ARCHITECTURE | GARDENS

Meiji-jingū (Meiji Shrine) is Tokyo's signature Shintō shrine. Set in a 70-hectare forest that literally offers a breath of fresh air, even though it's right in the thick of the city, it's a major tourist attraction that's also appreciated by locals: it is. A shrine visit is also a great way to participate in Japanese culture.

UINO/SHUTTERSTOCK ©

How to

Getting here The JR Yamanote line to Harajuku Station (west exit) or the Chiyoda line to Meiji-jingūmae (exit 2).

When to go As early as possible! The shrine is least crowded in the morning. It's open dawn until dusk, which can be rather early in Tokyo, especially in winter.

Cost Free!

Photo op The colourful sake barrels (gifted to the shrine from sake makers – sake and Shintō have a long connection).

MATT MUNRO/LONELY PLANET ©

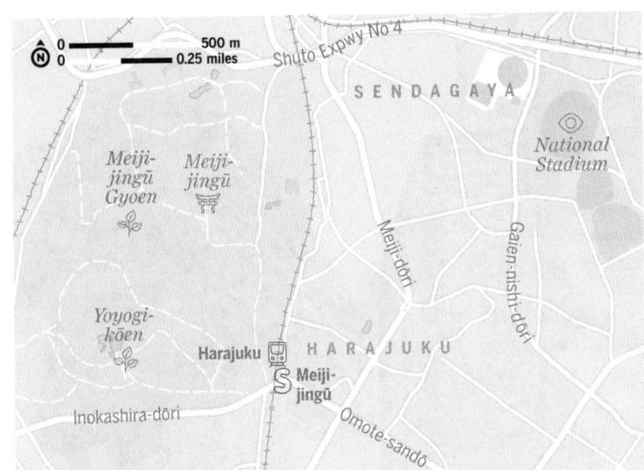

Above left *Torii*, Meiji-jingū
Below left Sake barrels, Meiji-jingū

Pass through the gates The shrine is at the end of a long (700m) gravel path. Along the way, you'll pass under three towering, wooden *torii* (shrine gates). These mark the boundary between the mundane world and the sacred world, and you'll see locals bowing here before passing through.

Purify yourself at the font Before the final *torii* is the *temizu-ya* (font), where it is the custom to purify yourself: dip the ladle in the water and first rinse your left hand then your right. Pour some water into your left hand and rinse your mouth, then rinse your left hand again. Make sure none of this water gets back into the font!

Make an offering In front of the main shrine building, with its cypress beams and copper-plated roof, there's a box for offerings. To make one (along with a wish), toss a coin – a ¥5 coin is considered lucky – into the box, bow twice, clap your hands twice and then bow again. (Note that you can't take photos here, or anywhere where there is a roof over your head.)

Relax in the gardens Most visitors bypass **Meiji-jingū Gyoen**, the garden on the shrine grounds (¥500 admission), which means it's usually quiet. It has all the elements of a classic Japanese stroll garden, with a pond and seasonal blooms – it's particularly famous for its irises in June.

Way of the Gods

Shintō, or 'the way of the gods', is the oldest extant belief system in Japan. Its innumerable *kami* (gods) are located mostly in nature (eg in trees, rocks, waterfalls and mountains), but also in the objects of daily life, like hearths and wells. Historically, extraordinary people could be recognised as *kami* upon death, such as the Emperor Meiji (1852–1912) who, along with his wife, is enshrined at Meiji-jingū.

Emperor Meiji's reign coincided with Japan's transformation from isolationist, feudal state to modern nation. But that doesn't mean visitors are here to worship the former emperor. People visit for all kinds of reasons: to pray for luck in love, business or exams; to connect with their culture; or to take a moment out of their daily lives.

02 Tokyo POP!

POP CULTURE | FASHION | SHOPPING

From Pokemon to streetwear, Studio Ghibli to lolita fashion, Japanese pop culture synthesises media into fashion while also creating works of art. Shinjuku and Shibuya are hubs where you can adopt some of Japan's coolest new trends.

DEREKTEO/SHUTTERSTOCK ©

How to

Getting to the Ghibli Museum, Mitaka Take the JR Chūō line to Mitaka Station. From here it's a 15-minute walk or a ride on the community bus. Buy bus tickets from a vending machine at bus stop 9.

Tips Entry tickets are highly limited; see ghibli-museum.jp for details.

Photography Not allowed except at the rooftop garden and cafe. At the former location, you can get a snap with a Laputa robot sculpture.

AGUSTIN ACOSTA/SHUTTERSTOCK ©

Ghibli Museum

Studio Ghibli, co-founded by directors Miyazaki Hayao and Takahata Isao, is consistently responsible for Japan's most critically acclaimed and commercially successful animated films – a rare combination. It's also responsible for turning out a whole generation of Japanophiles – those who fell in love with films like *My Neighbor Totoro* (1988) and *Spirited Away* (2001).

The **Ghibli Museum, Mitaka** (ghibli-museum.jp) captures the spirit of wonder that makes the films so enchanting. Located in the quiet yet charming city of Mitaka, the space is equally fun for adults and kids. There's also a small cinema here that screens original shorts directed by Miyazaki, Takahata and their protégés. Check the website for regular

PHOTOGRAPHER253/SHUTTERSTOCK ©

Gotcha Gashapon

Gasha-gasha is the onomatopoeia for the sound of the vending machine that *gashapon* capsules come from. Prizes are often highly detailed tiny key rings or figures. These can be cool anime characters to something as random as mini furniture. Grab a bunch to take home as fun and surprising souvenirs.

Above left Godzilla, Shinjuku
Left ACDC RAG, Takeshita Street (p49)
Above right *Gashapon* machines

updates on what's on. Naturally, the museum has an excellent gift shop.

Akihabara & Nakano

Tokyo's famous pop culture district, Akihabara ('Akiba') is filled with shops selling anime (Japanese animation), manga (Japanese comics) and gaming merch, neon-bright electronics stores, retro arcades, cosplay cafes and *gashapon* (capsule toy vending machines). The iconic SEGA buildings of the past have had a makeover and are now called GiGO. But they're still just as good if you want to try your hand at a claw machine or dance to the beat of a rhythm game. From Akihabara Station, take the Electric Town exit.

Less flash and bling than Akiba, Nakano a treasure trove for the nostalgic nerd. The highlight here is **Nakano Broadway**, a vintage 1960s shopping mall that's home to the original Mandarake Complex – the go-to shop for all things manga and anime. (There are other branches, including one in Akiba, but the one

Where to Find Cute Characters

Doraemon Future Department Store Test out the robot cat's most creative inventions and snag some cute mugs, key rings and Doraemon-shaped cookies. In Odaiba.

Shibuya 109 (shibuya109.jp) Home to all things Hello Kitty, Cinnamoroll, Kuromi and more. A visit is also an excuse to simply check out this buzzing mall, packed with mini-sized Japanese fashion shops.

Tokyo Character Street (tokyostationcity.com) Over a dozen small (and often-changing) shops covering a variety of characters, from Ultraman to Pretty Cure. Inside Tokyo Station.

Godzilla Store Tokyo Posters, figures, T-shirts and more. In Shinjuku.

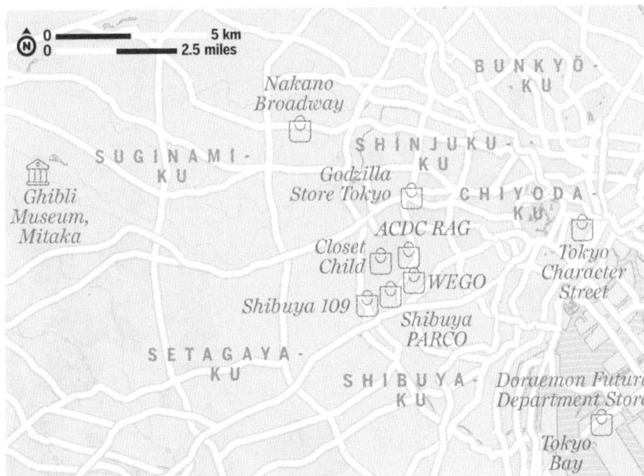

in Nakano, spread out over 25 tiny, niche shops, is the best.)

Eclectic Fashion

The key to shopping in **Harajuku** is to let creativity lead and become a walking work of art yourself. This is the place to survey independent boutiques and observe subculture trends that are taking off. **ACDC RAG** is unmissable for its bright-red awning and mannequins sporting funk-fantasy and gothic looks. **Closet Child** does lolita, punk and more, plus secondhand items so you can find bargains. **WEGO** carries basics but also quirky accessories like fidget toys and rabbit-ear hairbands. Take the JR Yamanote Line to Harajuku and follow signs for Takeshita Gate.

Shibuya PARCO (shibuya.parco.jp) represents the intersection of media and fashion. TORCH-TORCH and RADIO EVA STORE on the 5th floor are two labels bringing anime and gaming to the runway. On the 6th, you'll encounter the likes of Nintendo, Pokemon and Capcom, with their larger-than-life shops and photo-worthy character busts. Give some attention to the pop-up shops and cafes, as these often showcase the latest in video game merch. Most trains lead to Shibuya Station, which will be the closest stop to Shibuya Parco.

Left Hello Kitty shop, Tokyo Character Street **Below** Nintendo shop, Shibuya PARCO

Tokyo LANDMARKS

01 Hachiko

Tokyo's most famous loyal dog, who showed up daily to meet his master at Shibuya Station long after the man's death, is commemorated as a statue.

02 Tokyo Tower

Eiffel Tower-like in design, this 1958 broadcast tower symbolised Tokyo's rise from the ashes of WWII.

03 Asahi Flame

The Philippe Starck–designed headquarters for Asahi Beer in Asakusa is nicknamed the 'golden turd'.

04 Unicorn Gundam

This 19.7m-tall model of an RX-0 Unicorn Gundam comes from the wildly popular *Mobile Suit Gundam* anime franchise.

05 Kaminarimon

The 'Thunder Gate' at the entrance to Tokyo's oldest temple, Sensō-ji, is instantly recognisable for its enormous *chochin* (lantern).

06 Shibuya Crossing

Tokyo's most photographed intersection is rumoured to be the busiest in the world (and at least the busiest in Japan).

07 Tokyo Skytree

This sleek, mesh spire is Tokyo's current broadcast tower, completed in 2012 and standing 634m-tall. At night, it's illuminated in either blue or purple.

08 Shinjuku Toho Building

A 12m-tall Godzilla statue on the roof looks ready to bite into this building by Toho (the studio that produces the films).

09 Tokyo Station

Tokyo's central rail terminus, completed in 1914, was constructed when the vogue for European-style architecture was at its peak.

10 Nihombashi

This 1911 granite bridge, guarded by bronze lions and dragons, marks the geographical centre of Tokyo.

03 Hidden Dining ALLEYS

FOOD | DRINK | CITY LIFE

Scattered around Tokyo, often in the shadow of train tracks or wedged among skyscrapers, are clusters of alleys that house bars and restaurants so small they might not seat a dozen, sometimes with makeshift outdoor seating (folding tables and turned-over beer crates) tacked on. Tokyoites love them and the odds are you will too.

NAKANO-KU
SHINJUKU-KU
Omoide-yokochō
Shinjuku-gyoen
Meiji-jingū Gyoen
Jingū-gaien
Yoyogi-kōen
SHIBUYA-KU
Nonbei-yokochō
Ebisu-yokochō
0 1 km
0 0.5 miles

How to

When to go Early (around 5pm or 6pm) to grab a seat at popular places, or later in the evening, after 9pm. This is especially the case if you're a group (as space is limited); solo travellers (and sometimes pairs) can generally show up whenever and trust that space will be made.

Cost Many spots will charge a service fee (¥300 to ¥1000 per person); this is always the case if you're given a free appetizer.

Yokochō The word *yokochō* means 'side town' and is often used to describe these clusters of eating and drinking alleys. Many began as black markets after WWII, and still occupy the same hastily constructed wooden buildings. It's this look and feel of an otherwise long-gone Tokyo that endears them to locals. Note that it's considered bad form to linger past your last order, unless you're a regular customer.

Omoide-yokochō Tokyo's most famous (and photographed) *yokochō,* near Shinjuku Station. Many shops here specialise in *yakitori* (meats or vegetables grilled on skewers). Several

Right above Street restaurant, Omoide-yokochō
Right below *Yakitori*, Omoide-yokoch ō

MATT MUNRO/LONELY PLANET ©

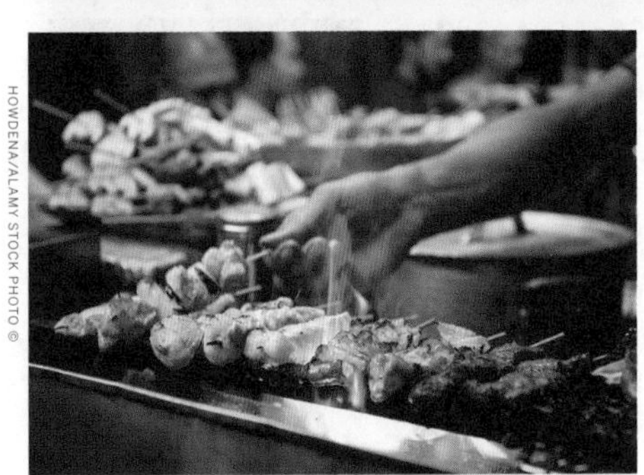

HOWDENA/ALAMY STOCK PHOTO ©

Yakitori

Yakitori is a *yokochō* staple, and *yakitori* restaurants can often be identified by their red *chōchin* (lanterns) hanging outside. You can order tasting sets *(moriawase)* or 'by the skewer', seasoned with salt *(shio)* or sauce *(tare)*. Sit at the counter and watch the grill masters at work.

have English menus, and open entrances mean you can easily see inside.

Ebisu-yokochō A covered shopping arcade refitted as an eating and drinking strip. There's a wider range of food on offer here than at Omoide-yokochō (and the quality is a bit higher), including seafood (grilled or served as sashimi). English menus are scarce but you can get a sense of what to order by seeing what everyone else is eating. Gets packed; in Ebisu.

Nonbei-yokochō Two lanes of bars, bistros and *izakaya* (Japanese pub-eateries) alongside Shibuya's elevated train tracks. You'll need some courage to open the doors as there's little indication of what to expect from outside.

04 Throwback: Edo CULTURE

HISTORY | ARTS | CRAFTMANSHIP

Futuristic Japan is often juxtaposed against tradition, and no era is more celebrated than the Edo Period. Thankfully, so much of Tokyo's history has been preserved through art, documentation and sacred practices. These highlights give curious travellers a look into the past.

How to

Getting here Take the Hibiya Line or Toei Asakusa Line to Higashi-Ginza Station. Kabuki-za theatre is connected and sits right above the station.

Top tip Kabuki-za sells one-act tickets for those who want to sample without committing to several hours of theatrics. These can be purchased online in advance at kabukiweb.net/about/ticket or by rocking up on the day. Head to the theatre entrance and look for a ticket window on the left side.

The Art of Kabuki

Also known as the Tokugawa Period, the Edo Period (1603–1868) marked a huge leap in Japanese history for cultural arts and economic growth. Part of this included the emergence of kabuki, a form of Japanese theatre that combines story with dance. It's easily recognisable by its striking makeup, heavily adorned costumes and exaggerated acting. While its origins can be traced back to kabuki founder, Izumo no Okuni's female dance troupe, the craft went on to become a male-only practice. Kabuki storylines often revolve around everyday stories with themes of romance, tragedy and moral virtue.

Tokyo's **Kabuki-za** (kabukiweb.net) is one of the principal theatres in Japan where you can still catch this 400-year-old art form.

Above left Kabuki-za
Left Kabuki poster

The building is also artistry in itself. First built in 1889 as a wooden structure, it has since undergone several reconstructions due to fire, natural disasters and WWII. What we see today was reopened in 2013 and is inspired by the baroque architecture styles of old Japanese fortresses.

Japan's National Sport

Yet another heirloom of the Edo period is sumo, a type of full contact wrestling. Two sumo wrestlers *(rikishi)* fight, with the victor succeeding by forcing his opponent out of the ring or into touching the ground with any body part other than his feet. Common strategies involve pushing, tossing and striking, all while manipulating an opponent with the limited space around them. *Rikishi* can weigh anywhere between 73kg and 288kg, all while following a regimented training schedule and diet. Even today, sumo still deeply embodies many rituals linked to Shintōism, such as the use of salt to purify the ring.

Common Phrases

Hanamichi A raised platform in a kabuki theatre that runs through the audience to the main stage. Allows for dramatic entrances and exits by the kabuki actors.

Onnagata Male kabuki actors who play female roles.

Rikishi The Japanese term for a professional sumo wrestler.

Dohyō The sumo ring in which the wrestling occurs. It's typically made with buried rice and bales of straw.

Shōgun The title given to Japan's military dictators from the 12th to the 19th century.

Kissaten Literally 'tea-drinking shop' but also acts as a quiet place to drink coffee and read. Popularised in early-20th-century Japan.

🎧 Kabuki Audio Guide

Non-Japanese speakers can rent a Simplified English audio guide to help explain the performance. These are available for a single act (¥800) or the full programme (¥1000). While they are not one-for-one translations, they are very helpful for providing the gist of what is happening.

Ryōgoku Kokugikan (sumo.or.jp) is the home of sumo. This arena has also seen its fair share of renovations, with its latest iteration completed in 1985. Tournaments at Kokugikan are held just three times a year, so it's best to plan ahead to incorporate it into your trip. Chair seating starts from around ¥3800 per seat, while floor-style seating *(masu-seki)* are approximately ¥38,000 for four; see sumo.or.jp/en. To get here, take either the JR Sobu line or the Toei Oedo line to Ryōgoku Station. The stadium is a three-minute walk away.

Time Capsules

Once the HQs of Japan's powerful shogunate, Edo-jō (Edo Castle) is now a serene site for **Imperial Palace** (sankan.kunaicho.go.jp), as well as public gardens and museums. Many of the buildings have burnt down, but the carefully preserved ruins will give a glimpse as to what once stood in this space.

Foray into **Yanaka**, a rare Tokyo neighbourhood that still has old wooden buildings, quiet temples, winding alleys and ateliers. It's popular with locals and visitors alike, who come to soak up the old Tokyo atmosphere. Come for the shaved ice from **Himitsu-dō** (instagram.com/himitsudo132) and linger at cafes like **Kayaba Coffee** (instagram.com/kayaba coffee).

Left Ryōgoku Kokugikan
Top right Kabuki-za actors
Bottom right Tennoji Temple, Yanaka

Karaoke

SING THE NIGHT AWAY, JAPAN-STYLE

Karaoke isn't just about singing: it's an excuse to let loose, bond, and keep the party going into the early hours. It's a way to express yourself – are you the type to sing the latest pop hit (dance moves included) or do you go all in on an emotional ballad?

Left Karaoke microphone
Centre Big Echo, Marunouchi branch
Right Karaoke performance

PETER MULLER/GETTY IMAGES ©

Trends come and go but karaoke (pronounced ka-ra-oh-kay) has been a fixture of Japanese culture for decades. It doesn't matter if you're a good singer or not, as long as you have heart.

In Japan, karaoke is usually sung in private rooms with friends, at establishments called karaoke boxes. A typical karaoke box has multiple floors with dozens of rooms of varying sizes. All major cities have them, in entertainment districts or around major train stations. Smaller cities often have one near the main train station, and it just might be the only after-dark entertainment option around.

Karaoke Basics

You enter a karaoke box as you do a hotel, heading first to the counter in the lobby. Reservations aren't required, though occasionally you may have to wait for a room to open up. Some chains may require a nominal membership, which someone in the group will have to sign up for (so make sure at least one person has ID on them). Otherwise, the first step is to tell the staff the size of your party.

Then you need to work out for how long you want to rent a room. Most places charge admission per person per 30 minutes, with a one-hour minimum. If you're not sure how long you want to commit, you can book the initial one hour and then choose to extend by 30 minutes or an hour indefinitely (so long as no one is waiting on an empty room and it's not yet closing time). Pricing varies by day and time of day, being most expensive on

TERENCE TOH CHIN ENG/SHUTTERSTOCK ©

BRONEK KAMINSKI/GETTY IMAGES ©

Friday and Saturday nights (around ¥500 per 30 minutes) and cheapest on weekend afternoons (around ¥150 per 30 minutes).

Alternatively, most establishments offer various packages, which may include unlimited drinks *(nomihōdai)* and/or room rental for a set number of hours (often called 'free time'). These packages are usually a much better deal than ordering drinks and food à la carte and paying by the hour.

> It doesn't matter if you're a good singer or not, as long as you have heart.

When you're inside your room, locate the console, which you'll use to select songs. In most chains, it's possible to switch the console into English and search songs alphabetically. If there's no English function, check the room (or ask staff) for a songbook – a huge paper directory of all the songs – that will list English-language songs in English (you enter the song code into the console). English songs will play with the lyrics in English on the screen.

Pro tip: queue up several songs so that you don't waste precious karaoke time mulling over what to sing next.

You can order food and drink via the telephone in the room. Staff will ring you around 10 minutes before your session is due to expire; you can extend or decide to call it a night. When your time is up, return to the lobby (taking the tab with you if there's one in the room) to pay.

Karaoke Boxes

Karaoke boxes are easy to spot: just look for the colourful, illuminated signs spelling out カラオケ (karaoke). Most are chains, and it's these that have the biggest songbooks, offer non-smoking rooms, and are most likely to have consoles and menus in English.

Big Echo (ビッグエコー; big-echo.jp) The biggest national chain and all-round good option.

Karaoke-kan (カラオケ館; karaokekan.jp) Ubiquitous, nationwide and cheap.

Uta Hiroba (歌広場; utahiro.com) Tokyo area with free soft drinks; look for the smiley face logo.

Jankara (ジャンカラ; jankara.ne.jp) Kansai area (Kyoto, Osaka, Nara etc) and Kyūshū; cheap all-you-can-drink packages.

05 The Future IS HERE

MODERN | GREENERY | ART

Cyberpunk is out and balance is back in. New spaces are cropping up in Tokyo that service modernity without sacrificing the pillars of community, art and nature. Step into Azabudai Hills, an oasis that imbues quiet luxury and the newly reborn teamLab Borderless. Both show us that the future is perhaps far greener than we could have ever imagined.

How to

Getting here Kamiyachō Station on the Hibiya line is the closest. From there it's a 2-minute walk.

Booking ahead teamLab Borderless tickets must be pre-purchased online at teamlab.art/e/tokyo. These can be booked up to two months in advance.

Crowds If lunching at Azabudai Hills arrive early to beat the office crowd on weekdays and everyone else on weekends. Aim for around 11am but check individual restaurant business hours just to be sure.

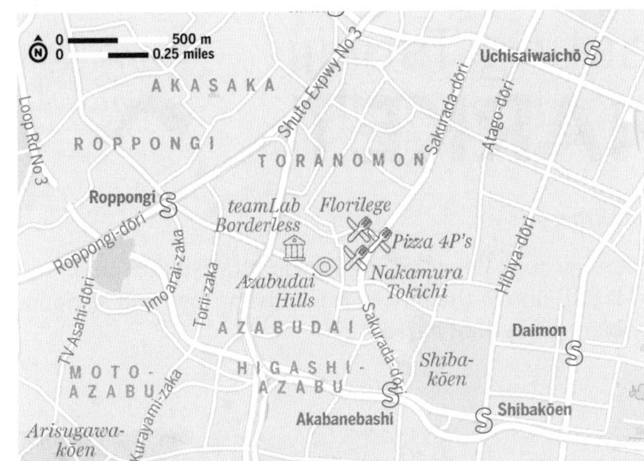

Lush Luxury

After more than 35 years in the making, **Azabudai Hills** has officially opened its doors. Leaning into the concept of a 'modern urban village', the development puts greenery at the forefront while incorporating retail, education, culture and residences. Developed by Mori Building, construction also involved the likes of César Pelli who designed the Bloomberg Tower in New York and the Petronas Towers in Kuala Lumpur.

Architecture aside, this is a stop worth making because it has it all. Indulge in a variety of culinary experiences, from cult-hit **Pizza 4P's** to 1854 *matcha* teahouse, **Nakamura Tokichi**. Even Michelin-starred **Florilege** has taken up an intimate 16-seater communal space, perfect for the fine diners. The outdoors of Azabudai Hills is its biggest draw, though. A central square, fruit orchard and vegetable garden make up the lush landscape, as does a 1.25km running route plotted through the development. Bring your running shoes and a water bottle; there's a free refillable water station just for this occasion.

Art collective **teamLab** has made waves across the globe and on social media with their immersive experiences. Now based at Azabudai Hills, the **teamLab Borderless** exhibit offers up installations themed around people, nature and expressions of philosophy. Each room and corridor is a photo op, as is **EN TEA HOUSE**, teamLab's tea house that projects art using digital technology onto your drinks.

Above left teamLab's *Universe of Water Particles on a Rock where People Gather* **Below left** Azabudai Hills

teamLab Tip

Sketch Ocean at teamLab allows guests to draw their own fish and then see them swim to life in the projection. Now you can capture these moments of delight as a truly personal trip memento at **teamLab Sketch Factory**; the factory saves all of the artwork drawn as part of the museum's installation and can turn them into badges, T-shirts and tote bags for you to take home.

When dining at **EN TEA HOUSE**, order the frozen green tea. Tea branches and flowers will sprout from it, attracting butterflies that will then flutter around the teacups of other guests.

06 Tasting Tsukiji MARKET

SEAFOOD | WALKING | SOUVENIRS

While the tuna auction has long departed for Toyosu, the Tsukiji Outer Market remains intact and is still one of the best places to trawl for fresh seafood, bite-sized snacks and the vibe of a bustling bazaar.

TAIYOU NOMACHI/GETTY IMAGES ©

How to

Getting here Ride the Hibiya line, getting off at Tsukiji Station. The market is a six-minute walk from there.

Getting around The market is densely packed. Walking is your friend.

When to go Weekdays and as early as you can wake up. Eateries open from 5am and close around 2pm.

Top tip A four-minute walk away is **Tsukiji Hongan-ji**, an impressive Jodo Shinshu Buddhist temple built in 1617.

Coffee Please

You'll need this for an early start. **Mako** (twitter.com/kissamaco) offers its speciality coffee blends with a side of *ozoni* (*mochi* soup typically served for New Year's). **Kunisuke Coffee** has everything from hot Americanos to ice *matcha* (powdered green tea) lattes. Combine coffee with Sri Lankan curry at **Tsukiji Peppers Cafe**.

04 **Tsukiji Itadori Bekkan** is on the expensive side when compared to the street snacks, but here you're paying for top-quality seafood bowls topped with fatty tuna and sea urchin.

03 Oysters are in the name for **Kakigoya**. Get them steamed or simply slurp them up raw. Don't go past their giant scallops either; these are cooked in sake, soy sauce and butter.

02 **East India Curry Company** combines a Japanese-Indian-European curry blend with chunks of meaty, deep-fried tuna. Located on the market's 2nd floor; keep an eye out for a colourful staircase to the left.

05 Hom-estyle *onigiri* (rice-ball snack) and sushi rolls can be found at **Onigiri Marutoyo**. Get the spicy cod roe for a flavourful bite with a kick. These hefty portions will definitely fill you up.

01 Many try to imitate it, but **Yamachō** is the original *tamago-yaki* (egg omelette) on a stick. Lightly sweetened and with the texture of pudding, it's the perfect kick-off snack.

Listings

BEST OF THE REST

Green Spaces & Scenic Views

Yoyogi-kōen

Not Tokyo's prettiest park but definitely its most popular. Weekends are full of picnickers, Frisbee games and the like; look for festivals at the plaza across the street. Free and open 24/7. In Harajuku, adjacent to Meiji-jingū.

Shinjuku-gyoen

With manicured lawns (dotted with cherry trees) this is one of Tokyo's classiest picnic spots. The greenhouse has spectacular orchids. In Shinjuku.

Rikugi-en

An elegant stroll garden with wooded walkways, stone bridges and a teahouse overlooking the central pond. Located in a quiet, north Tokyo residential neighbourhood, and rarely crowded.

Hama-rikyū Onshi-teien

Bayside landscape garden, once part of the shogun's summer villa. Highlights include the teahouse and a magnificent 300-year-old black pine tree. Central (near Ginza).

Tokyo Metropolitan Government Building

Tokyo's landmark city hall in Shinjuku has observatories (at 202m) atop both the south and north towers of Building 1 for views over the city. Free!

Art Museums

Mori Art Museum

Blockbuster shows featuring contemporary artists and movements from both Japan and abroad. Bonus: open late. In Roppongi (part of Roppongi Hills).

TOP Museum

Tokyo's principal photography museum, with an extensive collection of works by Japanese artists. Part of the Yebisu Garden Place complex in Ebisu.

Ukiyo-e Ota Memorial Museum of Art

Ukiyo-e (wood-block prints) presented in seasonal, thematic exhibitions (with English curation notes). Quality reproductions sold in the gift shop. In Harajuku.

Nezu Museum

A renowned collection of Japanese, Chinese and Korean antiquities in a gallery space designed by contemporary architect Kuma Kengo (with a garden out the back). In Aoyama.

Design Festa Gallery

A mish-mash of over 70 exhibition spaces, reflecting the zany creativity of Harajuku. This place is a great haunt to find emerging artists.

Markets

Aoyama Farmers Market

Get acquainted with local farmers and try

Bird and cherry blossoms, Shinjuku-gyoen.

their produce, baked goods and condiments. Open on the weekends; in front of the United Nations University.

Toyosu Market

Tokyo's central wholesale market, where the famous tuna auction is held most mornings. Check the website for access instructions. Tokyo Bay area.

Ameya-Yokochō

Old-school, open-air market (originally a post-WWII black market) with vendors selling everything from fresh seafood to vintage jeans. In Ueno.

Sushi & Classic Japanese

Tonki ¥

Tokyo *tonkatsu* (crumbed pork cutlet) institution for over 80 years. In Meguro; English menu.

Sushi Dai ¥¥

The classic spot for sushi breakfast at the fish market. Note: this is at the market in Toyosu, not Tsukiji. Come very early or expect to queue.

Sahsya Kanetanaka ¥¥

Approachable *kaiseki* (Japanese haute cuisine): elegant lunch sets of seasonal delicacies, with longer courses for dinner (reservations required). In Harajuku; English menu.

Tensuke ¥¥

Popular local tempura spot, famous for its egg tempura that's batter-crisp on the outside and runny in the middle. Expect to queue; in Koenji (west of Shinjuku).

sushi m ¥¥¥

Creative sushi paired with boutique wines and sake (including some truly rare bottles). A memorable splurge in Aoyama. Booking essential; English menu.

KORKUSUNG/SHUTTERSTOCK ©

Ameya-yokochō

Izakaya, Bistros & Gastronomy

Shinsuke ¥¥

Nearly 100-year-old *izakaya* (Japanese pub-eatery) with a long cedar counter, seasonal menu and premium sake. In Ueno. Reservations recommended; English menu.

Narukiyo ¥¥¥

Local favourite *izakaya* serving excellent renditions of all the classics with a side order of punk-rock cheek. In Aoyama. Reservations recommended.

Kabi ¥¥¥

Japanese-meets-Nordic cuisine with an emphasis on fermented ingredients, paired with natural wines and sakes. In Meguro. Reservations required; English menu.

Lodge Bistro Saru ¥¥

Cosy lodge-style bistro occupying a space in residential Meguro. This place specialises in hearty mountain cuisine that's bolstered by local Japanese produce.

Noodles & Sandwiches

Mensho ¥

The Tokyo ramen darling of the moment. Branches near Tokyo Dome City (Kasuga

Station) and in Shibuya (inside Shibuya Parco); vegan options in Shibuya. English menu.

Afuri ¥

Afuri's speciality is *yuzu-shio* ramen (a light, salty broth flavoured with *yuzu,* a type of citrus). Branches around town, but the original is in Ebisu. English menu.

Delifucious ¥

Deluxe fish burgers dreamed up by a former sushi chef. In Shibuya (inside Shibuya Parco). English menu.

Coffee & Tea

Turret Coffee ¥

Tokyo's best latte (get the Turret latte), in Tsukiji. Named for the three-wheeled trucks that used to cruise around the old Tsukiji Market (there's one in the shop).

Fuglen Tokyo ¥

Local hot spot with a cool mid-20th-century Scandi decor and perfect pours of the cafe's signature light-roast, single-origin beans. In Tomigaya (near Shibuya).

Sakurai Japanese Tea Experience ¥¥

Tasting courses that pair different styles and regions of Japanese tea with traditional sweets; reserve for courses. In Aoyama.

Drinks with a View

Two Rooms ¥¥

Tokyo's best terrace, overlooking Harajuku. Call ahead (staff speak English) to reserve a Friday or Saturday night spot under the stars.

New York Bar ¥¥¥

The definitive high-altitude Tokyo night spot, on the 52nd floor of the Park Hyatt in Shinjuku, with sweeping views from the floor-to-ceiling windows.

Craft Beer, Sake & Cocktails

Mikkeller Tokyo ¥¥

Beers from pioneer 'gypsy brewer' Mikkel Borg Bjergsø. In the side streets of Shibuya.

Another 8 ¥¥

Japanese craft beer and small-batch sake in a renovated garage in Meguro. Live DJs on most Friday and Saturday evenings.

Gem by Moto ¥¥

Gem specialises in boutique sakes. Bookings recommended. In Ebisu.

SG Club ¥¥¥

Creative cocktails in Shibuya from award-winning bartender Shingo Gokan. Reserve a seat in the speakeasy-like basement.

Home & Kitchen

Kama-asa

The place to get hand-forged kitchen knives, plus cast-iron cooking ware. Near Asakusa.

Imadeya

Small but mighty wine and liquor shop, with an excellent selection of sake and other made-in-Japan spirits. In the basement of Ginza Six mall.

COMME des GARÇONS

d47 design travel store

Showcase for exceptional regional Japanese artisanship from trendy lifestyle brand D&D Department. In Shibuya.

 Fashion & Vintage

Beams Japan

Several floors of curated Japanese fashion brands, plus original artwork and contemporary crafts. In Shinjuku.

Okura

Contemporary T-shirts and hoodies and also items that riff on older silhouettes, like the trailing sleeves of a kimono, all dyed with indigo. In Daikanyama.

COMME des GARÇONS

Flagship store for designer Kawakubo Rei's ground-breaking label. In Aoyama.

Flamingo

Stocks new and used '40s to '80s America-core pieces. The accessory section is particularly eye-catching. Branches in Harajuku, Shimokitazawa and Kichijoji.

House @Mikiri Hassin

Hidden deep in the side alleys of Harajuku, House stocks an ever-changing selection of experimental Japanese fashion brands. Look for 'ハウス' spelled vertically in neon.

RagTag

This consignment shop is stocked with labels loved by Harajuku shoppers: Vivienne Westwood, Junya Watanabe and more.

 Malls & Department Stores

Coredo Muromachi

Spread over several buildings, with a focus on homewares and gourmet shops. In Nihombashi, one of Tokyo's oldest neighbourhoods.

PICTURE CELLS/SHUTTERSTOCK ©

Coredo Muromachi

Ginza Six

High-end mall with art installations and a branch of Tsutaya Books (with many art, design and travel titles in English).

Mitsukoshi

Classic Ginza department store with an excellent homewares floor and basement gourmet food hall.

 Onsen & Spas

Spa LaQua

Huge spa complex with indoor and outdoor baths fed by natural hot springs, plus a variety of saunas. Part of the Tokyo Dome City complex in central Tokyo (Suidobashi Station).

Kamata Onsen

Old-school public bathhouse famous for its mineral-rich black water, courtesy of underground springs seeped in volcanic ash. In Kamata, a suburb south of Tokyo.

07 Day Trip to NIKKŌ

CULTURE | ADVENTURE | AUTUMN

An unforgettable getaway awaits a mere two-hour train ride from Tokyo. The historic town of Nikkō and neighbouring Kinugawa Onsen are among the best places to embrace nature in the Kanto region, and whether you're looking for culture, action or relaxation, there's plenty to experience. Here's where to begin.

How to

Getting here The Tōbu Nikkō line connects central Tokyo's Asakusa Station directly to Nikkō and Kinugawa Onsen.

When to go Wonderful all year round, but autumn in November gets a special mention.

How much Tōbu Railway (tobu.co.jp/en) offers a variety of travel passes from ¥2040. A night at a ryokan starts from ¥10,000 per person.

Afternoon snack Pop by Nikkō Sakaeya near Tōbu Nikkō Station for *ageyuba manjū* (bean paste wrapped in tofu skin), a local fried delicacy.

0 — 5 km
0 — 2.5 miles
Nikkō National Park
Kinugawa Line Kudari
Kinugawa Onsen
Nantai-san
Tōshō-gū
Chuzenji-ko
Nikkō
Shin-kyō
Imaichi
Kegon-no-taki

Pick Your Path

Worship Set against the backdrop of a lush forest, **Tōshō-gū** is the final resting place of Tokugawa Ieyasu, founder of the Tokugawa shogunate. This Shintō shrine is one of the most elaborate and beautiful in the country and features the best traditional architecture and artisanship.

Nature's wonders Kegon-no-taki is a sight to behold. An hour away by bus from Nikkō Station, visitors can stand on a platform and witness one of Japan's three most beautiful waterfalls cascade 97m from a lake

Above right Tōshō-gū shrine
Right Kegon-no-taki

MOROZ NATALIYA/SHUTTERSTOCK ©

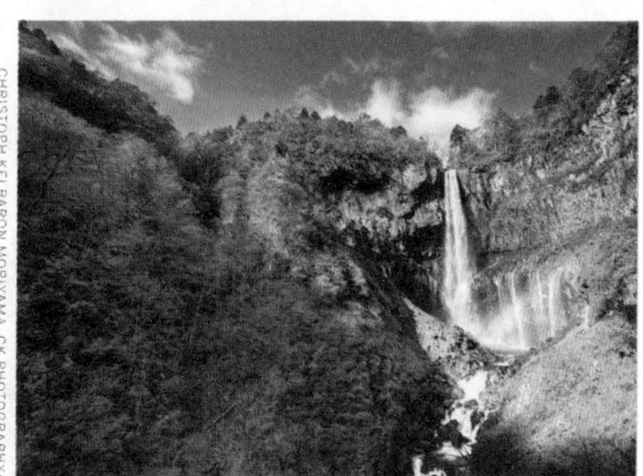

CHRISTOPH KEI BARON MORIYAMA, CK PHOTOGRAPHY/GETTY IMAGES ©

Shin-kyō

In Nikkō, look out for a red arched footbridge extending from the main road towards a forested area. Known as **Shin-kyō** ('sacred bridge') and said to have existed prior to 1636, this Nikko landmark is among the finest bridges in Japan. Snap some photos, or make a trip across and back for a small fee (¥500).

down to the rocks below. Surrounding trees paint the area a different colour each season, and the waterfall freezes solid in winter.

Unwind Relax after a day of sightseeing and trekking at **Kinugawa Onsen**, a hot-springs town near Nikko. Flowing through the centre of town is the long, rocky Kinu-gawa, flanked by hotels and ryokan. Take a dip in the natural hot springs, and enjoy a *kaiseki* (Japanese haute cuisine) dinner with exceptional service.

Set sail Kinugawa Line Kudari offers boat tours, where you'll strap on a safety vest and hop on to a long wooden boat for a drift down the Kinu-gawa. High above are colourful forests and jagged cliffs. The river itself is mostly calm, but sometimes choppy, so you're in for an exciting ride.

08 Side Trip to MT FUJI

HIKING | NATURE | CULTURE

Mt Fuji (3776m) is Japan's tallest mountain, a perfectly formed volcanic cone rising above the clouds, and historically an object of worship. Climbing it is a summer rite of passage, and something most Japanese feel they should do once in their lifetime.

DAILY TRAVEL PHOTOS/SHUTTERSTOCK ©

How to

Cost ¥2000 per climber is required to cover maintenance.

Resources Check news and weather updates (fujisan-climb.jp). Attempting a climb in bad weather can be miserable (at best) and dangerous (at worst).

When to go The climbing season runs from 1 July to 10 September. Try to avoid climbing on weekends and public holidays. Only 4000 climbers are allowed per day.

Connect Mountain huts on the Yoshida Trail have free wi-fi.

JAMOO/SHUTTERSTOCK ©

The Trails

Mt Fuji is divided into 10 'stations' from base to summit, but the main hiking trails start halfway up, at the fifth station (as far as the roads go). There are four routes: Yoshida, Subashiri, Fujinomiya and Gotemba. Of these, the **Yoshida Trail**, which starts from the Fuji Subaru Line 5th Station, is by far and away the most popular route, as it's the one that is most easily accessed via public transport from Tokyo. It also has the most amenities en route (toilets, first aid stations, huts from which to buy water etc), and it is also the most crowded. For this trail, allow six to eight hours to summit and three to four hours to descend.

The **Subashiri Trail** is famous for its *sunabashiri* ('sand run') descent from the seventh station (sunglasses and a

DOWRAIK/SHUTTERSTOCK ©

Trail Access

During climbing season, there are direct buses from Shinjuku Bus Terminal (2½ hours) and Kawaguchi-ko Station (one hour) to the Fuji-Subaru Line 5th Station (for the Yoshida Trail). Access for the Subashiri and Gotemba Trails is via bus from Gotemba Station; for the Fujinomiya Trail, buses run from Mishima Station.

Above left Mt Fuji and Kawaguchi-ko **Above** Reaching the summit on the Yoshida Trail **Left** Hiking the Subashiri Trail scarf or bandana to protect from dust are recommended). The **Fujinomiya Trail** is the shortest, and convenient if you're travelling from or onwards to points west (such as Kyoto). The **Gotemba Trail** has the distinction of being the longest and the least crowded (with the fewest amenities).

Note that the descending trail is often different from the ascending one. The mountain is well signposted in English, though fog at the top can make it easy to miss signs.

The Climb

Most of the climb takes place above the tree line, on ground scoria ranging in hue from dark brown to a fiery red. As you get higher, the trail becomes steeper, at points requiring hikers to scramble over boulders.

Mountain Huts

Breaking up the hike with a stay in a mountain hut is highly recommended, especially to help acclimatise to the altitude. Two popular

What to Pack

Conditions can change dramatically on Mt Fuji and it can be freezing (literally) on the summit. Pack clothes appropriate for cold and wet weather; gloves can also protect your hands from sharp rocks. If you're walking at night, you'll need a headlamp. While rare, falling rocks have caused deadly accidents; free helmet rentals are available at the sixth-station Mt Fuji Safety Guidance Center on the Yoshida Trail. Huts, located at each station, sell food and water (¥500 per 500mL bottle; cash only); they also have toilets (¥200; toilet paper, but not soap, is provided) and free wi-fi. Rubbish must be taken away.

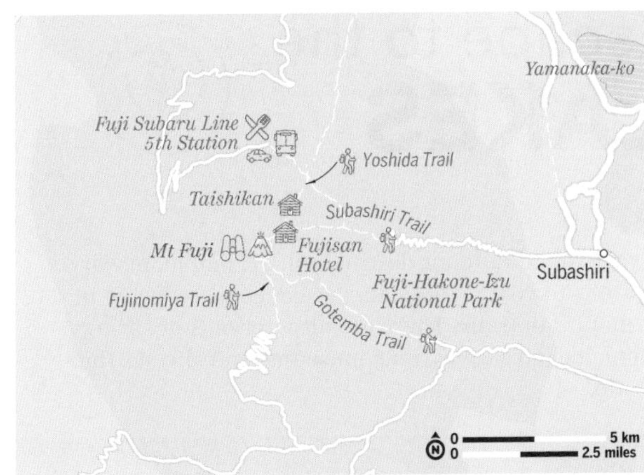

Left Sunrise at Mt Fuji's summit
Below Mountain huts at Mt Fuji's 7th Station

ones are **Fujisan Hotel** (fujisanhotel.com); at the Original 8th Station, where the Yoshida and Subashiri Trails meet; and **Taishikan** (mfi.or.jp/taisikan) at the lower 8th Station on the Yoshida Trail). The latter can do vegetarian and halal meals. Bookings essential.

Sunrise at the Summit

For many climbers, the goal is to see *goraiko* (the rising sun) from the summit, which happens sometime between 4.30am and 5.30am. Pre-dawn, the mountain is at its most crowded and walking slows to a crawl on the Yoshida Trail, especially above the eighth station. To account for this, you'll need to start out from the fifth station at 8pm or 9pm. Or, if you're staying at a mountain hut, depart from the eighth station around midnight or from the Original 8th Station (Hon-Hachigome) at 2am.

Still, it's often too foggy at the summit to see much. It's also cold and windy. Clearer views (with fewer crowds) are likelier from the stations below. Weather permitting, sunrise is visible from anywhere on the Yoshida Trail above the sixth station.

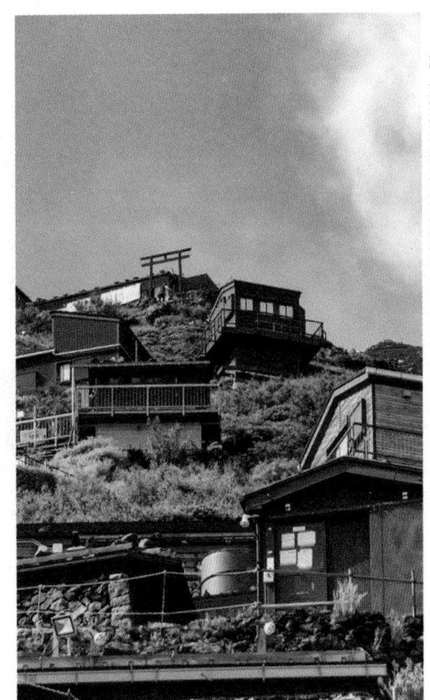

09 Escape to the LAKES

HIKING | NATURE | CULTURE

Fuji Five Lakes is a year-round outdoor destination. Mt Fuji looms large here, as one of the main reasons to visit is to see its perfect cone, reflected in the lakes or from surrounding mountain trails. There are also onsen (hot springs) and other natural phenomena like lava caves, plus museums and shrines that bring the history of Fuji to life.

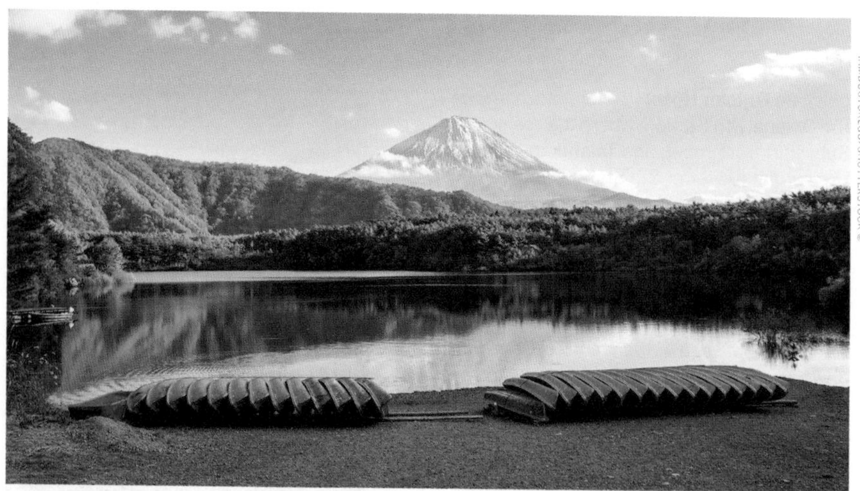

IAMDOCTOREGG/SHUTTERSTOCK ©

How to

When to go Year-round. Fuji Five Lakes is most crowded during the Golden Week holiday (late April to early May), summer season and late autumn (when the leaves change colour). In winter, snow is possible at higher elevations on some hiking trails.

Getting around If you are relying on public transport, be sure to check bus schedules in advance as some routes run infrequently.

DARKZ DIESEL/SHUTTERSTOCK ©

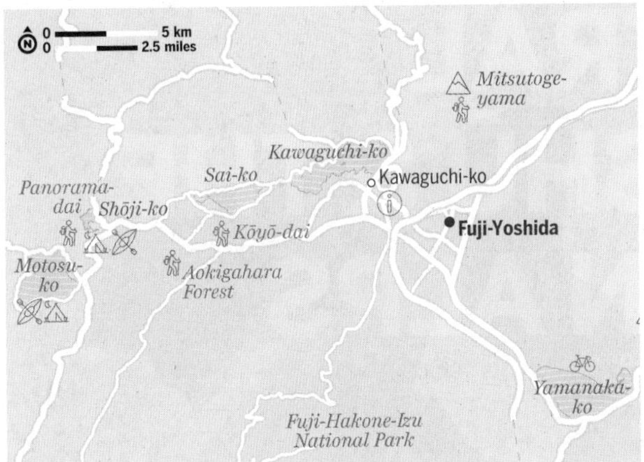

Above left Autumn colours at Sai-ko
Below left Cycling the shores of Yamanaka-ko

The Lakes

Kawaguchi-ko The most developed of the lakes is Kawaguchko. It is the easiest to reach by public transport and the best place to base yourself if you don't have a car. Many hiking trails are reachable here by bus, and there are good views of Mt Fuji from the north shore of the lake.

Sai-ko Just west of Kawaguchi-ko, Sai-ko is quieter and the jumping-off point for visiting caves formed by ancient lava flows, and the **Aokigahara Forest**. A flat, 3km trail through Aokigahara Forest connects two caves, Sai-ko Komoriana and Fugaku Fukestu.

Further west still is **Shōji-ko** (the smallest of the lakes) and **Motosu-ko** (the deepest). It's very quiet out this way, with just a handful of small hotels and campsites, many of which rent canoes or kayaks in the summer. While swimming is prohibited in all of the lakes, because of extremely cold temperatures just below the surface, Shoji-ko does have a small sandy beach where you can dip your toes.

The views of Mt Fuji reflected in either Shōji-ko or Motosu-ko are stunning; it's the view from Motosu-ko's northwest shore that is depicted on the back of the ¥1000 banknote.

Yamanaka-ko The largest lake is Yamanaka-ko, which is east of Kawaguchi-ko. Like Kawaguchi-ko, it has a lot of development, especially on the southern shore. One fun thing to do here is rent a bicycle and cycle the 14km bike path around the lake.

Best Hikes

Panorama-dai (1328m) A short, all-level hike (6km) with a dead-on view of Mt Fuji at the top. The trail starts at the Panorama-dai-shita bus stop, on the shore of Shoji-ko.

Kōyō-dai (1165m) A half-day trek (12km) with undulating elevation changes and views of Fuji, Aokigahara and Sai-ko. It's particularly recommended in late autumn, when Aokigahara's trees blaze red. Nearest bus stop: Koyo-dai-iriguchi.

Mitsutoge-yama (1785m) A local favourite hike through pretty native broadleaf forest, with views of Mt Fuji and over Kawaguchi-ko from the summit. There are a few trails, including one that picks up from the Fuji Viewing Platform, so you can tailor this one to your level.

CENTRAL HONSHŪ & THE JAPAN ALPS

OUTDOORS | HIKING | HISTORY

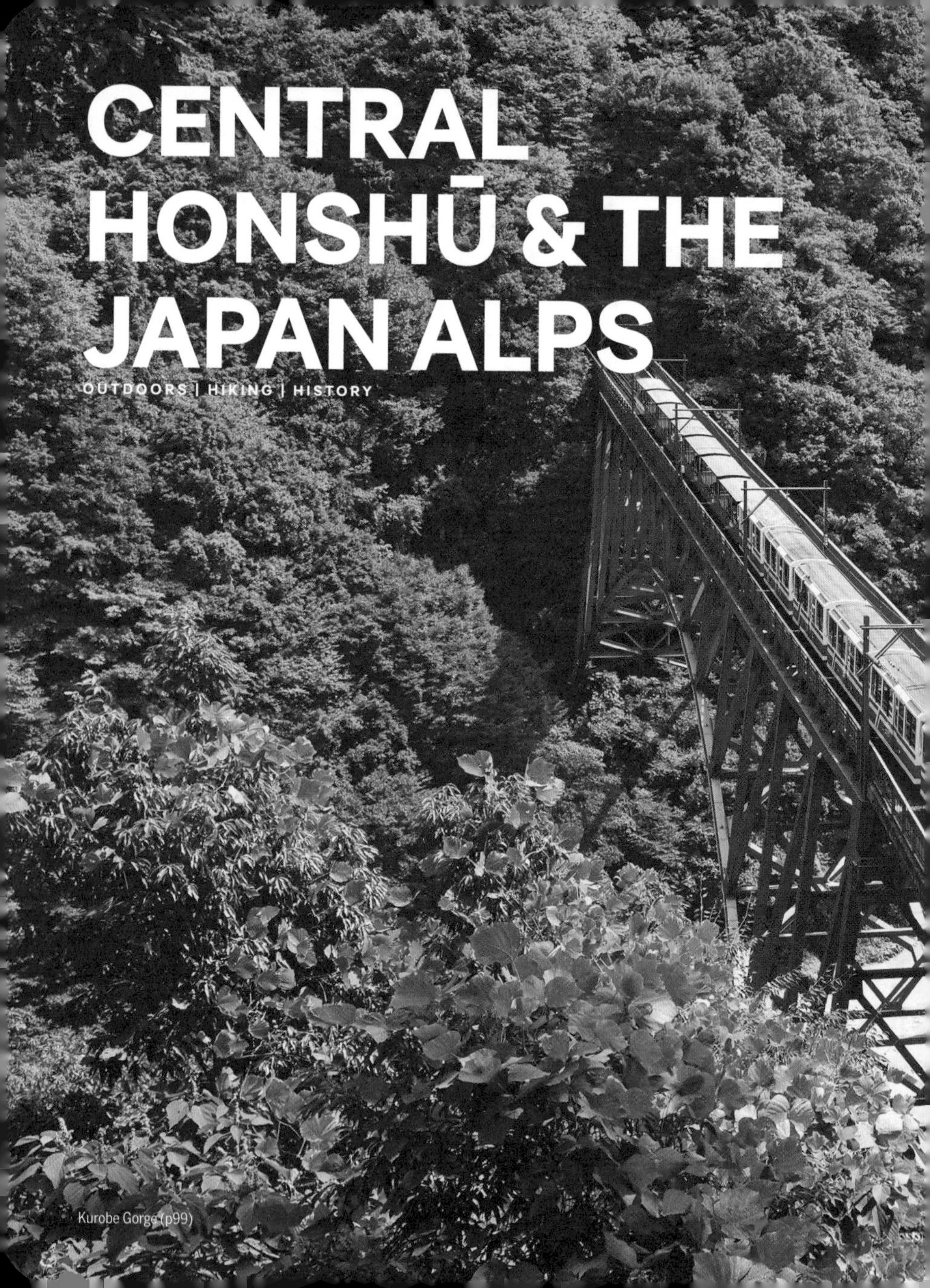

Kurobe Gorge (p99)

Journey to the remote villages at the foot of the Alps: **Ainokura** and **Suganuma** (p93)
About 2hrs by train and bus from Kanazawa

Visit **Ogimachi village** for the winter light-up event (p93)
1½hrs by bus from Toyama

Spend a night at a thatched-roof hut in **Shirakawa-gō** (p90)
1½hrs by bus from Toyama

CENTRAL HONSHŪ & THE JAPAN ALPS

Trip Builder

Escape the bustling cities and go on an adventure into the Japan Alps. Witness the centuries-old, unchanged beauty of Japan when you trek along old forest paths, climb mountains and visit Edo-period villages.

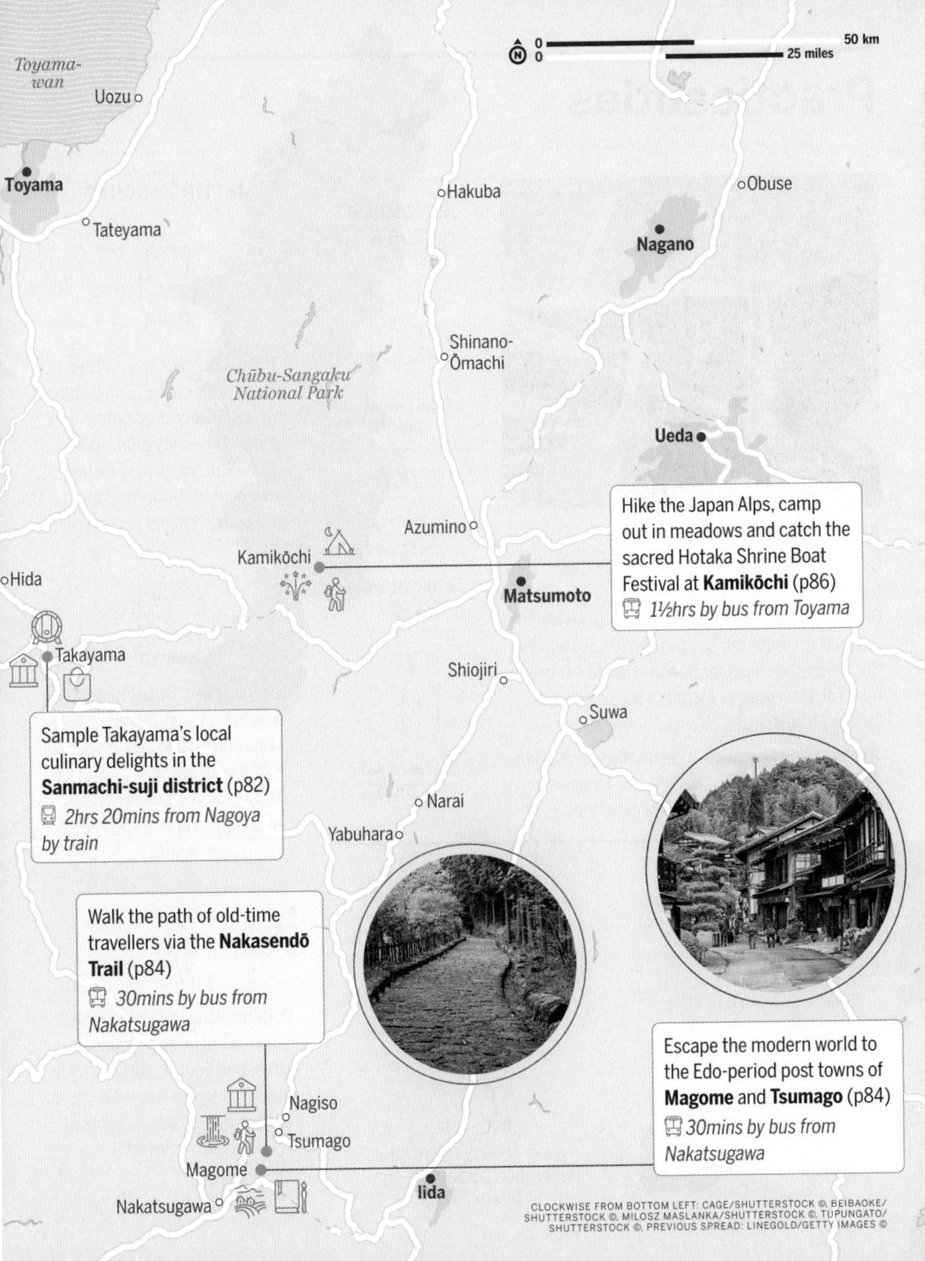

Hike the Japan Alps, camp out in meadows and catch the sacred Hotaka Shrine Boat Festival at **Kamikōchi** (p86)
1½hrs by bus from Toyama

Sample Takayama's local culinary delights in the **Sanmachi-suji district** (p82)
2hrs 20mins from Nagoya by train

Walk the path of old-time travellers via the **Nakasendō Trail** (p84)
30mins by bus from Nakatsugawa

Escape the modern world to the Edo-period post towns of **Magome** and **Tsumago** (p84)
30mins by bus from Nakatsugawa

Practicalities

WIRE DOG/SHUTTERSTOCK ©

ARRIVING

Central Japan International Airport Get to central Nagoya by bus (¥1200, 80 minutes) or train (¥1230, 30 minutes). Buy tickets upon arrival; no reservation required. The bus arrives at Meitetsu Bus Terminal – ideal for transferring to a highway bus. The train goes to Meitetsu Nagoya Station for easy transfer to JR trains.

JR Nagoya Station Reach destinations around the Japan Alps from here by transferring to express trains and shinkansen (bullet trains; pictured).

HOW MUCH FOR A

Set meal ¥1500

Coffee at a cafe ¥500

Bottle of sake ¥2000

WHEN TO GO

MAR–MAY
National parks reopen in April; cherry-blossom season is from late March.

JUN–AUG
Cool and temperate, ideal for outdoor activities; some crowds in late summer.

SEP–NOV
Fine weather with cool breeze; see autumn leaves from late October.

DEC–FEB
Heavy snowfall from late December; busiest season at Shirakawa-gō.

GETTING AROUND

Train A quicker way to travel across prefectures. Timetables are easily accessed online and a spot is usually guaranteed. However, trains may be less frequent in more rural areas and some walking is required.

Highway bus Buses can often take you straight to your destination. Shirakawa-gō and Kamikōchi are best accessed by bus. Some buses can't be reserved, so arrive early to get a spot.

Walking A fair bit of walking is required between stations, bus stops and your destination. All public transport will leave right on the dot, so allow plenty of time to head back.

EATING & DRINKING

Takayama This is the food heart of the Alps, where you can have beautifully marbled Hida beef (pictured), followed by exquisite locally brewed sake. Save space in your stomach, because with the variety of delicious street food here, you'll be eating all day.

Yaki-zakana A common dish found across the region is *yaki-zakana* (grilled fish; pictured). You'll find it served whole, head and all, and sometimes skewered on a stick. Many traditional restaurants circle the skewered fish around an *irori* (hearth), giving it a woody, charred flavour.

Must-try street food

Hida Kotte-ushi (p98)

Best soba noodles

Keiseian (p98)

CONNECT & FIND YOUR WAY

Wi-fi Get free wi-fi at stations, visitor centres and most tourist sites. To stay connected, rent a pocket wi-fi or buy a prepaid SIM card from the airport or online at Japan Wireless (japan-wireless.com).

Navigation Use Google Maps for detailed public transport schedules and walking routes. Large maps are common around town if you need to get oriented.

REGIONAL TRAVEL PASS

Get unlimited rides on JR trains using the Alpine-Takayama-Matsumoto Area Tourist Pass (¥23,800; touristpass.jp). It's valid for five days and available through travel agents or major JR stations.

WHERE TO STAY

You may be checking in and out of hotels on your trip through the Alps – stay at accessible towns to keep that to a minimum.

Place	Pros/Cons
Nagoya	Major transport hub, with a range of hotels and guesthouses to suit any budget.
Takayama	Accessible from Nagoya; good base for taking the bus to Shirakawa-gō and Gokayama.
Kamikōchi	A selection of camping grounds, lodges and hotels are located within the national park.
Shirakawa-gō	*Gasshō-zukuri* (thatched-roof huts) offer a special stay in the quiet countryside.
Magome or Tsumago	Rest and relax here if walking the Nakasendō Trail.

MONEY

Shops in rural areas seldom accept cards, although some might. Carry at least ¥10,000 in cash at all times. Head to the visitor centre in any area to look for tourist discount tickets and transport passes.

10 Tastes of TAKAYAMA

SIGHTS | FOOD | CRAFTS

A gateway to the Japan Alps, Takayama is a small city bursting with character, history and number of local culinary specialities, from fragrant sake to world-class beef. A stroll through Takayama's old-fashioned and picturesque streets is a feast for all the senses. Here is what you can see, taste and discover in one of central Japan's prettiest cities.

PIXHOUND/SHUTTERSTOCK ©

How to

Getting here Takayama is easily accessible from Nagoya, Kyoto and Osaka on the JR Hida Limited Express. From Tokyo it is four or five hours by train, or you can take the train to Matsumoto and then a bus.

When to go Takayama Festival, in mid-April and mid-October, is one of Japan's best; sake lovers should visit in March for the Nombe Festival.

Sanmachi-suji district The beautifully preserved old district is full of shops and historical buildings dating from the Edo period.

BLANSCAPE/SHUTTERSTOCK ©

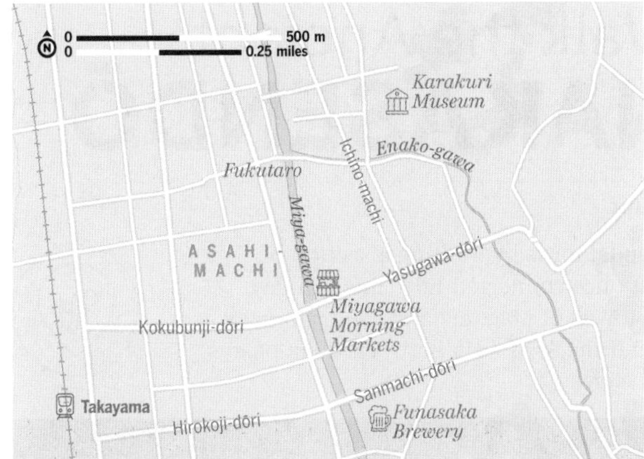

Fine (rice) wine Clear water collected from the northern Japan Alps and locally harvested rice go into every batch of the exceptional sake brewed in Takayama. There are six individual breweries within the town, each offering tasting sessions for their signature sake; **Funasaka Brewery** is one of the more popular. To spot a brewery, look out for a *sugidama* out the front.

Street food The aroma of charcoal fires and food on the grill wafts through Takayama, a place that is every street-food lover's dream. Must-try items include Hida beef skewers and *goheimochi* (rice cakes slathered in sweet miso served on a popsicle stick). Look out for some other treats too: juicy Hida beef buns, crispy beef croquettes and adorable cat-faced *manjū* (buns filled with sweet-bean paste). The **Miyagawa Morning Market** is a good place to get your fill.

Woodcarvings and lacquerware Lacquerware unique to Takayama is known as *Hida shunkei* – dinnerware coated in a clear lacquer that draws out the natural beauty of the wood underneath. Wooden ornaments can be found in shops around the city too, hand-carved by artisans out of yew using only chisels in a method called *ichii ittobori*.

Clockwork puppets Takayama's **Karakuri Museum** is a testament to the town's artisanship. Each *karakuri ningyō* puppet housed here has a clockwork mechanism, and depicts a well-known figure from Japanese history and mythology. See them in action at the museum, or catch them on a float during the **Takayama Festival** in spring and autumn.

Above left Sanmachi-suji district
Below left Takayama Festival

Spotting a Sugidama

A fairly common sight in Takayama, a large sphere hanging above the entrance to a building is how you identify a sake brewery, but the *sugidama* is significant in one other way. Fashioned out of fresh cedar sprigs, the *sugidama* starts out bright green when it's first put in place. The eye-catching ornament is a brewery's way of signalling to passers-by that the year's brewing is complete and that it's time to enjoy fresh sake. Once put up, the *sugidama* is left for a year, slowly turning brown until it's replaced at the same time next year.

11 Walk the Ancient NAKASENDŌ

HISTORY | WALKING | NATURE

Travel the way of feudal lords by walking a section of the Nakasendō, a trail that once connected Edo (modern-day Tokyo) to Kyoto. The post towns of Magome and Tsumago have been lovingly preserved, and the 8km walk between them passes through forest and countryside.

THIRAWATANA PHAISALRATANA/SHUTTERSTOCK ©

How to

Getting here Easiest access to the Kiso Valley is from Nagoya on the JR Chūō line. From Nakatsugawa Station, it's a 30-minute bus ride to Magome.

When to go Any season, but winter may require extra gear.

Easy trekking Head from Magome towards Tsumago for a mostly downhill walk. A luggage-forwarding service is available at ¥1000 per piece.

A memento Buy a special card (¥300) at Magome's visitors centre and get it stamped in Tsumago for a certificate of your journey.

What are Post Towns?

Post towns, or *shuku-ba,* played a crucial role during the Edo period, when travel was slow and rest stops were vital. They were also responsible for forwarding goods and letters onwards. Because *shukuba* means 'a place of lodging' in Japanese, the name of each town is followed by the suffix *-juku* (eg Magome-juku).

05 Finally, you will arrive at **Tsumago**, another pretty post town with many wonderful historic buildings, shops and inns; some of them can be booked online (japaneseguesthouses.com) if you want to lodge in the old-fashioned way.

04 Carry on downhill along cobblestone paths, slipping through serene forests dotted with ancient monuments. Later pass the gushing **Odaki** and **Medaki** waterfalls, where there are also toilets.

01 Start at the town of **Magome**, soaking in the old-town atmosphere as you wander its beautiful quaint streets lined by well-preserved shops, inns and teahouses, and prepare for the three-hour walk ahead.

03 From here it is a short and gentle climb up to **Magome Pass**, which at 790m is the highest point of the walk. A rustic teahouse serves noodles and refreshments.

02 After exploring the town, it's time to get moving. The walk begins at the eastern edge of the settlement and the **Magome Lookout**, with sweeping mountain views.

0 — 1 km
0 — 0.5 miles

FUKEZ84/SHUTTERSTOCK ©

12 Adventures at KAMIKŌCHI

ALPINE VIEWS | NATURE | HIKING

The term 'Japan Alps' was coined right here at Kamikōchi, where snowy mountain vistas, reflective ponds and green meadows converge to create an otherworldly paradise. Pack your outdoor gear and hiking boots – it's time to climb mountains, splash in the rivers and camp out under the stars right in the heart of the Japan Alps.

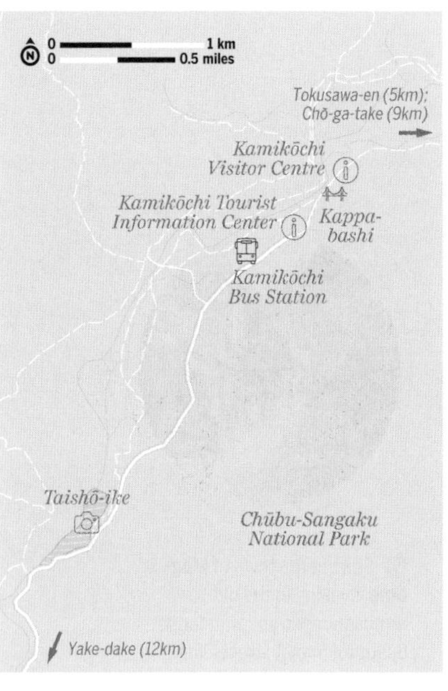

How to

Getting here Catch a direct bus from Nagano Station (2½ hours). A bus trip from Takayama is also possible, stopping first at Hirayu Onsen (1½ hours).

When to go During the cool, verdant summer; the park is open April to November.

Bundle up Temperatures can dip below 10°C, even in summer. Pack a warm jacket and rain gear.

Where to stay Set up camp at designated areas, or book a nearby lodge or hotel.

Mirror ponds, alpine views Kamikōchi's nature will take your breath away. The sky and the mountains are reflected in perfect symmetry at **Taishō-ike**, formed with the eruption of Yake-dake. Take your time walking across **Kappa-bashi**, an iconic bridge on the sparkling Azusa-gawa near the bus terminal – spectacular alpine views unfold on either side.

Hiking the Japan Alps Beginner and expert hikers alike can attempt the many trekking routes in this vast national park. Those inexperienced can make a leisurely trek to **Tokusawa** to see an alpine meadow and a

Above right Hiker, Japan Alps
Right Taishō-ike

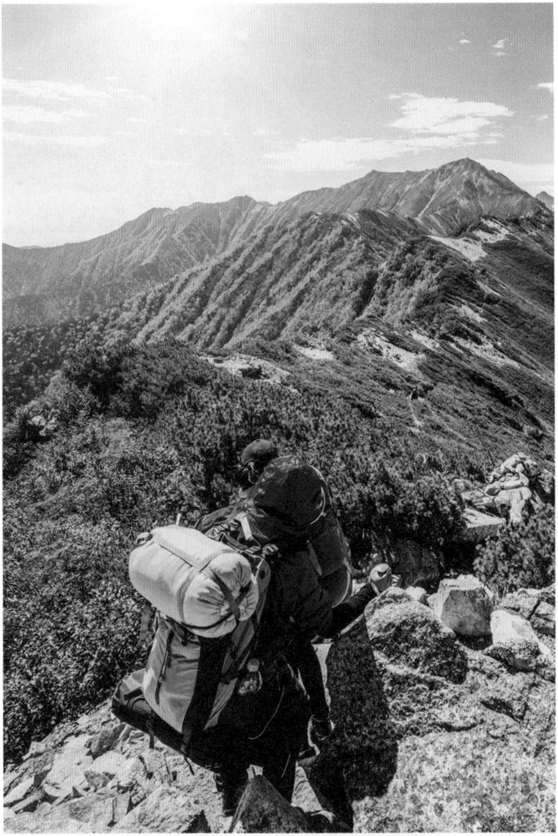

 **Expert Tips**

Those looking for a more rigorous hike can try the journey up to the **Karasawa Col**. Come in early spring with crampons!

Adventurous travellers can try the **Yari-ga-take ascent**, followed by a hair-raising traverse of the **Daikiretto ridge**. Technical climbers will also enjoy rock climbing at the **Byōbu Iwa rock face**.

■ **Tips by William Habington**
freelance writer, translator and expert on Kamikōchi. @nokori3byo

side of rocky Mae-hotaka-dake. Seasoned hikers can try climbing **Chō-ga-take** or **Yake-dake**, among other peaks. More advanced trails require an overnight stay in a tent or cabin, plus filling out a trekking itinerary (go-nagano.net/climbing).

Festivals The most notable events are the **Kaizansai** (mountain opening) ceremony in April, when the park first opens to visitors, and the **Myōjin-ike Ofune Matsuri** (Hotaka Shrine Boat Festival) in October, when ceremony boats sail across the pond of Myōjin-ike. Both are Shintō ceremonies, performed to pray for safe passage through the mountains and to give thanks.

Hiking in Japan

STRAP ON YOUR BOOTS AND EXPLORE JAPAN'S OUTDOORS

Over 70% of Japan is mountainous and criss-crossed with walking trails, making it one of the world's great hiking destinations – a surprising backdrop to the country's densely populated cities. From remote wilderness treks in Hokkaidō to gentle nature trails near Tokyo and the other big cities, there are hikes to suit all abilities.

Left Tateyama Kurobe Alpine Route
Centre Kamikōchi (p86)
Right Mt Minami summit

While the majority of Japan's population now lives in the cities, nature and an appreciation of the outdoors remain an important facet of Japanese culture, and for many people hiking is a popular pastime, allowing them to escape the cramped confines of urban life and enjoy the fresh air and scenic views that Japan's many mountains offer in abundance. Mt Fuji is of course familiar to most; at 3776m it is Japan's tallest peak, a national icon and a hiking goal for many serious (and casual) peak-baggers, both from at home and abroad. However, the official hiking season is short (July to early September) and, in all honesty, it is far from Japan's most scenic or enjoyable hike – many argue that it is better viewed from afar than actually climbed.

Central Japan is home to the North (Kita), Central (Chūō) and Southern (Minami) Alps, three large mountain ranges collectively known as the Japan Alps, which stretch north–south across the width of the main island, from the Sea of Japan all the way to the Pacific coast. These ranges are home to all of Japan's highest peaks (other than Mt Fuji) over 3000m in altitude, and offer a great variety of landscapes, including steaming volcanoes, rocky knife-edged ridges, perennial snowfields and glaciers, secluded forest valleys and wildflower-covered plateaus. Takayama and Matsumoto are the main gateway cities to the Alps, with the small alpine resort of Kamikōchi (p86) a popular base for adventures deeper into the mountains. Hikes in the Alps range from short day walks to intense multiday trips, and while some of the trails are very rugged and remote, there is a good network of mountain huts that provide shelter, food and respite from the elements.

SUCHART BOONYAVECH/SHUTTERSTOCK ©

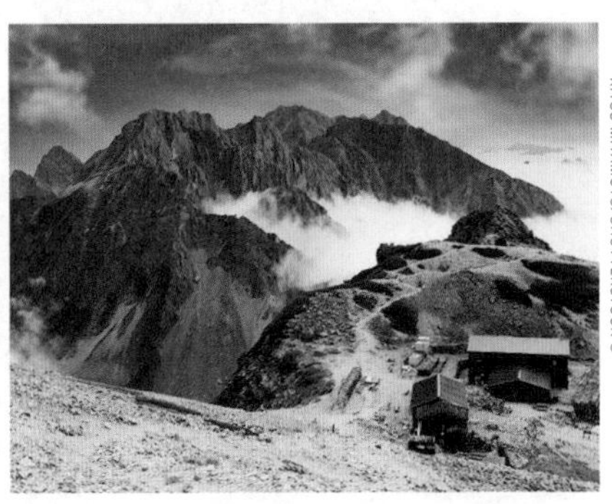
RITSU MIYAMOTO/SHUTTERSTOCK ©

The Japan Alps are undoubtedly one of Japan's premier hiking hot spots, but almost anywhere you travel in the country there are excellent hikes to be had; Hokkaidō offers true wilderness experiences in Daisetsuzan and Shiretoko national parks (p205); Tōhoku is dotted with shapely lone peaks; Kantō (Tokyo area) has many interesting and easy-to-access day hikes; Kansai (Kyoto and Osaka) and the Kii Peninsula (p144) are famous for the ancient Kumano Kodō pilgrimage trails; and in the far southwest of the country, Kyūshū is home to numerous volcanoes and onsen, and the forested island of Yakushima (p186) is home to some of Japan's oldest *sugi* (cedar) trees. The *hyakumeizan* – or Japan's 100 Famous Mountains – is a list of venerated peaks spread across the country, each one notable for either its shape, history or character, and climbing them all is a goal for many Japanese hikers.

The Japan Alps are undoubtedly one of Japan's premier hiking hot spots, but almost anywhere you travel in the country there are excellent hikes to be had.

The best seasons in Japan tend to be spring and autumn, as unless you get up high into the alpine zone, summers tend to be uncomfortably hot and humid below around 2500m. Hiking in the snows of winter is only for those with the correct knowledge, gear and experience. The Yamap app is useful and popular for downloading trail maps and checking recent trip reports; *Hiking and Trekking the Japan Alps and Mt Fuji* (Cicerone Press) is a recommended guidebook for detailed information.

Mountain Huts

Japan has a fairly extensive network of *yama-goya* (mountain huts), particularly in the Japan Alps. They come in many guises, ranging from unstaffed and basic emergency shelters to large, staffed and relatively luxurious lodgings with bedding and meals. In the Alps huts are open from around May to October, and cost between ¥6000 and ¥12,000 for one night with breakfast and dinner; it is usually advisable to book ahead either by phone or sometimes email. Huts operate on 'mountain time', so check-in is early afternoon, dinner is served from 5pm, lights out at 8pm, and many hikers are up at 3am!

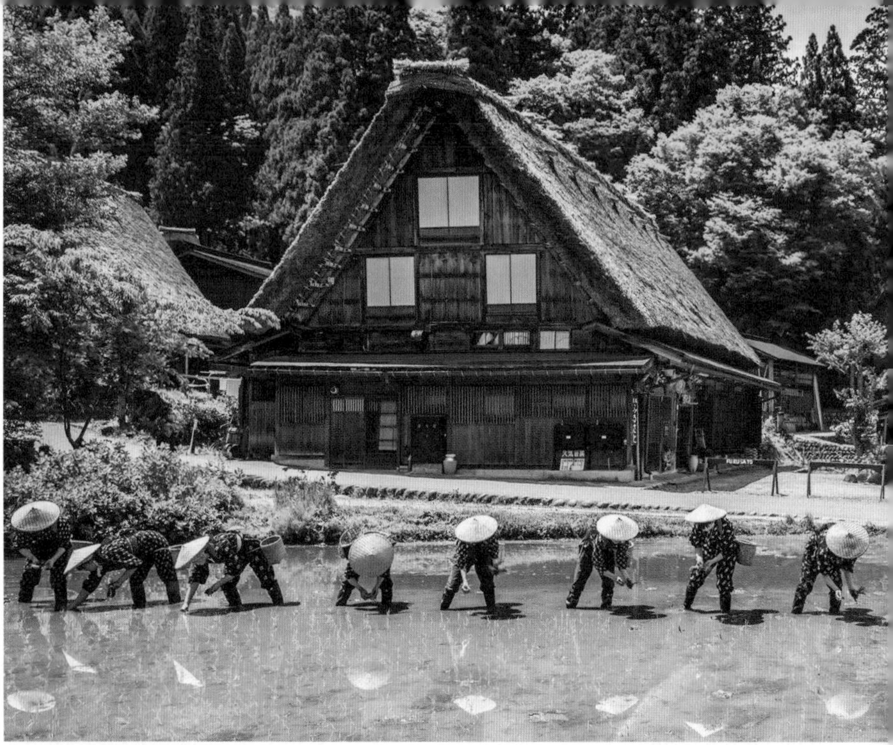

13 A Slice of Mountain VILLAGE LIFE

Nestled in a valley in the mountainous areas of Shirakawa-gō and Gokayama are thousand-year-old villages with picture-perfect countryside views and rustic architecture. Stay under the sloping roofs of the *gasshō-zukuri* huts and get a taste of the quiet life in this remote region.

RPBAIAO/SHUTTERSTOCK ©

How to

Getting here & around Shirakawa-gō is accessible by bus from Nagoya, Takayama, Toyama and Kanazawa. Buses also go from Shirakawa-gō to Gokayama.

When to go Visit in winter (December to February) for spectacular snowy scenery, or in summer (June to August) when the climate is cool and comfortable.

Coffee and crafts Shop for local crafts and warm up with a coffee at **Shingedō** in Ogimachi village.

JOINTSTAR/SHUTTERSTOCK ©

Fascinating Farmhouses

The remote mountain villages of **Shirawkkawa-gō** and **Gokayama** lie nestled in the foothills of the mighty Haku-san, one of Japan's three sacred peaks, and are famed for a unique building style found only here. Known as *gasshō-zukkuri*, these large wooden farmhouses have steep thatched roofs, designed to withstand and shed the large dumps of snow common in this region. Constructed without using any nails, the roof space was traditionally used for cultivating silkworms, and some of the area's remaining houses are more than 250 years old. Some of the farmhouses now operate as family-run guesthouses (called *minshuku*), and a stay at one can make your trip that extra bit special – **Kidoya** is both cosy and welcoming.

What's in the Name?

The steep sloping thatched roofs of the village farmhouses are the only ones of this kind found in Japan. The houses derived their name from the word *gasshō,* which in Japanese means 'prayer hands', implying that the buildings resemble two hands pressed together in prayer.

JOMNICHA/SHUTTERSTOCK ©

Above left Rice farmers, Shirawkawa-gō
Left Winter light-up event, Shirawkawa-gō
Above *Gasshō-zukuri hut*, Shirawkawa-gō

Stay the Night

Spend the day exploring the villages, then check in at your chosen farmhouse and warm up by the flaming *irori* (hearth) while your host prepares a dinner with ingredients fresh from the river and fields nearby. You may share the farmhouse with other guests and the host's family – it's a chance to make conversation over dinner around the hearth. At night, curl up on a futon laid out on tatami mats. Wake up to the sound of birds and splendid mountain views. All *gasshō-zukuri* houses retain their traditional, rustic interior, but most are fitted out with modern Western-style toilets and good bathing facilities. All guests are limited to a night's stay at each farmhouse, and all payments must be made in cash; you can make reservations online (japaneseguesthouses.com).

World Heritage Villages

Three villages around the border between Gifu and Toyama prefectures make up one of

Local Cuisine

River-fish shioyaki Freshly caught fish from the nearby Shō-gawa, skewered whole, generously salted and grilled on a traditional *irori* (hearth).

Goheimochi Rice dumplings slathered in a locally produced, sweet-tasting miso paste, skewered and grilled over charcoal. Sweet, salty and fragrant, all at the same time!

Hōba-miso Meat and vegetables covered in sweet miso paste, set atop a dried mulberry leaf and placed over a small charcoal burner to cook. A must-try.

Hida beef Beautifully marbled, melt-in-your-mouth beef from prized cattle raised within the region. Try it grilled, as *sukiyaki* hotpot or with *hōba-miso*.

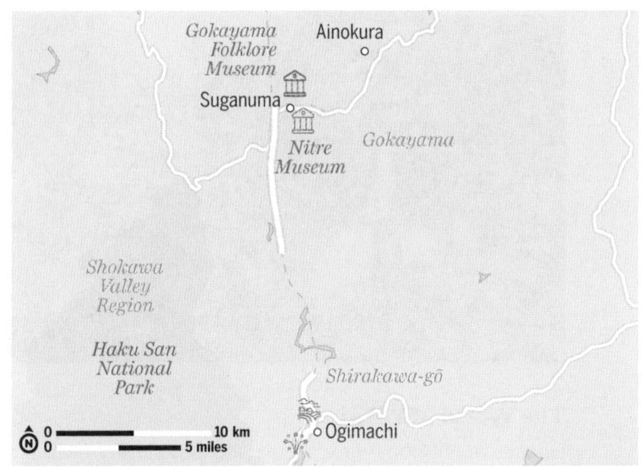

Left *Hida beef* on *hōba-miso*
Below Gokayama

Japan's most prominent UNESCO World Heritage Sites. The most famous is Ogimachi village, located in Shirakawa-gō district, while the villages of Ainokura and Suganuma belong to the Gokayama area.

Ogimachi village has the largest number of *gasshō-zukuri* huts, and is also the most visited. The region is a popular place to visit throughout the year, but particularly in winter when the snow makes everything look more magical; it's also nice in summer and autumn when the villages are a little quieter. A winter light-up event takes place in Ogimachi on select weekends in January and February. Demand is high and reservations are required, but spending a night at a farmhouse in Ogimachi village guarantees you a spot.

Ainokura is the largest – with around 20 farmhouses – and most remote of the villages in the Gokayama area. Here you can observe the art of making traditional Gokayama *washi* (handmade paper), as well as making your own *washi* in a workshops; no reservation required.

Suganuma is a quiet village with nine *gasshō-zukuri* houses. The **Gokayama Folklore Museum** has exhibits showcasing daily life in the village, and the **Nitre Museum** houses tools used for nitre production, a former major industry in Gokayama.

The Mythical Creatures of Japan

DIVE INTO THE MYSTERIOUS WORLD OF YŌKAI

At the centre of Kamikōchi is a stately wooden bridge, Kappa-bashi. When it was built is unclear, but it was immortalised in the 1927 novel, *Kappa,* by Ryūnosuke Akutagawa. A creature that dwells in the watery depths, the *kappa* is but one of Japan's spirits of the unknown.

Left *Tanuki*
Centre Illustration of *Yotsuya kaidan,* a 19th-century ghost story
Right *Kappa*

KUREMO/SHUTTERSTOCK ©

The World of Yōkai

Ghostly apparitions, inexplicable phenomena, animals that maybe aren't what they seem – these are what Japan calls *yōkai*. Every culture has its own ghosts and spirits, but it isn't an exaggeration to say that Japan seemingly has a *yōkai* version of everything, from completely made-up monsters to everyday objects and furry critters.

Haunted Objects

The popularity of *kaidan,* or the telling of ghost stories, was believed to have emerged during the Edo period. It was represented in written stories, drawings and *ukiyo-e* (wood-block prints). Stories of possessed daily objects were commonplace – a lantern that looks a little ghostly? It might be a *chōchin-obake,* with eyes, an open mouth and a lolling tongue. Umbrellas can be *yōkai* too; a popular character through the ages is the *kasa-obake,* a cyclops umbrella with two arms and a leg. Unlike some monsters that still carry an air of mystery, very little suggests that people believed these apparitions to be real, and they were possibly not even meant to frighten but merely entertain.

Animal Spirits

Even animals are not exempt from gaining *yōkai* status. A popular animal that is sometimes considered a *yōkai* is the Japanese racoon-dog, *tanuki*. It's a shape-shifting creature known for mischief, and there are tales of *tanuki* changing into tea kettles, humans and even Buddhist monks. Prominent folk tales like 'Kachi-kachi Yama' and 'Bunbuku Chagama' feature a *tanuki* playing pranks on people or generally being up to no good.

ARTOKOLORO/ALAMY STOCK PHOTO ©

AKSARA.K/SHUTTERSTOCK ©

Ghostly Apparitions

No ghost story is complete without haunting apparitions, and popular Japanese stories both modern and old are full of these. A woman with long flowing hair in a white kimono drifting alone on a cold winter night is *yuki-onna* (snow woman), ready to lure men into their cold graves. Horror-movie favourite Sadako from *The Ring* can also trace her origins back to a kind of Japanese ghost called *onryō*, a vengeful spirit crawling back from the afterlife to exact revenge.

> Japan seemingly has a *yōkai* version of everything, from completely made-up monsters to everyday objects and furry critters.

Fictitious Monsters

The *kappa* is perhaps the most popular example of a *yōkai*, appearing as a sometimes cute and mostly harmless character in anime and video games, as well as being Kappa-bashi's namesake. Often described as a slimy water creature with a beak, a shell on its back, and a dish on its head (plus a penchant for cucumbers), the *kappa* might not sound very frightening – until you hear of the sordid affairs it gets up to. It's said to have sucked the soul out of humans, drowned adults and children, and even consumed their flesh. So how was a bridge in picturesque Kamikōchi named after this creature? Legends say that a *kappa* used to dwell in the waters under the bridge, though whether that's true remains a mystery.

Yōkai in Media

Yōkai can be found everywhere in books and media. The manga *GeGeGe no Kitarō* by Shigeru Mizuki is a beloved series that brought *yōkai* to modern audiences. More recently, the video game and anime series *Yo-kai Watch* has gained a popular following among schoolchildren.

For a taste of traditional Japanese ghost stories in English, the books *Kwaidan* and *In Ghostly Japan* by scholar of Japanese culture Lafcadio Hearn are the best places to start. Prime examples of *yōkai* can also be seen in animated films from Studio Ghibli, including the shape-shifting old lady Yubaba from *Spirited Away*, and the ghostly little Kodama from *Princess Mononoke*.

14 Spirit Yourself Away to GHIBLI PARK

THEME PARK | ANIME | ATTRACTION

A household name with movie buffs and animation fans worldwide, Studio Ghibli has been creating whimsical worlds and memorable stories for decades, and this relatively new park (opened in 2022), just east of Nagoya, is where fans can come to see their favourite scenes and settings brilliantly brought to life.

COWARDLION/SHUTTERSTOCK ©

How to

Getting here From central Nagoya, take the Higashiyama subway line for 30 minutes to the final stop, Fujigaoka. Then transfer to the Linimo elevated train and get off after 15 minutes at Aichikyūhaku-Kinenkōen.

When to go The park is open daily from 10am to 5pm (from 9am on weekends and national holidays); it's closed Tuesdays (or the following day if it's a national holiday).

Ticket prices Regular passes cost ¥3500, while premium passes are ¥7300 and give access to additional attractions; kids are half price.

TINARCETA/SHUTTERSTOCK ©

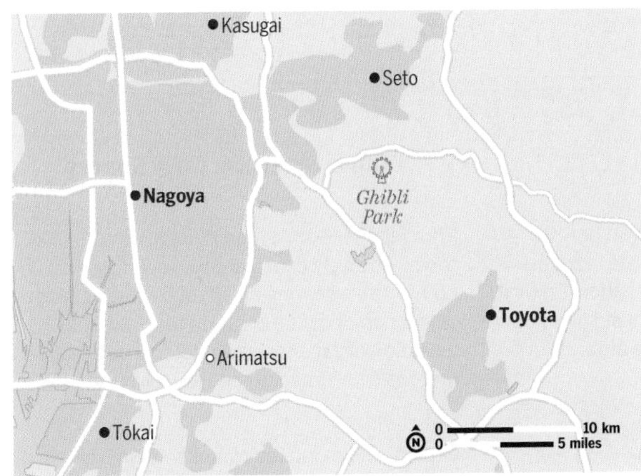

Following the Fantasy

Central park Situated 30km east of Nagoya in the expansive, forested grounds of Aichi Commemorative Park (which hosted the World Expo in 2005), Ghibli Park consists of five main areas, each differently themed and featuring various attractions. **Ghibli's Grand Warehouse** is the park's centrepiece where you can watch exclusive short movies, and enjoy exhibitions showcasing locations from numerous iconic Ghibli movies. Many of these have interactive elements where it feels like you're the star and have stepped into the movie; the *Arrietty* (2010) attraction, for example, allows visitors to experience the world of giant plants from the perspective of the film's tiny protagonist.

Enchanting worlds The **Hill of Youth** features places from various Ghibli movies, including the Elevator Tower from *Laputa: Castle in the Sky* (1986) and *Howl's Moving Castle* (2004), and a charming house from *Whisper of the Heart* (1995). Fans of *My Neighbor Totoro* (1986) will want to make a beeline for **Dondoko Forest**, where you can find Satsuki and Mei's famous house from the classic animation. Nestled in the northern end of the park is **Mononoke Village**, where you can explore the historical landscapes from *Princess Mononoke* (1997); kids will enjoy sliding down the back of the boar god Okkoto-nushi. The park's newest area (opened in 2024) is the **Valley of Witches**, which includes themes from *Kiki's Delivery Service* (1989) and the eponymous castle from *Howl's Moving Castle*.

Above left Ghibli Park
Below left Totoro cream puffs

Getting Tickets

Unlike many other theme parks where you can just turn up on the day, at Ghibli Park tickets must be purchased in advance. Due to the popularity of the franchise, daily visitor limits are imposed so that the park does not get overcrowded, and visitors can have a more enjoyable experience. Currently, tickets can be booked online on set days two months in advance, but be warned: they usually sell out within 30 minutes. Also there are a couple of different pass types, so check the details carefully before purchasing. See the website (ghibli-park.jp) for booking information.

Listings

BEST OF THE REST

Local Flavours

Hida Kotte-ushi ¥

Juicy and fatty Hida beef is served here as *nigiri-zushi* atop a homemade rice cracker, topped with chives and special sauce. Enjoy it as you stroll around Takayama's old town or find a spot in the casual seating area.

Tōhoen ¥

Buy some cat-faced *manjū* at this confectionery shop in Takayama's old town. A small box contains five *manjū*, each filled with a different flavoured sweet-bean paste. Great for gifts!

Irori ¥¥

Try the famous *hōba-miso* and other hearty and delicious *teishoku* (set meals) in this eatery located within Ogimachi village.

Kamonji-goya ¥

Have *iwana* (river trout) grilled on a traditional hearth at this Kamikōchi landmark, established over 140 years ago. There's also a signature sake, served together with grilled fish in a bowl.

Gosenjaku Kitchen ¥¥

Family-friendly dining area with a great view of Kappa-bashi in Kamikōchi. The signature dish is *sanzokuyaki*, a platter with fried chicken cutlet, but diverse menu options are available. It's inside Hotel Kamikōchi; go for an early or late lunch to avoid crowds.

Keiseian ¥

Dine on fresh handmade soba noodles in this rustic Edo-style building in Magome with a traditional hearth at its centre.

Coffee, Sweets & Cosy Spaces

Cafe Ao ¥

This Japanese-style cafe in Takayama's old town has lovely courtyard views. Enjoy the comfortable seating and a relaxed atmosphere with a cup of coffee or green tea. Excellent selection of Japanese sweets; try the creamy *matcha* (powdered green tea) roll cake.

Cafe Kappe ¥

Quaint cafe along the Nakasendō in historical Magome, with outdoor seating and mountain views as you refresh yourself with matcha ice cream or tea with traditional sweets.

Chabō Ebiya ¥

Cafe in an old-style building in Tsumago serving drinks and an array of Japanese confectionery. Drop by in summer for *kakigori* (shaved ice flavoured with syrup).

Cafe Grindelwald ¥¥

Warm lighting, a classic European aesthetic, and a giant mantelpiece complete with crackling firewood make this the cosiest space in Kamikōchi. Stop by for afternoon tea and cake; it's inside Kamikōchi Imperial Hotel.

Hida Folk Village

Traditional Stays

Shiroyama-kan ¥¥¥

This ryokan in Ogimachi village, built in the Meiji period, is now run entirely by one family. The ryokan only houses four groups of guests at a time, so advance booking is recommended.

Jyuemon ¥¥

A 300-year-old *gasshō-zukuri* house providing farmstays in a quiet area at the very end of Ogimachi. Spend an evening by the hearth with other guests and enjoy a *shamisen* (three-stringed instrument) performance.

Fujioto ¥¥

Edo-period ryokan in Tsumago with cypress baths and rooms that overlook a gorgeous Japanese garden.

Outdoor Thrills

Kurobe Gorge Canyoning

Slip, slide, glide and dive into the blue waters at Kurobe Gorge with half-day canyoning tours, available April to November at Unazuki Onsen. Pack a swimsuit!

Satoyama Experience

See rivers, *sakura* (cherry blossoms) and rice fields against the mountains of Gifu Prefecture with Satoyama Experience. Join a guided cycling tour in the warmer months, or trek through thick layers of snow in winter. Tours depart from Hida-Furukawa near Takayama.

Historical Vibes

Hida Folk Village

Traditional houses from across the Hida region can all be seen in one place at this open-air museum in Takayama. Try your hand at local crafts by joining some of the workshops; no reservation required.

MOREGALLERY/SHUTTERSTOCK ©

Takayama Shōwa-kan

Takayama Shōwa-kan

Slip back in time to Japan's Showa period at a Takayama museum. It's laid out like a small town, with recreated shops, restaurants and even a classroom.

Nagiso Town Museum

This museum in Tsumago is made up of three sections: two historical inns (*honjin* and *waki-honjin*) and a history museum. The *waki-honjin* – built using cypress wood, which was once banned from harvest – is especially popular.

Magome Waki-honjin Museum

A former secondary inn, meant for lower ranking travellers, now displays items that tell of Magome's history as a post town.

Tajima House Museum of Silk Culture

The only building in Ogimachi village of Shirakawa-gō with exhibits pertaining to sericulture – the cultivation of silk worms. An informative look at what the *gasshō-zukuri* houses were actually used for.

KYOTO

HISTORY | CULTURE | ARCHITECTURE

Women wearing *yukata* (light cotton kimono)

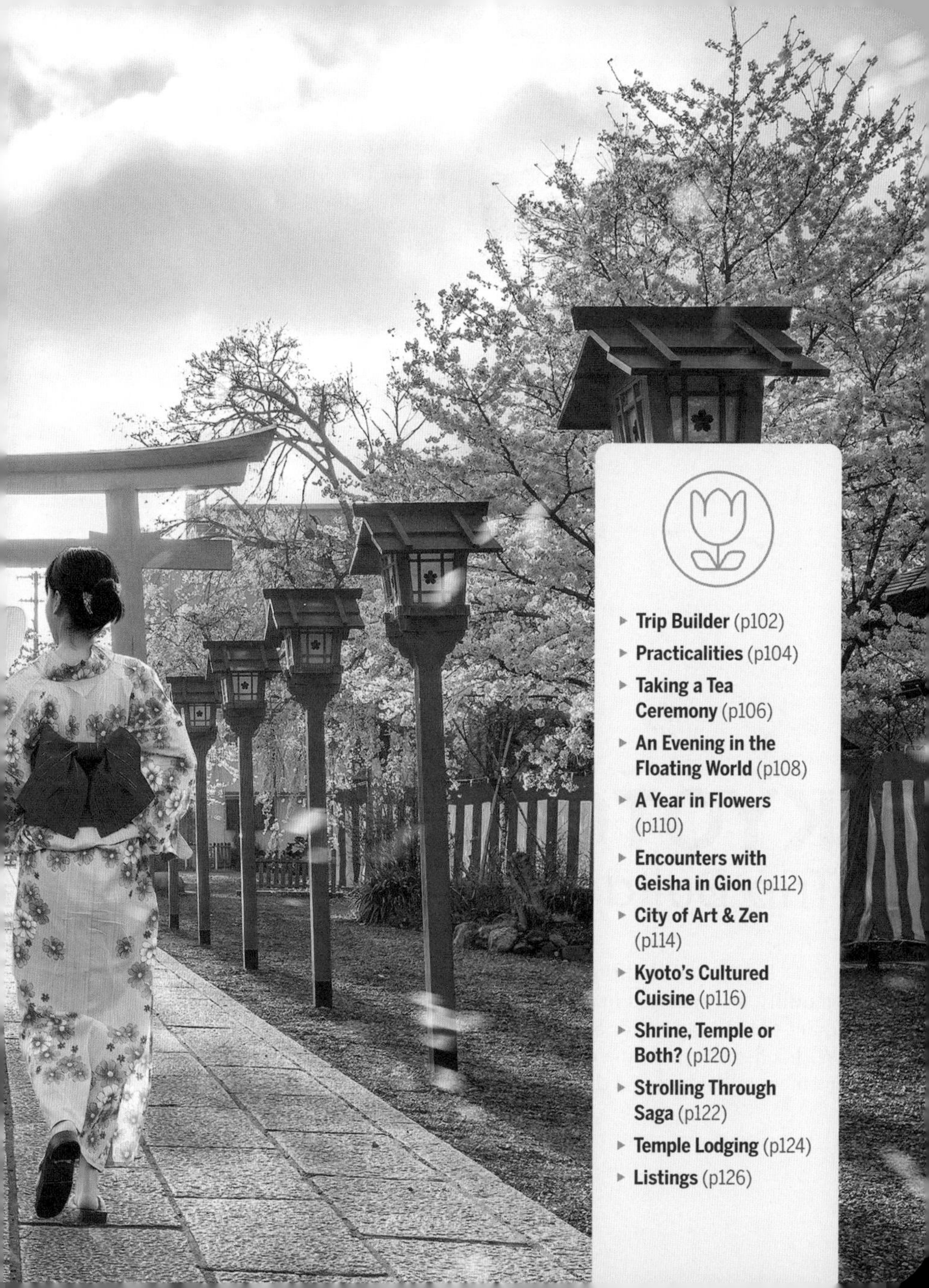

Take time to wander around **Kinkaku-ji** and Kyoto's other famous sites (p115)
40mins by bus from Kyoto Station

KYOTO
Trip Builder

Kyoto's old traditions epitomise delicacy and gentility, as expressed in a grand *kaiseki* dinner, a quiet temple garden, or an evening with a geisha. With a history spanning over 1000 years, the former capital remains the cultural heart of Japan.

Plan your stay around Kyoto's **food culture**: elaborate *kaiseki*, rustic *obanzai-ryōri* and simple *shōjin-ryōri* meals (p116)
15mins by subway from Kyoto Station

Ponder the seasons on the **Path of Philosophy** (p115)
35mins by bus from Kyoto Station

See the world in a bowl of **tea**, in its birthplace (p106)
10mins from Kyoto Station by subway

Practicalities

LEXOSN/SHUTTERSTOCK ©

ARRIVING

Trains Depart Kansai Airport twice an hour for the 75-minute trip to Kyoto, costing about ¥3600. Tickets can be purchased adjacent to the boarding gates (no reservations required). Shinkansen (bullet trains; pictured) from Tokyo Station make the trip for ¥14,000 in just over two hours. From Osaka, express trains depart frequently for the 30-minute, ¥500 trip. Kyoto has two subway lines, the Karasuma line and the Tōzai line, which criss-cross the city north–south and east–west.

HOW MUCH FOR A

***Matcha* ice cream**
¥350

***Bentō* box**
¥900–1200

Temple visit
¥500

WHEN TO GO

DEC–FEB
Winters in Kyoto are notoriously cold; pack accordingly.

MAR–MAY
The warming days bring an array of flowers; probably Kyoto's best season.

JUN–SEP
Kyoto is one of the hottest places in Japan; hot and very sticky.

OCT–NOV
A very pleasant time to visit, but occasional typhoons.

GETTING AROUND

Suica and Pasmo Rechargeable, prepaid Suica and Pasmo cards work on all Kyoto trains, subways and buses. Purchase from any touchscreen ticket-vending machine. Both require a ¥500 deposit, which is refunded (along with any remaining charge) when you return the pass to any ticket window.

Bicycle Kyoto's limited train service, crowded buses and flat terrain make the city ideal for cycling. Bicycles can be rented from numerous locations throughout the city for ¥1000 per day. Many hotels offer free bicycles to guests.

Taxi Taxis are numerous in Kyoto. Most drivers don't speak English, but as GPS location can be entered by telephone number, have this on hand for those difficult-to-find destinations.

EATING & DRINKING

Sanjō Bridge Hundreds of restaurants can be found on the main boulevards and side streets to the west of Sanjō Bridge. Let the menus and plastic food on display be your guide.

Pontochō This narrow alley is lined with little eateries that offer views over the river. If visiting in summer, be sure to take a meal on the wooden *yuka* decks built above a cooling stream. One of the best is Karyū, offering affordable *kaiseki* (haute cuisine) in a restored teahouse.

Must-try snacks
Tofu doughnuts at Nishiki Market (p117)

Best *matcha* ice cream
Just about everywhere

WHERE TO STAY

One of the world's top travel destinations, Kyoto has no shortage of accommodation for every budget. Split your stay between a quaint Airbnb and one of the city's classic hotels.

Neighbourhood	Pros/Cons
Gion	Traditional geisha quarter. Somewhat crowded, but with plenty of restaurants and quiet streets after dark.
Karasuma	Home to numerous hotels, close to bustling nightlife and along the convenient Karasuma subway line.
Kyoto Station area	Convenient for those making day trips to Osaka, Kobe or Nara. No shortage of restaurants and shopping nearby, but a bit busy.
Arashiyama	This popular area on Kyoto's western edge empties out after dark. An early-morning walk in the bamboo forest promises photos free of crowds.
Higashiyama	For a longer stay, rent an Airbnb in semi-rural Higashiyama and live like a local.

CONNECT & FIND YOUR WAY

Wi-fi The free KYOTO_WiFi can be found at over 600 hot spots throughout the city. However, users must send an email in order to get an access code, so be sure to register before coming to town.

Navigation Built on a grid, Kyoto is one of the easier cities to navigate.

BEAT THE CROWDS

Most temples and many shrines open early, so visit before the crowds. Sites tend to be clustered, so divide the city into grids and walk.

MONEY

Cash is king in Japan, and often the only option, though cards are beginning to be more widely used. Have lunch at local neighbourhood shops, before splurging at dinner.

15 Taking a Tea CEREMONY

ART | CULTURE | DRINK

As much of Kyoto culture developed around tea, teahouses can be found throughout the city, and taking tea is a must for visitors. Enjoy the host's hospitality, as *matcha* (powdered green tea) is whisked into a froth with incredible speed, accompanied by sweets to balance the flavour. The experience offers a refreshing break from the outside world.

How to

Arranging a tea experience While many Kyoto hotels can arrange a tea experience, a handful of places in town can be contacted directly for a more authentic experience, offered in English.

How much A typical one-hour ceremony costs around ¥3000, or ¥6000 if a kimono option is offered.

Top tip A highly caffeinated burst of green *matcha* in the late afternoon is a wonderful way to refresh you for the nightlife ahead.

At its most simple, a tea gathering entails drinking hot *matcha* tea after eating Japanese sweets. Yet the experience is highly refined: reflected in the way a guest holds a bowl, or how the host prepares the boiling water and handles the utensils.

As the Japanese of the past had no access to museums, the tearoom became a repository of Japanese art itself, and even today, the flowers, incense and hanging scrolls are carefully chosen, often to reflect the season. At its most refined,

Above right Japanese sweets
Below right Tea ceremony

KEI SHOOTING/SHUTTERSTOCK ©

Tea on the Go

Kyoto is filled with shops catering to tea culture. **Ippōdō** is perhaps best known, with roots going back to 1717. Three-hundred-year-old **Marukyū Koyamaen** sells tea grown at its estate in Uji. **Yamashita** on Teranouchi-dori has been selling tea ceremony utensils that are works of art since 1850.

the process becomes meditative. Randy Channell Soei, owner of Ran Hotei, states: 'Both host and guest strive to grasp the essence of harmony, respect, and purity, allowing one to experience tranquillity, while sharing a bowl of tea.' Yet he feels that it should be enjoyable rather than formal: 'I hope that people will consider tea more than just a drink. Ideally it is sharing time with others and appreciating the moment.'

Maikoya Kyoto leads the kimono-clad guest to make their own cup of tea, with a variety of displays that explain tea culture. **Nagomi** offers an accessible, simpler affair held at various times throughout the day. **Ran Hotei** allows for a more relaxed, tailored experience in a full-on cafe that offers food, drink and original teas to take home.

TUUL AND BRUNO MORANDI/ALAMY STOCK PHOTO ©

■ **With expert insights from Peter MacIntosh**
Peter is a Kyoto-based Canadian photographer, artist, entrepreneur and geisha culture guru. petermacintosh.com, @kyotopmac

An Evening in the Floating World

TAKE A DEEP DIVE INTO A CLASSIC JAPANESE TRADITION

Much like Kyoto itself, part of the appeal of the geisha is the cultivated mystique. It's possible to share an evening with these classical performers, though whether that entails dinner or simply drinks is based on the dimensions of your wallet.

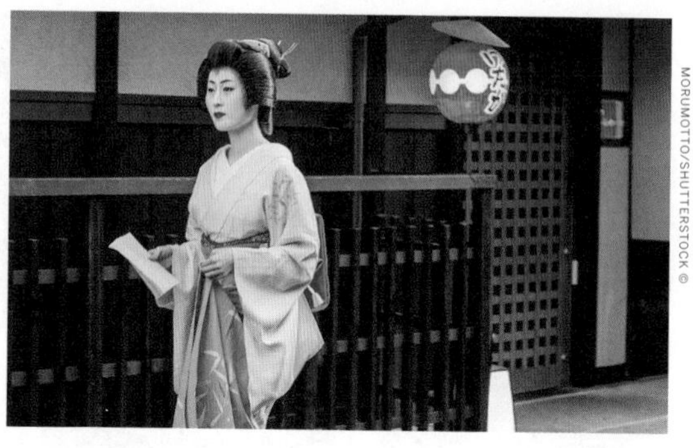

MORUMOTTO/SHUTTERSTOCK ©

Recognised as an integral symbol of Kyoto, geisha are referred to locally as *geiko*, with their younger apprentices being called *maiko*. Divided between the city's five geisha districts, known as *hanamachi* (flower towns), the current population stands at about 240.

The term *gei* means performance, and training begins after finishing junior high school. The initial five-year curriculum consists of dance, music, poetry and calligraphy, but studies continue throughout their career. For a young Japanese woman, it's the best way to get such a comprehensive understanding of her own culture.

Access to the floating world was once incredibly exclusive, permissible only via an introduction. Besides private parties at teahouses and restaurants, geisha could be hired for big social events. Because of recent economic difficulties, restrictions have loosened to keep the tradition alive.

So where can the visitor see geisha? A chance encounter with anyone in a city of 1.5 million is obviously difficult, but if you stroll any of the *hanamachi* in the early evening you'll have the best chance of catching a glimpse of a *geiko* or *maiko* as they head out to their first engagement. There has been a backlash against foreign tourists crowding the women, so be sure to give them space. You can tell a *maiko* from a *geiko* as the former wear colourful kimonos with longer sleeves and ornate hairpins. *Geiko* wear simpler kimonos with shorter sleeves, and fewer accessories in their hair.

The most affordable way to see a performance is to attend one of the five annual Dance Festivals, usually in spring and autumn. *Maiko* also perform daily at the Gion Corner.

Left *Geiko*, Gion
Centre *Maiko*, Gion
Right *Maiko* performance during *ozashiki*

PR IMAGE FACTORYE/SHUTTERSTOCK ©

IRINA WILHAUK/SHUTTERSTOCK ©

An evening of geisha entertainment for two – over a private *ozashiki* dinner – starts at around ¥90,000, and includes one *maiko*, one *geiko* and a *shamisen* player. Peter MacIntosh says 'People say geisha entertainment is expensive, and they are right. These women are highly trained professionals dedicated to the arts and they are expensive to hire. You get what you pay for.' Some inns offer a more affordable two-hour group dinner with a *maiko* for about ¥20,000 per person.

> *Maiko* wear colourful kimonos with longer sleeves and ornate hairpins. *Geiko* wear simpler kimonos with shorter sleeves, and fewer accessories in their hair.

Most geisha *ozashiki* take place in a formal setting so it's important to dress smartly but comfortably. 'To enjoy geisha entertainment as a foreign visitor, you must put aside any preconceived ideas you have from movies and books and let the women take you into their world where you, the customer – whether it be man, women or child – will get a glimpse into the floating world and traditional culture,' MacIntosh says.

A *kaiseki* meal is the first order of business, throughout which your entertainer will make small talk. Performances follow, usually songs and dances often seen in traditional Japanese theatre arts. But the most memorable part of the evening is certain to be the traditional party games involving wordplay and penalty drinking. MacIntosh says his 'customers always comment on how much fun the entertainment was and how they were surprised by how the *maiko/geiko* were so down to earth and not overly formal'.

Best Geisha Books

While Arthur Golden's novel *Memoirs of a Geisha* is the best known, *Geisha of Gion*, the autobiography of his research subject Mineko Iwasaki, is far more accurate. *Geisha* by American anthropologist Liza Dalby details her immersive experience performing in an unofficial capacity at an *ozashiki*. Lesley Downer's *Geisha: The Remarkable Truth Behind the Fiction* was written from the perspective of living in Miyagawa-cho, one of Kyoto's five geisha districts. *Madame Sadayakko,* also written by Downer, tells the story of Japan's most celebrated geisha, who entertained European statesmen and royalty of the early 20th century, before retiring to tour the world as a travelling actress.

A Year in FLOWERS

01 Plum blossoms
(late Feb–early Mar)
The first floral harbinger of spring, *ume* can be found nationwide, but popular spots include Kyoto's Kitano Tenman-gū, and Kyū Shiba Rikyū in Tokyo.

02 Cherry blossoms
(late Mar–early Apr)
Japan's unofficial national flower can be widely seen everywhere. One favourite spot is along the Meguro-gawa in Tokyo.

03 Wisteria
(late Apr–early May)
Often seen climbing the trellises of many parks. Try Tokyo's Kameido Tenjin, or Byōdō-in in Kyoto.

04 Hydrangea
(mid-Jun–mid-Jul)
These multicoloured gems line the paths of Mimuroto-ji in Kyoto, Hasedera in Kamakura, and Yatadera Temple in Nara.

05 Lotus
(mid-Jul–mid-Aug)
Buddhism's favourite flower can be best seen at Shinobazu-ike in

Tokyo, Hōkongō-in in Kyoto, or Mizunomori Water Botanical Garden beside Biwa-ko.

06 Irises
(late May–Jul)
Favourite spots include Nezu Museum and Meiji-jingū in Tokyo, and Kenroku-en in Kanazawa.

07 Cosmos
(late Aug–early Oct)
These dot the rural landscape. Try Hama-rikyū in Tokyo and around Mt Fuji, particularly Yamanaka-ko.

08 Chrysanthemum
(Sep–mid-Nov)
The best place to see this symbol of Japan's Imperial Family is at Shinjuku-gyoen in Tokyo.

09 Autumn foliage
(late Nov–early Dec)
Coloured maples can be seen throughout the hillsides nationwide. Yellow gingko line the boulevards of many major cities.

10 Winter peonies
(late Nov–mid-Feb)
For a bit of colour in the winter season, try Ueno-kōen or Hama-rikyū in Tokyo.

16 Encounters with Geisha IN GION

HISTORY | THEATRE | ARCHITECTURE

Gion is Kyoto's famous geisha district and traditional entertainment quarter, where streets are crammed with wooden-latticed *machiya* (townhouses), shops, restaurants and *ochaya* (teahouses). If you're lucky, you might glimpse a kimono-clad *geiko* (the Kyoto word for geisha) or *maiko* (apprentice geisha).

PAUL ATKINSON/SHUTTERSTOCK ©

How to

Getting there Gion-Shijō on the Keihan Main Line is the nearest station; buses run there too.

When to go Early evening is the best time to experience the magic of Gion, when the roadside lanterns are lit up and geisha may be seen slipping by.

Save your yen Most of the attractive *machiya* in this area house expensive restaurants and exclusive clubs, but Gion is a great place for an evening stroll without spending a single yen.

JURI POZZI/SHUTTERSTOCK ©

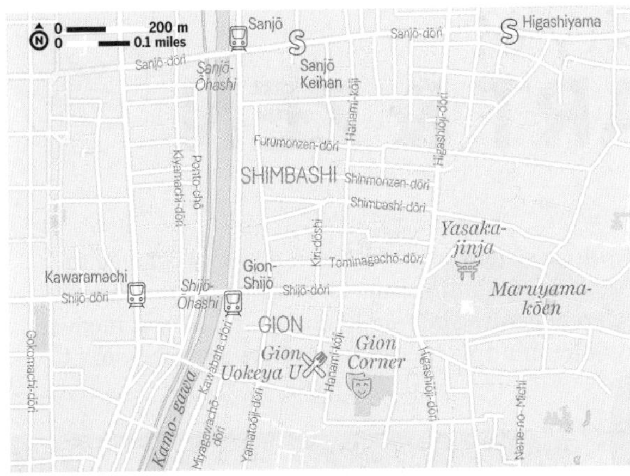

Early Evening Strolls

Entertainment district Gion originally grew as a drinking and entertainment district due to its proximity to **Yasaka-jinja**; *ochaya* or teahouses were built to cater for visitors to the shrine, and in the mid-18th century, Gion was officially developed as Kyoto's teahouse quarter. Geisha and *maiko* would provide evening entertainment for patrons to the teahouses, and the district blossomed as Kyoto's main nightlife hub, with over 500 *ochaya* at its booming peak.

Main street One of Kyoto's most scenic streets, **Hanami-kōji** is Gion's main pedestrian thoroughfare; walking down it feels like you've been transported back to late Edo- or Meiji-era Kyoto, with beautiful wooden *machiya* lining the streets lit up by atmospheric roadside lanterns. You can follow the foot traffic southwards, but it is worth veering off the main road to explore some of the enchantingly pretty back alleys and side streets, where every turn feels like it could lead to a hidden teahouse, secluded private garden or rustic Michelin-starred restaurant, such as **Gion Uokeya U**, which specialises in grilled eel.

Picturesque scenes Aside from the main area, Gion has some other exceptionally pretty spots. On the north side of Shijō-dōri is a district called **Shimbashi** (or Shirakawa Minami-dōri); here you can wander along the flagstone paved streets lining the Shirakawa ('White River') and soak up the old-fashioned atmosphere – in the evenings it looks like something from a film set. During cherry-blossom season the streets are pastel pink and stunningly pretty.

Above left Hanami-kōji, Gion
Below left *Maiko*

See the Sights

Gion is Kyoto's most famous geisha district, and interactions with them tend to be fleeting. To experience a full evening's entertainment in the company of a geisha usually costs serious money and requires deep connections, but at the annex theatre at **Gion Corner** (kyoto-gioncorner.com) you can get a taste of geisha dancing and other cultural mainstays in the daily hour-long evening shows.

While Gion's streets and buildings (and its geisha) are extremely photogenic, it is important to respect any signs prohibiting photography, always ask before taking someone's photo, and be careful not to trespass on private property.

17 City of ART & ZEN

ARCHITECTURE | ART | RELIGION

To many, the name Kyoto is synonymous with Zen. The city is home to over 1600 Buddhist temples (and 400 Shintō shrines), with many internationally renowned for their gardens, architecture and fine Buddhist art. To visit them all and see everything would require multiple lifetimes, but here are a few select choices to start with.

F11PHOTO/SHUTTERSTOCK ©

How to

Getting around A relatively flat city, Kyoto is ideal for bicycling or walking. Many of the sights are in clusters, so your visit can be broken into zones. Get a Kansai Thru Pass if using public transport to go further afield.

When to go Any time, although some temples are only open in certain seasons.

Top tip Many temples house their most precious art and artefacts in a separate treasure hall; entry usually requires a small extra fee.

COWARDLION/SHUTTERSTOCK ©

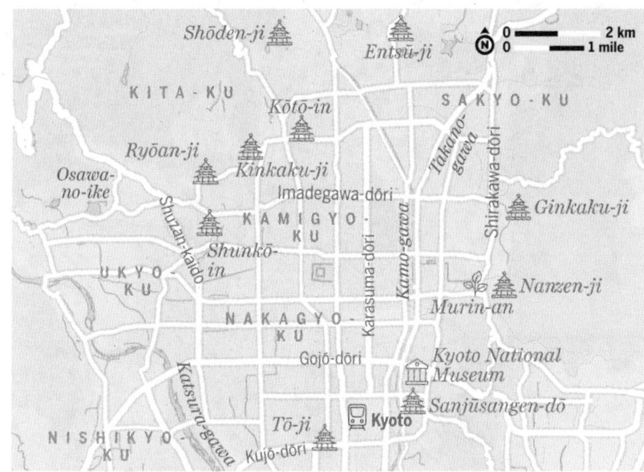

Treasure Hunting

Where to start Kyoto's real beauty lies in its religious sites, and your visit will inevitably revolve around them. While the major places can be crowded, they're still worth a visit, and are quietest an hour or two after opening, or late in the afternoon. Try to pace yourself and don't schedule too many sites in a day, as some visitors find themselves getting templed out.

Temples as art Kyoto's poster child is inevitably **Kinkaku-ji**, the Golden Pavilion, famous not only for the eponymous villa standing regally above a reflective pond but also for its stroll garden of water and moss. A short walk away is **Ryōan-ji**, famed for its deceptively simple courtyard garden of sand and stone. The stroll garden above the Silver Pavilion at **Ginkaku-ji** offers picturesque views, while inside houses Edo- and Meiji-era paintings and exceptional sliding screens. Continue down the Path of Philosophy's quiet canal to **Nanzen-ji**, unmissable due to its towering gate. The famous pagoda of **Tō-ji** has its own treasure hall packed with priceless art; it is open for a few weeks twice a year, in spring and autumn.

Among the gods **Sanjūsangen-dō** is one of Kyoto's most mesmerising sights – 1001 life-size statues of Kannon stare back at you, and the temple hall itself is Japan's longest wooden structure. The nearby **Kyoto National Museum** is a treasure trove of art masterpieces.

Above left Kinkaku-ji
Below left Kōtō-in

Smaller Treasures

Be sure to visit a few of the quieter, lesser-known sites too – these will have modest entry fees and you may have the place to yourself.

Daitoku-ji's sub-temple of **Kōtō-in** (sometimes closed to visitors) is a riot of colour in autumn, and offers a contemplative respite for most of the year. Higashiyama's 36 peaks serve as borrowed scenery at **Shōden-ji**, hovering above a pristine rock garden. Nearby **Entsū-ji** presents a similar effect, though in this case the mountainscape is emulated within the garden moss. Visitors entering **Murin-an** (murin-an.jp/en) villa may feel the surrounding city drop away, before disappearing completely during the walk along the Kurodani/Yoshida hill.

18 Kyoto's Cultured CUISINE

FOOD | MARKETS | RESTAURANTS

Kyoto is a city for food lovers, with a culinary legacy dating back centuries. The birthplace of *kaiseki* (Japanese haute cuisine), which is celebrated for its seasonality and refinement, Kyoto also boasts vibrant food markets and restaurants to suit all tastes and budgets.

BEATRICE SIRINUNTANANON/GETTY IMAGES ©

How to

Getting around Kyoto has two subway lines linking many neighbourhoods north–south and east–west. Buses and bicycles help reach more out-of-the-way places.

When to go Any time! Much of Kyoto's finest food is seasonal, so find out what's on the menu during your trip.

Top tip Eating out can be expensive, but some of the best restaurants also offer a more affordable lunch service.

COROSUKECHAN3/SHUTTERSTOCK ©

Downtown Eats

You can find exceptional food almost anywhere you go in Kyoto, but for the widest spread of choices, head downtown. A highlight of any foodie itinerary, **Nishiki Market** is a narrow, covered and bustling pedestrian shopping street, popular with both locals and tourists. Crammed with over 100 shops, stalls and restaurants, and known colloquially as 'Kyoto's Kitchen', it is the place for seeing and sampling the many unique ingredients of Kyoto cuisine. Stretching for about five blocks across the centre of town, the market has origins dating from the 14th century, and is home to a mix of traditional shops – many of which have been run by the same family for generations – and more modern vendors.

Kyo-yasai

Kyo-yasai (Kyoto vegetables) developed back when Kyoto was the capital; there was strong demand for high-quality produce, but as the city is surrounded by mountains and far from the sea, it became imperative to source most food locally. Hence the cultivation of unique *kyo-yasai* developed; these vegetables are suited to and shaped by the local environment.

SINSEEHO/SHUTTERSTOCK ©

Above left Seafood, Nishiki Market
Left Nishiki Market **Above right** *Kyo-yasai*

A visit to the market is a real culinary adventure. Sample the sweet or sour crunch of *tsukemono* (Japanese pickles), delicately flavoured *wagashi* (traditional Japanese sweets), *kyo-yasai* (Kyoto vegetables), tea, fresh seafood and lots more. One of the market's most famous street foods is *tako-tamago;* these tiny red octopuses are cooked and marinated in a mixture of mirin, sugar and soy sauce, stuffed with a quail egg and skewered – a strange savoury delicacy.

Fine Dining

Kaiseki or *kaiseki ryōri*, is the pinnacle of Japanese high-end cuisine. Its origins can be traced its origins back to the imperial courts of the Heian period (794–1159), when Kyoto first became the nation's capital. These multi-course banquets are enjoyed over several hours and feature ornately arranged dishes of fish and vegetables, and sometimes meat. *Kaiseki* is a full sensory experience, with the presentation of each beautifully arranged dish

Best Dining Experiences

Kikunoi Honten Located in a secluded spot not far from Maruyama-kōen, this Michelin-starred *kaiseki* restaurant is one of the finest in all of Kyoto, with exemplary food and service.

Kiyama Michelin-starred *kaiseki* restaurant serving exquisite multi-course seasonal dishes; the lunch menu is more affordable but no less divine. Reservations online.

Tōsuirō Marvel at the number of varied tofu-based dishes on offer at this specialist tofu restaurant on Kiyamachi-dōri. Lovely Japanese setting, and outdoor riverside seating in the summer.

Menami Friendly establishment specialising in home-style *obanzai-ryōri*. Plenty of small fish, vegetable and meat dishes. Enter through a sliding door near an elevator.

Left Small dishes, Kikunoi Honten
Below *Yuba*

just as important as the multitude of tastes and textures; the ingredients focus predominantly on local produce and reflect the seasons, so dishes and menus are constantly evolving. You can try *kaiseki* at many fancy restaurants and ryokan throughout the city, and if your budget allows, it is a culinary experience that you should try at least once during your trip – budget around ¥12,000 to ¥22,000 per person for an evening meal.

Foodie Favourites

Tofu is one of Kyoto's signature foods and has been made here for many generations, making use of the city's high-quality groundwater. Dishes include *yudōfu,* which is tofu warmed in a *konbu* (seafood) broth and eaten with a variety of condiments including soy sauce, *ponzu* and *togarashi* (powdered seasoning with chilli peppers). *Yuba* is made from the skin that forms when soybean milk is heated during the tofu-making process – it can be eaten fresh or dried and is a Kyoto mainstay.

Another local speciality is *obanzai-ryōri,* which comprises various small homemade-style dishes featuring mostly local ingredients – far more humble and hearty than the snobby refinery of *kaiseki*. At some temples you can also try *shōjin-ryōri,* the traditional vegetarian cuisine eaten by Buddhist monks (p124).

Shrine, Temple **OR BOTH?**

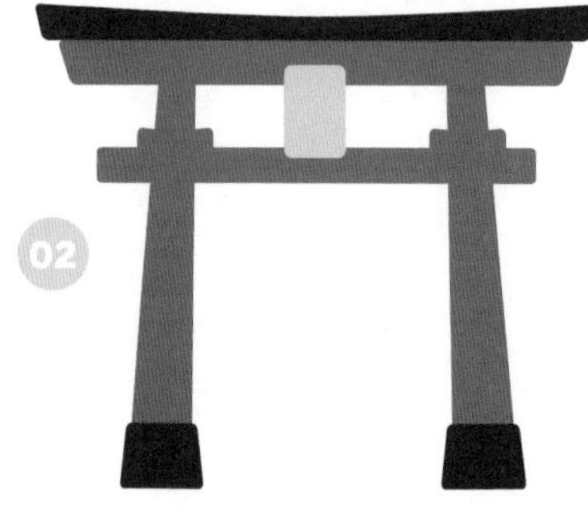

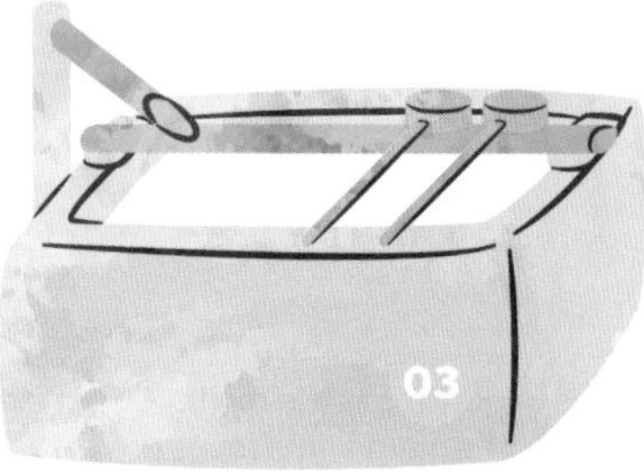

01 Goshuin

Unique stamps available for a small fee at many (but not all) temples and shrines, collected in a book called *goshuinchō*.

02 Torii

The traditional gate of a Shintō shrine, marking the boundary between the ordinary world and the sacred.

03 Chōzuya

A trough of water used to purify your hands and mouth before entering a shrine.

04 Shimenawa

A woven rope of straw or hemp used in Shintō to denote a place or object that is sacred.

05 Komainu

A pair of statues in the shape of lion-dogs that guard shrines from evil.

06 Ema

Originating from Shintō but now used by Buddhist temples too; wooden plaques on which visitors can write their prayers and wishes.

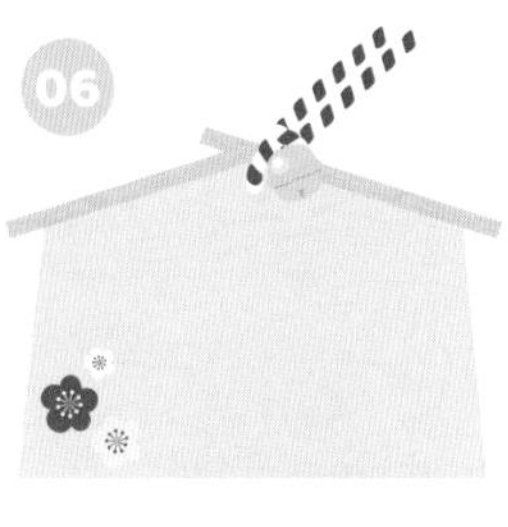

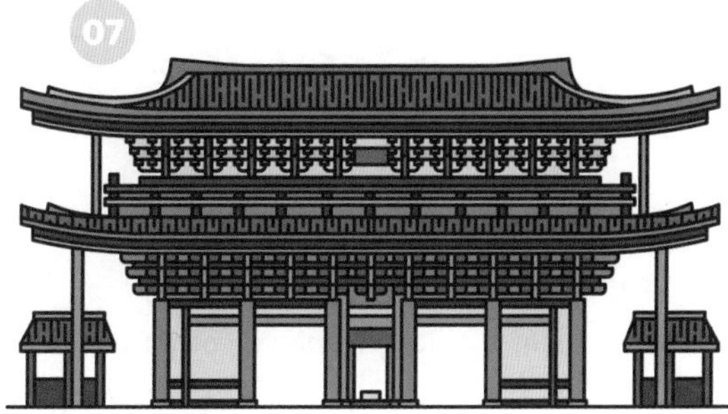

08

07 Sanmon

The largest and most important gate of a Buddhist temple. It is usually located between the *sonmon* (outer gate) and the main hall.

08 Bonshō

A large bronze bell used in ceremonies at a temple; it is rung 108 times for the New Year.

09 Niō

A pair of fierce-looking guardian carvings or statues that protect Buddhist temples from evil.

10 Jizō

This jovial-appearing Buddhist statue represents a god who protects children and travellers and is a favourite deity in Japanese culture.

11 Omamori

These small charms can be purchased from shrines to protect you from various misfortunes or grant you luck in specific situations.

19 Strolling Through SAGA

WALKING | NATURE | CULTURE

Wander this lesser-known corner of town, along rural lanes lined with thatch houses, popping into the lush grounds of temples along the way. Skirt the edge of the renowned bamboo forest, before lunching beside Katsura-gawa's quick-moving water.

7MARU/SHUTTERSTOCK©

How to

Getting there JR runs a frequent rail service to Saga Arashiyama from Kyoto Station. The most interesting approach is through the Kyoto suburbs on the little Keifuku Randen Arashiyama tram that departs from Ōmiya Station. Buses to Otagi-mae depart hourly from both Randen-Saga and Saga-Arashiyama Stations.

Top tip In summer, do this course in reverse and cross through a haunted tunnel to enjoy a swim beside Kiyotaki village.

Sleepy Sagano

This corner of Kyoto city is hardly city at all. There is a definitive rural feel in the thatched-roof teahouses, maple-infused temple grounds and family-run shops specialising in pottery and bamboo. Pleasantly free of crowds, this half-day walk serves as a refresher, before dropping down into buzzing Arashiyama.

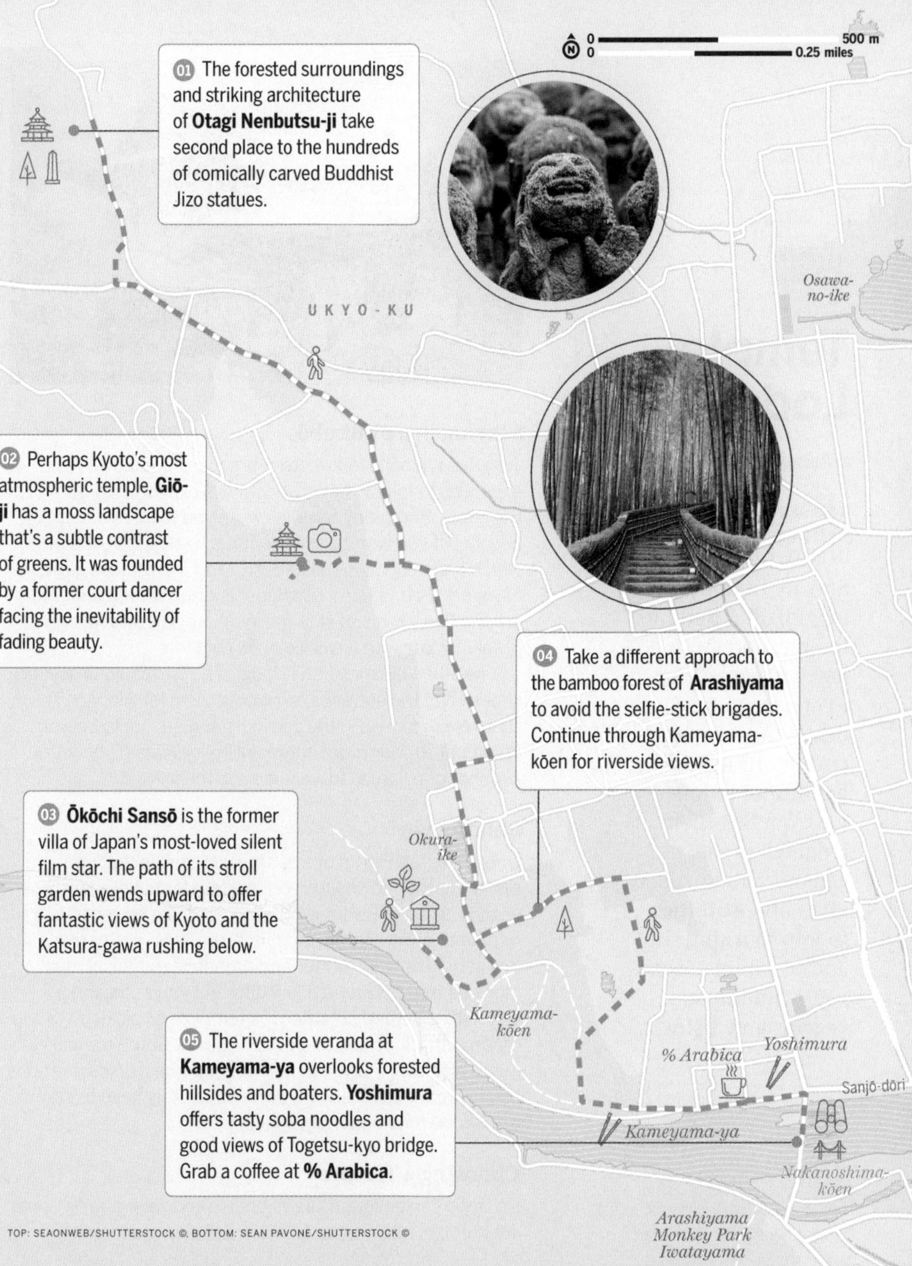

TOP: SEAONWEB/SHUTTERSTOCK ©, BOTTOM: SEAN PAVONE/SHUTTERSTOCK ©

Temple Lodging

SEE A BUDDHIST TEMPLE FROM THE INSIDE OUT

Stay in a *shukubō,* a lodging at a Buddhist temple, and go beyond sightseeing to engage more deeply with Japanese culture. In Kyoto a handful of temples have opened their lodgings to the general public. A stay gives opportunities to join morning rites and to sample *shōjin-ryōri* (Buddhist vegetarian cuisine).

Left Ninna-ji **Centre** Buddhist monks, Chishaku-in **Right** Bell tower, Ninna-ji

COWARDLION/SHUTTERSTOCK ©

Staying in a Shukubō

Temples typically follow strict timelines and guests are expected to follow them. Check-in is expected by 5pm at the latest, and many temples want you to inform them in advance if you won't arrive on time. A few will hold dinner, which typically happens at 6pm. Morning prayers generally start around 6am. Breakfast is often served just after, around 7am. You can skip morning prayers and roll up to breakfast late, but it will likely be cold.

Like other Japanese-style lodgings, you should take your shoes off at the entrance, swapping them for slippers. The slippers are for use in the corridors and are not to be worn on tatami. In your room, there will be a *yukata* (light cotton kimono) or pyjamas to wear around the temple.

Shōjin-ryōri

One of the highlights of any *shukubō* stay is that you can try authentic *shōjin-ryōri;* perfect for vegetarians or vegans, Japan's Buddhist cuisine contains no meat, fish or animal products, or pungent aromatics (like garlic). It is served at both dinner and breakfast. A typical meal includes tofu prepared a few different ways; seasonal vegetables served steamed, as tempura or pickled; a soup made with a kelp-based broth; and rice. Some temples in Kyoto also serve lunch to non-staying guests (reservations usually required) – so you don't absolutely have to stay in a *shukubō* to experience *shōjin-ryōri*.

Choosing a Temple

Shukubō can be found all over Japan and vary greatly. Some are humble, with shared facilities and sliding screens to

SUWIPAT LORSIRIPAIBOON/SHUTTERSTOCK ©

NUI7711/SHUTTERSTOCK ©

partition rooms. Others may have en suite bathrooms, lifts and garden views. Sleeping is typically on futons (quilt-like mattresses) laid out on tatami, though there are some temples that offer Western-style beds. Most allow visitors to observe the monks' morning prayer rituals. Some also offer meditation experiences.

One of the temples offering overnight stays in Kyoto is Mouro Kaikan in **Ninna-ji** (ninnaji.jp), with its beautiful gardens (including a five-storey pagoda) and morning chanting; a stay with breakfast and dinner included costs from around ¥15,000 per person. Not far from Sanjūsangen-dō is **Chishaku-in**, a large temple with accommodation facilities featuring comfortable, modern rooms; guests get an exclusive tour of the temple's treasure room.

One of the highlights of any *shukubō* stay is that you can try authentic *shōjin-ryōri;* perfect for vegetarians or vegans.

Mountain Temples

Aside from Kyoto, the mountain monastery town of **Kōya-san** in southern Kansai is the most popular place to experience a *shukubō*. There are over 50 here and some are especially accommodating towards overseas guests, with English-speakers who can explain some of the monks' practices and beliefs. Prices are fixed: the most basic rooms start at ¥9900 per person for one night and two meals, based on double occupancy. Most temples charge a surcharge for solo travellers. The **Koyasan Shukubo Association** (eng-shukubo.net) can assist with making reservations.

Best Temple Stays in Japan

Ekō-in (ekoin.jp) The best all-around temple in Kōya-san, managed by a team of English-speaking monks.

Shōjōshin-in (shojoshinin.jp) Atmospheric temple with a thatched roof and humble (but comfortable) rooms. In Kōya-san.

Ichijō-in (itijyoin.or.jp) Kōya-san temple, known for its beautifully presented, gourmet *shōjin-ryōri*.

Shunkō-in (shunkoin.com) Excellent place for a *shukubō* experience in Kyoto. The head priest speaks English, and you can try Zen meditation.

Saikan Atop Mt Haguro, one of the three sacred peaks that make up Yamagata's Dewa Sanzan, historically this is a place of pilgrimage for mountain ascetics.

Listings

BEST OF THE REST

Natural Escapes

Hiei-zan

Kyoto is notorious for its sweltering summer, so head for a cooling walk beneath towering cedars, among the Enryaku-ji buildings spread throughout the forest.

Isshū Trail

Descend from the overlook above Fushimi Inari-Taisha's red gates down the Kyoto Isshū Trail. Make your way towards Tōfuku-ji's famous temples, passing stone gods that flank hidden waterfalls.

Kyoto Botanical Gardens

One of the city's less-visited gems, with 12,000 species of plants offering a wide display of seasonal colours, a bustling avian community and lush paths perfect for strolling.

Imperial Palace Grounds

Former home to the Imperial family, this 100-hectare park at the centre of the city is one of the best places to let the kids work off excess energy.

Daimonji-yama

Undertake the one-hour climb up this mountain's kanji-carved face to watch the setting sun light up the temple roofs below as well as Osaka's far-off skyscrapers.

Pulses of the City

Fushimi Sake Village ¥¥¥

The spirit(s) of Fushimi, Japan's second-largest sake district, is honoured at this restaurant that offers a sampler of each of the town's 18 breweries. A food accompaniment is highly advised.

Gekkeikan Sake Ōkura Museum

Perhaps the gem of the Fushimi district, this museum guides you through the making of its famous sake, topped off with a tasting. You even get a complimentary one for the train home.

Kyoto Taiko Center

Find the heartbeat of Japan by having a go at playing *taiko,* traditional Japanese festival drums. Held within the hall of Chomyo-ji temple, you will surely rouse the deities.

Kyoto Sights & Nights

Enjoy a walking lecture around Kyoto's geisha districts led by an expert on geisha culture. Also available are drinks with a *maiko* or a geisha dinner party.

Dine-in

Nishiki Market ¥

Graze as you go, sampling many of the facets of Kyoto's internationally renowned food culture. A mere five blocks long, Nishiki's hundreds of shops offers everything from octopus skewers to tofu doughnuts.

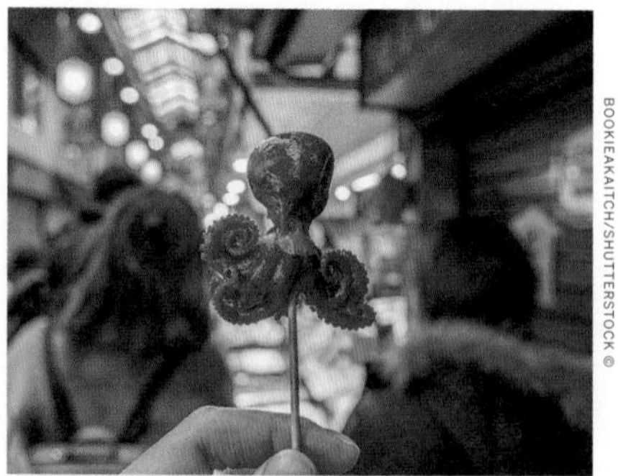

Octopus skewer, Nishiki Market

Dragon Burger ¥

Chef Adam Rawson created his award-winning burgers with the Japanese palate in mind. Try a sampler of wasabi burger, *yuzu-kosho* burger and cacao barbecue sliders, along with a local beer.

Dining room you ¥¥¥

Tucked away in a quiet neighbourhood, Dining room you is a subdued introduction to *izakaya* (Japanese pub-eatery) culture. Best known for its *obanzai-ryōri* and seasonal oysters, and for its vast choice of sakes.

Ganko Nijō-en ¥¥

The Kiyamachi location of the popular franchise is set within an L-shaped 1611 villa with a spacious garden and a quieter vibe than the usual *izakaya*.

Men-Bistro Nakano ¥¥

This unique shop serves ramen with a French vibe. The original flavour of the soup reflects the chef's training in Continental cuisine. Not to mention the fine selection of wines.

Ponto-chō Karyū ¥¥¥

The best choice for *yuka* (wooden deck) dining, eaten above a cooling stream for a respite from Kyoto's relentless summer heat.

Souvenirs & Treasures

Robert Yellin Yakimono Gallery

Marvel at the diversity that pottery can take at this picturesque gallery, run by one of the top foreign experts of Japanese ceramics. Be sure to email or call before visiting.

Hakuchikudō

For those visiting in the heat of summer, a folding fan is a must. Choose from the artistic treasures at the Hakuchikudō atelier, which has been making fans since 1717.

F11PHOTO/SHUTTERSTOCK ©

Fushimi Inari-Taisha

Shōgo-in Yatsuhashi Sohonten Kyoto

Born in 1689, the sweet bean-filled cinnamon confectionery known as *yatsuhashi* has gone on to become one of the city's favourite edible souvenirs. Also try the uncooked *cannelle* style.

Funahashiya

The speciality of this charming centuries-old shop near Sanjō Bridge is the dried-bean candies called *goshiki-mame*, sold in an array of flavours such as *yuzu* (citrus), cinnamon and plum.

Cultural Experiences

Camellia

Join a simple yet elegant tea ceremony with an English-speaking host, and learn all about the refined art of *sadō;* it includes a bowl of *matcha* and traditional sweets.

Gion Matsuri

Japan's most famous summer festival takes place in downtown Kyoto in July, and is a multiday celebration with enormous floats, food stalls and a vibrant atmosphere.

KANSAI

FOOD | CITY LIFE | SIGHTS

Shin-Sekai (p135)

安心と信頼の日立グループ
日本一の串かつ
横綱
酒処

KANSAI
Trip Builder

Kansai has a little bit of everything. Grittier than Tokyo, Osaka is Japan's 'second' city and food capital, Nara and Himeji are home to magnificent historic landmarks, and on the Kii Peninsula you can follow ancient pilgrimage trails through beautiful mountainous landscapes.

Discover a wealth of culinary delights at **Kuromon Ichiba** (p137)
20mins by train from Osaka Station
Delve into the world of tech stores and anime in **Den Den Town** (p135)
15mins by train from Osaka Station
Go deer-spotting in the green expanse of **Nara-kōen** (p140)
1hr by train from Osaka
Feel humbled in front of the giant Buddha at Nara's **Tōdai-ji** (p140)
1hr by train from Osaka
See the bright neon lights of **Dōtombori** (p134)
15mins by train from Osaka Station
Walk ancient and remote pilgrimage trails on the **Kumano Kodō** (p144)
2hrs by train from Osaka
Nagoya
Kuwana
Yokkaichi
Kyoto
Otsu
Kusatsu
Uji
Mino
Kawanishi
Osaka
Nara
Sakai
Haibara
Kishiwada
Sennan
Hashimoto
Iwade
Koya-san
Kii-nagashima
Owase
Kumano
Hongu
Sea of Kumano
Takijiri-oji
Kii Peninsula
Tanabe
Shingu
Nachi-Katsuura
Kii-Katsuura
Kushimoto
Shiono-misaki

Practicalities

ARRIVING

Kansai International Airport There are two train lines into Osaka: Nankai is better for Namba (40 minutes, ¥1500); and JR for Osaka (Umeda) or Shin-Osaka (one hour, ¥2400). Buses cost ¥1600 and take about 1½ hours (kate.co.jp). Taxis are very expensive (¥18,000).

Itami Airport Mostly handles domestic flights; a monorail connects with trains to central Osaka.

Shin-Osaka Station If arriving by shinkansen (bullet train), change to the JR line for Osaka or the Midō-suji subway line to reach downtown.

HOW MUCH FOR A

Tray of *tako-yaki*
¥600

Bowl of ramen
¥750

Craft beer
¥800

WHEN TO GO

MAR–MAY
Warm in the day, cool at night; cherry blossoms peak in April.

JUN–AUG
Rainy season from June to mid-July, then stiflingly hot and humid.

SEP–NOV
Hot until October; autumn colours from late November.

DEC–FEB
Cold and dry; most places close around New Year.

GETTING AROUND

Train The JR loop line is useful for accessing most of Osaka's main areas, with major stops including Osaka (Umeda) and Tennōji. Nara, Himeji and the Kii Peninsula can all be reached by train from Osaka.

Subway The Osaka metro has many lines, the most handy for visitors being the Midō-suji (red) line that runs north–south through the city.

IC Card Osaka's top-up transport card is called ICOCA and saves the hassle of buying tickets for every journey. It can be used throughout Kansai (and also in Tokyo) for trains (both JR and private lines), subways and some buses. Buy at JR ticket machines (preload with ¥2000, including a ¥500 refundable deposit).

EATING & DRINKING

Best areas Osaka has the best choice of places to eat and drink; Umeda and especially Namba are great for restaurants and bars. Other foodie districts include Fukushima (ramen shops), Tsuruhashi (Korean town and *yakiniku*) and Tenma with its labyrinth of back-alley restaurants and the Tenjinbashi-suji shopping street. Nara and Himeji have good options too.

Specialities Osaka's signature dishes are *tako-yaki* (fried octopus balls; pictured) and *okonomiyaki* (a kind of cabbage pancake), hearty soul foods made from a batter base.

Must-try ramen
Menya Jōroku (p148)

Best *okonomiyaki*
Ajinoya Honten (p137)

CONNECT & FIND YOUR WAY

Wi-fi Free in some areas; see ofw-oer.com/en.

Navigation Osaka is divided into two main areas: Umeda or Kita (north) centres on JR Osaka Station, while Minami (south) comprises the bustling downtown districts of Namba, Shinsaibashi and Dōtombori. You can find tourist offices at large stations throughout Kansai.

DISCOUNT CARDS & PASSES

Osaka Amazing Pass allows unlimited use of trains and buses, plus entry to attractions and other discounts; see osaka-info.jp/en. **Kansai Area Pass** offers unlimited travel across Kansai.

WHERE TO STAY

Osaka has many accommodation options, especially around Umeda and Namba, ranging from budget hostels and capsule hotels to five-star establishments. Smaller cities have more limited choices.

Place	Pros/Cons
Namba	Great for food, entertainment and nightlife, but also big crowds.
Umeda	Busy transit hub with plenty of shopping and dining options.
Tennōji	Good train links, if slightly out of the way. Near some of Osaka's seedier neighbourhoods.
Nara	A few options around JR Nara and Kintetsu Nara stations and the city centre. Quiet at night.
Himeji	Some hotels north and south of the station, although many visitors come as a day trip and stay elsewhere.
Kii Peninsula	Limited options, and mostly basic B&Bs in the mountain areas. Some hot spring inns in the larger towns.

MONEY

Always carry a good wad of notes, as although cashless payment is becoming more common, not everywhere accepts cards. Travel cards and passes can save you money.

20 Osaka Neon NIGHTS

CITY WALK | SIGHTSEEING | LANDMARKS

This evening walking tour takes in most of downtown Osaka's main sights and interesting neighbourhoods, all of which showcase the lively vibe and famous lights of the city, with plenty of opportunities for food and pit stops along the way.

CHRISTIAN MUELLER/SHUTTERSTOCK ©

How to

Getting around The full walk covers at least 4km, but it's possible to hop on and off the train or subway anywhere.

When to go Year-round, although summer evenings (July, August and early September) are hot.

Highlight Hit Dōtombori in the evening to see the riverside lights at their neon best.

Top tip If you don't fancy walking then rent a bicycle; check hubchari.com for rentals across the city.

Time it Right

If you're in Japan around early April for *hanami* (cherry-blossom viewing) season, then don't miss evening light-ups at **Osaka-jō**. Flea-market enthusiasts can browse for bargains at **Shitennōji** on the 21st and 22nd of every month. The **Nipponbashi Street Festa** is a cosplay festival held each March in Den Den Town.

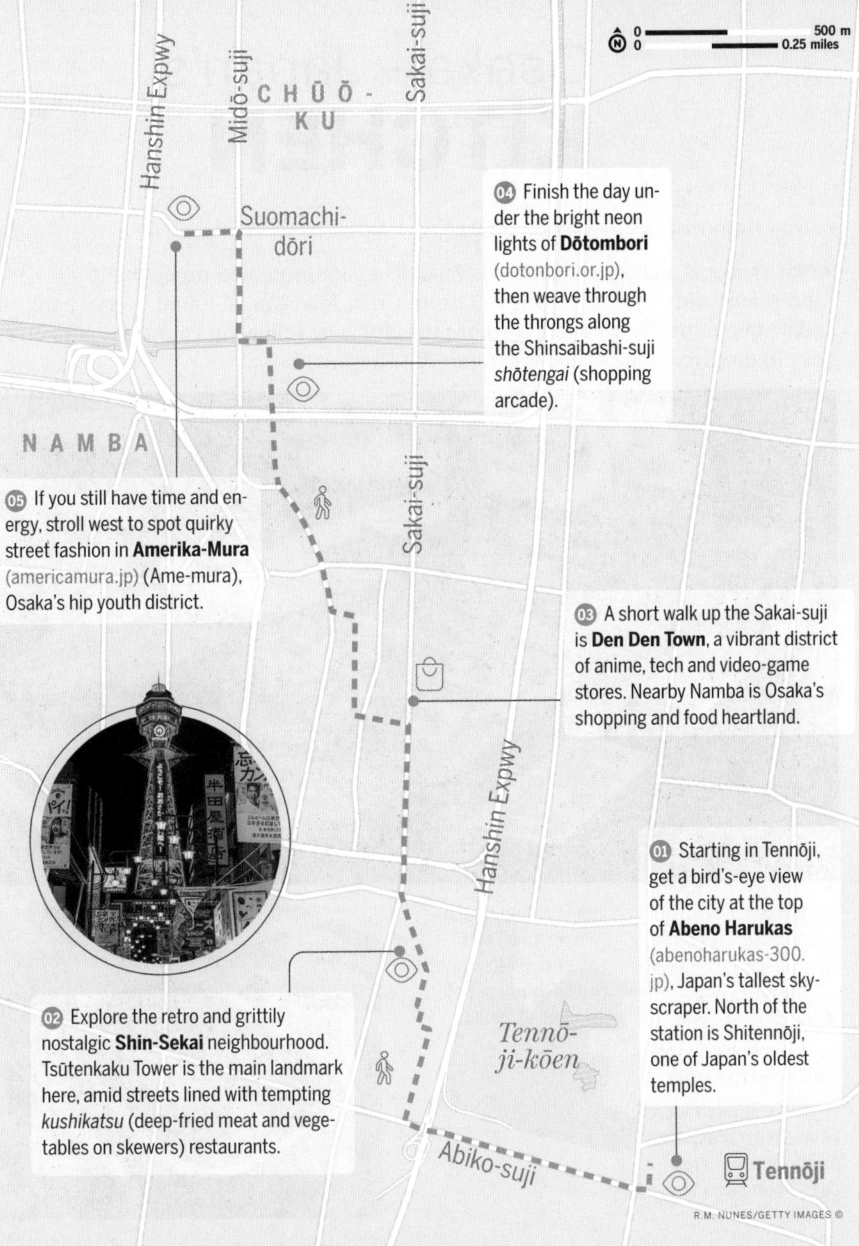

R.M. NUNES/GETTY IMAGES ©

21 Osaka – Japan's KITCHEN

FOOD | MARKET | LOCAL SPECIALITIES

Osaka is a city with a serious food obsession, summed up by the local expression *kuidaore* – 'eat until you drop'. Great food can be found everywhere, and so one of the best ways to explore the city is by following your eyes, ears and nose to discover some of the most mouth-watering bites.

YULIA GRIGORYEVA/SHUTTERSTOCK ©

How to

Getting around Most of Osaka is very walkable, and you can eat and drink until late as the trains and subways run until around midnight.

When to go Year-round, although many establishments close for a few days around New Year.

Fun fact Cup ramen (pot noodles) and *kaiten-zushi* (conveyor-belt sushi) were both invented in Osaka.

PAIKONG/SHUTTERSTOCK ©

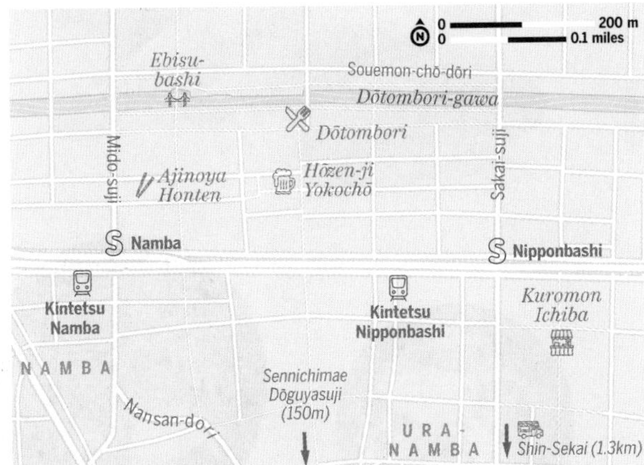

Downtown dishes The bright lights and lively buzz of **Dōtombori** make it Osaka's most popular hangout spot, especially around the famous **Ebisu-bashi** bridge and giant Glico 'running man' sign. The streets are lined with *tako-yaki* vendors, ramen bars and a barrage of colourful shops and signage, so grab some street food and soak up the sights and sounds. The area is also chockful of restaurants – just south of the bridge, **Ajinoya Honten** is one of the best places for *okonomiya,* while the atmospheric and old-fashioned cobbled alleyways of **Hōzen-ji Yokochō** are home to cosy *izakaya* (Japanese pub-eateries) that come alive at night.

Food shopping At the heart of Osaka's culinary scene, **Kuromon Ichiba** (Kuromon Market) is home to numerous shops selling fresh seafood, meat, fruit, vegetables and sweets – many have stalls out the front that cook food on the spot. A few blocks west is **Sennichimae Dōguyasuji**, a covered shopping street dedicated to kitchenware, with great foodie souvenirs.

Deep-fried delights An early-20th-century Osaka invention, *kushikatsu* is skewered meat, seafood and vegetables coated in breadcrumbs, deep fried and served with a dark, tangy dipping sauce. The antiquated and charmingly shabby streets of **Shin-Sekai** are rammed with *kushikatsu* restaurants, so take your pick and enjoy with a cold beer.

Above left Kuromon Ichiba
Below left *Kushikatsu*

Local Specialities

Osaka is called the 'nation's kitchen' because as a merchant city it became a literal storehouse of goods, like a kitchen in the home – while in culinary terms the city is known for its hearty local dishes.

Tako-yaki is Osaka's most famous street food; these golf-ball-size dollops of hot gooey batter are stuffed with octopus *(tako)* and cooked until crispy on the outside, then topped with a savoury sauce, mayonnaise, powdered seaweed and bonito fish flakes.

Okonomiyaki is another Osaka staple – savoury pancakes crammed with shredded cabbage and your choice of meat, seafood and vegetables, often cooked at your table.

Tastes of JAPAN

01 Sushi
Vinegared rice topped with raw fish and sometimes wrapped in *nori* (seaweed), served with soy sauce and wasabi.

02 Ramen
Wheat noodles in a rich broth from a meat or fish-based stock. Toppings include sliced braised pork, vegetables and eggs.

03 Udon
Thick white noodles made from wheat flour, usually served in a light broth with a variety of toppings.

04 Soba
Thin noodles made from buckwheat, either eaten cold with a dipping sauce, wasabi and spring onions, or in a hot broth.

05 Yakiniku
Literally 'grilled meat'; slices of beef or pork cooked on a charcoal grill and eaten with rice and dipping sauces.

06 Japanese curry
Generally sweet and mild rather than eye-wateringly spicy. Also called *kare-raisu* (curry rice), it is eaten with a spoon.

07 Nabe

A broad term for meat/seafood and vegetables cooked in a hotpot; variations include *shabu-shabu* and sukiyaki.

08 Yakitori

Bite-size pieces of chicken on a skewer, cooked over charcoal and seasoned with salt or a *tare* (sauce).

09 Kushikatsu

Small pieces of meat, seafood and vege-tables that are skewered, battered in panko bread crumbs and deep-fried, then dipped in a dark sauce.

10 Tonkatsu

Pork cutlet coated in breadcrumbs and deep-fried, served with rice, shredded cabbage and a tangy *tonkatsu* sauce.

11 Tempura

Thinly sliced meat, seafood or vegetables covered in a light and crispy batter, sometimes eaten with a dipping sauce.

12 Okonomiyaki

A savoury pancake made of a wheat-flour batter mixed with cabbage, meat or seafood, and cooked on a *teppan* (iron hotplate).

22 Doting on Deer IN NARA

ARCHITECTURE | NATURE | HISTORY

Nara-kōen is a lovely green and verdant space with a number of interesting sights, where you can stroll and perhaps even be accompanied by the resident deer. Nearby, the Daibutsu (Great Buddha) of Tōdai-ji is the highlight of any trip to Nara; the 15m-tall bronze statue is a magnificent sight, and sits inside one of the world's largest and most beautiful wooden buildings.

LUCIANO MORTULA - LGM/SHUTTERSTOCK ©

How to

Getting here Nara-kōen is a 15-minute walk from JR Nara Station or five minutes from Kintetsu Nara Station. Alternatively, frequent buses run to the park for ¥220. Tōdai-ji is another 10 minutes beyond the park.

When to go Weekends and holidays are busy, but the park has many quiet spots. Tōdai-ji is open year-round, from 7.30am to 5.30pm April to October and 8am to 5pm November to March.

Top tip Festival days are particularly interesting, but be prepared for crowds.

KHONG KATESORN/SHUTTERSTOCK ©

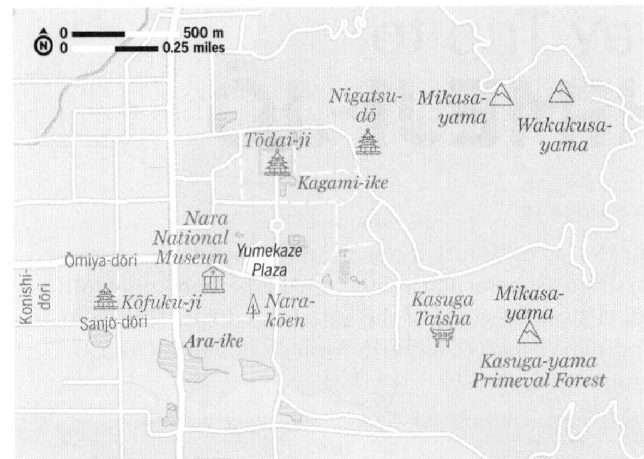

Above left Tōdai-ji
Below left Daibutsu

Treasures of the Park

Into the woods The highlights of Nara-kōen should take one unhurried day. Upon entering the park, you'll likely be confronted with herds of friendly, and occasionally feisty, deer. To the east rises **Wakakusa-yama**, a green hill that offers a short climb for good sunset views. Nearby you will also find **Kasuga Taisha**, an ancient Shintō forest shrine festooned with 3000 lanterns; when lit up at dusk they create a truly mystical aura.

Spectacular sights On the north side of the park is **Tōdai-ji**. Dating back to 752, the enormous wooden temple building took two million workers over 15 years to complete, although the current structure, rebuilt in 1709, is two-thirds the size of the original. Inside is the imposing yet kind-faced 15m-tall **Daibutsu**, a bronze Buddha statue made from over 500 tonnes of metal, and a truly mesmerising sight. Adjacent to Tōdai-ji is **Nigatsu-dō**, which in late winter is awash in flame at the Shuni-e Ceremony. Founded in 752, the temple's main hall is a National Treasure.

Among giants Back in the park, the **Nara National Museum** houses a tremendous collection of Buddhist art, with many exhibits dating from the 8th century. Strolling across the grounds of the adjacent **Kōfuku-ji**, you'll pass Japan's second-tallest wooden pagoda, and the unique Octagonal Hall at the far end of the courtyard. Descend the steps here to Sarusawa-ike pond.

Oh Deer!

Nara-kōen's 1500 deer are a highlight in themselves. According to legend, the deity of Kasuga Taisha rode into the park on a white stag. Deer also symbolise the Buddha's most essential teachings. As such, they were considered sacred, and until 1637 it was a capital offence to kill one. Now they wander around the park with gay abandon and exhibit little fear of humans – be careful not to have your clothes or bags nibbled! Small shops and stalls sell *senbei* (crackers) to feed them; some deer have learnt to bow in order to coax more food.

23 Day Trip to HIMEJI-JŌ

HISTORY | CASTLE | WORLD HERITAGE

Known as the 'White Heron' or 'White Egret' thanks to its dazzling white exterior, Himeji-jō is Japan's most spectacular castle. Sitting perched on a hill overlooking Himeji, a small city on the coast of the Seto Inland Sea, Himeji-jō is easily accessed by rail and makes a great day trip from Osaka and Kyoto, or a convenient stop-off if heading further west.

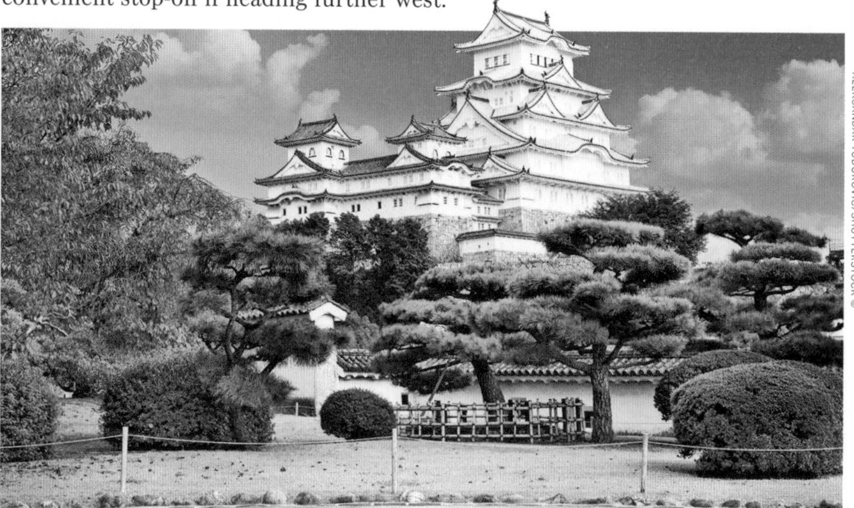

ALEKSANDAR TODOROVIC/SHUTTERSTOCK ©

How to

Getting here It's 30 minutes (¥3280) from Shin-Osaka on the shinkansen or one hour from Osaka Station on JR Special Rapid trains. The castle is a 15-minute walk north of Himeji Station, or a five-minute bus ride (get off at Ōtemon-mae stop, ¥100).

When to go Open all year (except 29–30 December); avoid busy times such as weekends and national holidays.

How much Entry is ¥1000 for adults, ¥300 for under 18s, preschool children free.

CYRUS_2000/SHUTTERSTOCK ©

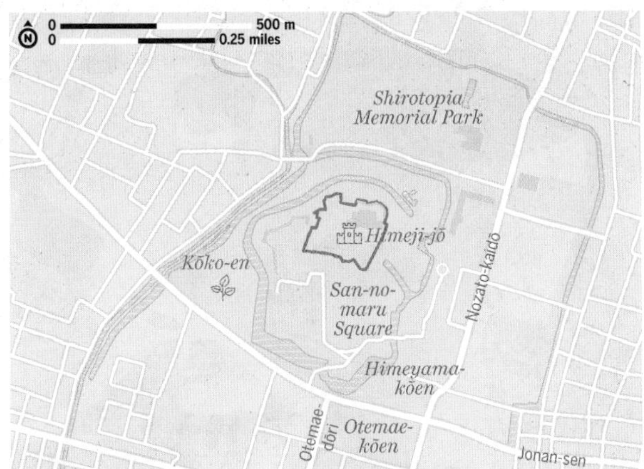

Deep history Designated as a National Treasure and one of only 12 original castles remaining in Japan (most are modern reconstructions), Himeji-jō is famed for its magnificent form, size and maze-like castle grounds. The site has been home to fortifications since 1333, and the current castle was built in 1580 by Toyotomi Hideyoshi, enlarged 30 years later by Ikeda Terumasa, and then home to generations of feudal lords. Himeji-jō saw little conflict, but has survived earthquakes and WWII bombings. The castle reopened in 2015 after five years of refurbishment; its walls and eaves were covered in traditional white plaster to restore the castle to its original beauty.

Explore the castle The grounds are divided by stone walls, gates, moats and other buildings and can be explored at leisure, while the seven floors of the towering main keep require you to take off your shoes (to protect the wooden floors) and clamber up multiple sets of excitingly steep and narrow stairs. The arrow-marked route through the castle takes about 1½ hours to complete, and the keep is inaccessible for people in wheelchairs and with strollers.

Hidden surprises Keep your eyes peeled for lots of easy-to-miss details such as the various-shaped small openings for firing bows and guns, tiny hiding holes in the corners of the keep, and carved numbers and letters on wooden beams (used to aid construction).

Above left Main tower, Himeji-jō
Below left Interior, Himeji-jō

Beyond the Castle

Just west of the castle is **Kōko-en**, nine exquisitely reconstructed Edo-period homes and gardens, including the lord's residence (complete with pond and waterfall), a teahouse and a bamboo grove.

Many historical TV dramas have been filmed here, and it's a lovely place to sip *matcha* (powdered green tea) or enjoy a *bentō* (boxed meal) in peaceful surroundings. Entry is ¥310/150 for adults/children (¥1050/¥360 with combined castle ticket).

Be sure to try the Himeji speciality *anago* (conger eel); nowhere does it better than the small and smoky **Yamayoshi** near the station. It's also on the menu at **Kassui-ken** in Kōko-en.

24 In the Footsteps OF PILGRIMS

HIKING | NATURE | CULTURE

The Kumano Kodō is a network of trails deep in the interior of the Kii Peninsula, first mapped centuries ago by mountain ascetics seeking spiritual enlightenment. There are gentle day hikes and more serious treks, plus onsen, shrines and scenic vistas.

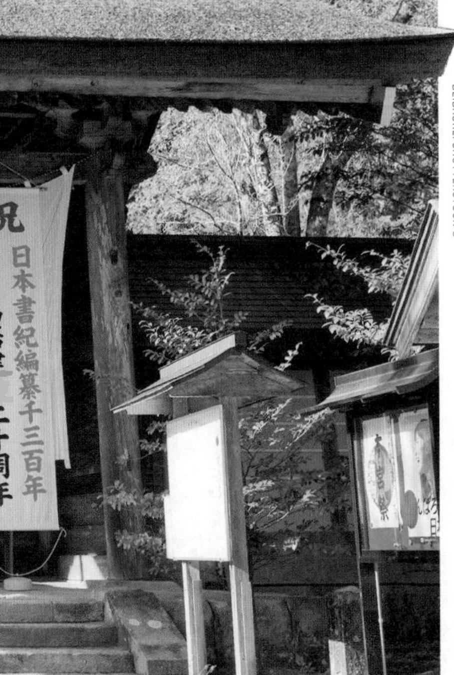

BEIBAOKE/SHUTTERSTOCK ©

How to

When to go It's possible to hike the Nakahechi route year-round, though bear in mind that you'll have fewer daylight hours to work with in winter, so plan accordingly (it's a good idea to have a headlamp).

Getting around You'll use a combination of legwork, buses and maybe a boat – how much of each is up to you. The Nakahechi Trail starts at Takijiri-ōji, a 40-minute bus ride from Kii-Tanabe Station.

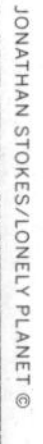

JONATHAN STOKES/LONELY PLANET ©

Shrines The great shrines of Kumano Hongū Taisha (p147), Kumano Hayatama Taisha (p147) and Kumano Nachi Taisha (p147) are the big draw for pilgrims on the trails; each is located at a deeply spiritual spot. The Nakahechi Trail runs between them, spanning (almost) the Kii Peninsula from west to east.

EIKO TSUCHIYA/SHUTTERSTOCK ©

Planning your hike Most travellers access the trails via Tanabe (Kii-Tanabe Station), a small city on the west coast of the peninsula, and finish at one of the cities on the east coast: Shingū or Nachi-Katsuura (Kii-Katsuura Station). **Kumano Travel** has an office in Tanabe, which is a great place to get current trail information, pick up maps and bus schedules and meet other travellers; they can also arrange luggage storage and shipping.

The Kohechi Trail

Experienced hikers can tackle the Kohechi Trail, which runs between Kōya-san and Hongū. It's 70km long, with major elevation changes, and typically done over four days, with overnights in Omata, Miura-guchi and Totsukawa Onsen. Only passable April to November.

Above left Kumano Hongū Taisha (p147)
Above right Kumano Kodō trail guide
Left Kumano Kodō

Walking the Nakahechi Trail The trail is broken down into numerous sections, bookended by small settlements where there are simple guesthouses to spend the night and get hot meals. The settlements also join the road, and you can pick up the bus at each, and also at some '*ōji*' – small temples that function as trail markers. Clearly signposted in English, the well-maintained trail is a mix of paved paths, packed earth and stone worn smooth from centuries of pilgrims treading them; the latter can get quite slippery when wet – poles can be a good hedge for balance. There are public toilets every few kilometres.

Takijiri-ōji to Hongū A good intro to the Nakahechi is the two-day trek from Takijiri-ōji to Hongū. This covers 38.5km, with some ups and downs, and includes overnighting midway in either Takahara or Chikatsu-yu (or both). For a short taste, consider the last 7.5km to Hongū (starting at Hosshinmon-ōji),

Kumano Culture

Starting around the 9th century, the wilds of the Kii Peninsula incubated a syncretic belief system, called **Shugendō**, that combined an early form of Shintō and Esoteric Buddhism with elements of folk religion, Taoism and shamanism.

In Shintō, *kami* (gods) are located in (among other things) impressive natural phenomena, such as mountains and waterfalls – of which Kii has many.

In Shugendō, these *kami* are also believed to be *gongen*, manifestations of the Buddha or bodhisattva. The practice of Shugendō includes acts of physical endurance, like hiking through the mountains, which is how the Kumano trails came to be.

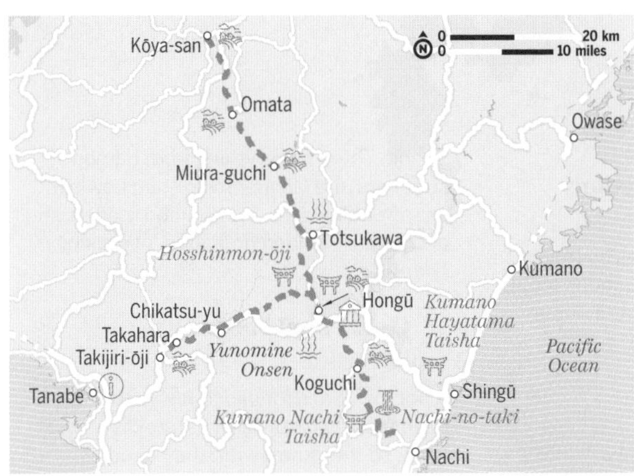

Left Nakahechi Trail
Below River cruise, Kumano-gawa

which takes two to three hours, is mostly downhill and passes through farmland and forest. Hongū is the trail's biggest hub, where **Kumano Hongū Taisha** is located. In Hongū, a short (2km) but steep trail, called **Dainichi-goe**, runs to the hot-spring settlement **Yunomine Onsen** – perfect for a post-hike soak. Buses also make the short trip between Hongū and Yunomine Onsen.

Ridgeline views or a river cruise From Hongū, there are a couple of options: continuing on the two-day hike (26.8km) to **Kumano Nachi Taisha**, with an overnight stay in Koguchi. This part of the trail is considered more challenging, and includes a steep section in the middle, but the pay off is some fantastic ridgeline views. Or you can do as many pilgrims of old did: take a 90-minute river cruise on a sampan down the Kumano-gawa, which finishes right near **Kumano Hayatama Taisha** in Shingu. You'll need to take a bus form Hongū to the pier; book through Kumano Travel and request an English-speaking guide.

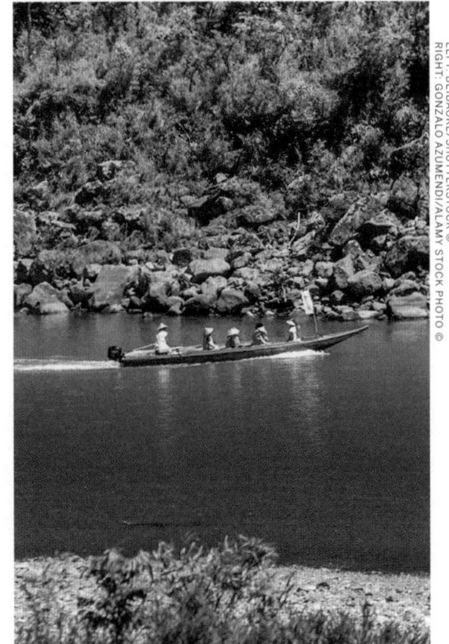

Listings

BEST OF THE REST

Popular Osaka Attractions

Universal Studios Japan

Popular theme park 10 minutes by train from Osaka Station. Rides and attractions for all ages, including Harry Potter– and Super Nintendo–themed worlds. Can get busy, so avoid weekends and holidays.

Umeda Sky Building

An Umeda landmark, two 40-storey towers connected at the top by a large observatory and outdoor viewing deck offering great nighttime city views. A 15-minute walk from JR Osaka Station.

Osaka Aquarium Kaiyūkan

One of the largest aquariums in Japan, 30 minutes by train from central Osaka. See a staggering array of fish and other marine life including sea otters, penguins and whale sharks.

Sumiyoshi Taisha

Founded in the 3rd century, Sumiyoshi Taisha is one of the oldest shrines in Japan and famous for its beautifully arched red bridge. Just 10 minutes by train south of Namba.

Osaka Museum of Housing & Living

Spend an hour or two exploring detailed and evocative recreations of streets and buildings from yesteryear Osaka at this compact but fascinating museum, located directly above Tenjinbashisuji-chōme Station.

Dōguya-suji Arcade

This long arcade sells just about anything related to the preparation, consumption and selling of Osaka's principal passion – food. There's everything from bamboo steamers and lacquer miso soup bowls to shopfront lanterns, plastic food models and, of course, moulded hotplates for making *tako-yaki*.

Osaka Soul Foods

Okonomiyaki Mizuno ¥

A popular place for *okonomiyaki* that has been making Osaka's signature dish since 1945, so they know what they're doing. Located halfway between Namba and Nipponbashi metro stations.

Takoyaki Wanaka ¥

It's not hard to find *tako-yaki* in Osaka, but this well-known chain serves up crispy yet delightfully gooey-on-the-inside octopus balls. Quick and friendly service. There's a branch in Osaka-jō park.

Menya Jōroku ¥

Celebrated ramen shop in Namba, specialising in bowls using a rich chicken-based stock. Don't miss the *chūka soba*, its signature soy-sauce ramen. Small place so there's usually a queue, but it's worth it.

Osaka Museum of Housing & Living

Ramen Jinsei JET ¥

Popular ramen restaurant a short walk north of JR Fukushima Station, in northwest Osaka, serving hearty bowls of chicken ramen in a thick broth. Order from the vending machine outside (staff can help).

Dōtombori Imai Honten ¥¥

An oasis of calm among the downtown hubbub, this udon restaurant one minute from Ebisu-bashi bridge is a long-running Osaka institution known for its top-notch food and old-style ambience.

Genrokuzushi ¥

The first *kaiten-zushi* (conveyor-belt sushi) in the world, now with restaurants across the city – the Sennichimae branch is probably the best. Decent, affordable sushi and English menus.

Endō Sushi ¥¥

Amazingly fresh top-grade sushi at this family-run restaurant next to Osaka Central Wholesale Fish Market. Popular with locals and tourists; expect to wait even early in the morning. Cash only.

Restaurants Around Kansai

Mizuya Chaya ¥

After seeing the sights of Nara, head to this lovely thatched-roof teahouse at the edge of the park for a bowl of udon or green tea and *wagashi* (Japanese sweets).

Hirasō ¥¥

Tucked away in the backstreets of Nara, this cosy establishment is the place to try local dishes such as *kakinoha-zushi* (sushi in persimmon leaf) and *chagayu* (rice porridge with green tea).

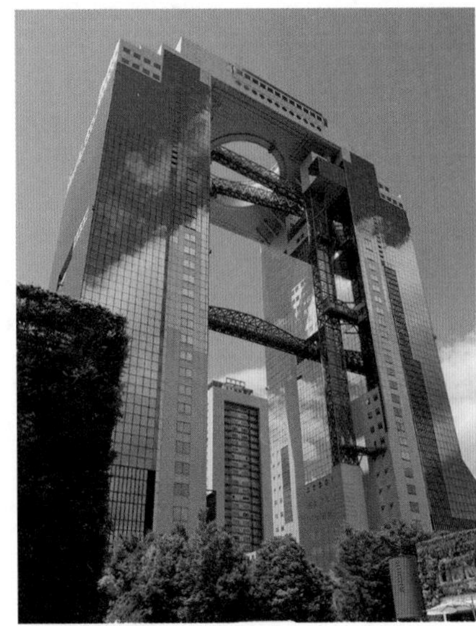

HIROSHI H/SHUTTERSTOCK ©

Umeda Sky Building

Takata-no-Baba ¥¥

A stone's throw from Himeji-jō, this combined shop and restaurant has tasty lunch sets, and boasts pavement seating with views of the castle.

Bononsha ¥¥

Chill vegetarian cafe in Kōya-san. Come after 11am for the excellent daily lunch plate, served until they run out. Good coffee and chai too. English menu.

HIROSHIMA & WESTERN HONSHŪ

CYCLING | ISLANDS | HISTORY

Shimanami Kaidō cycle path (p166)

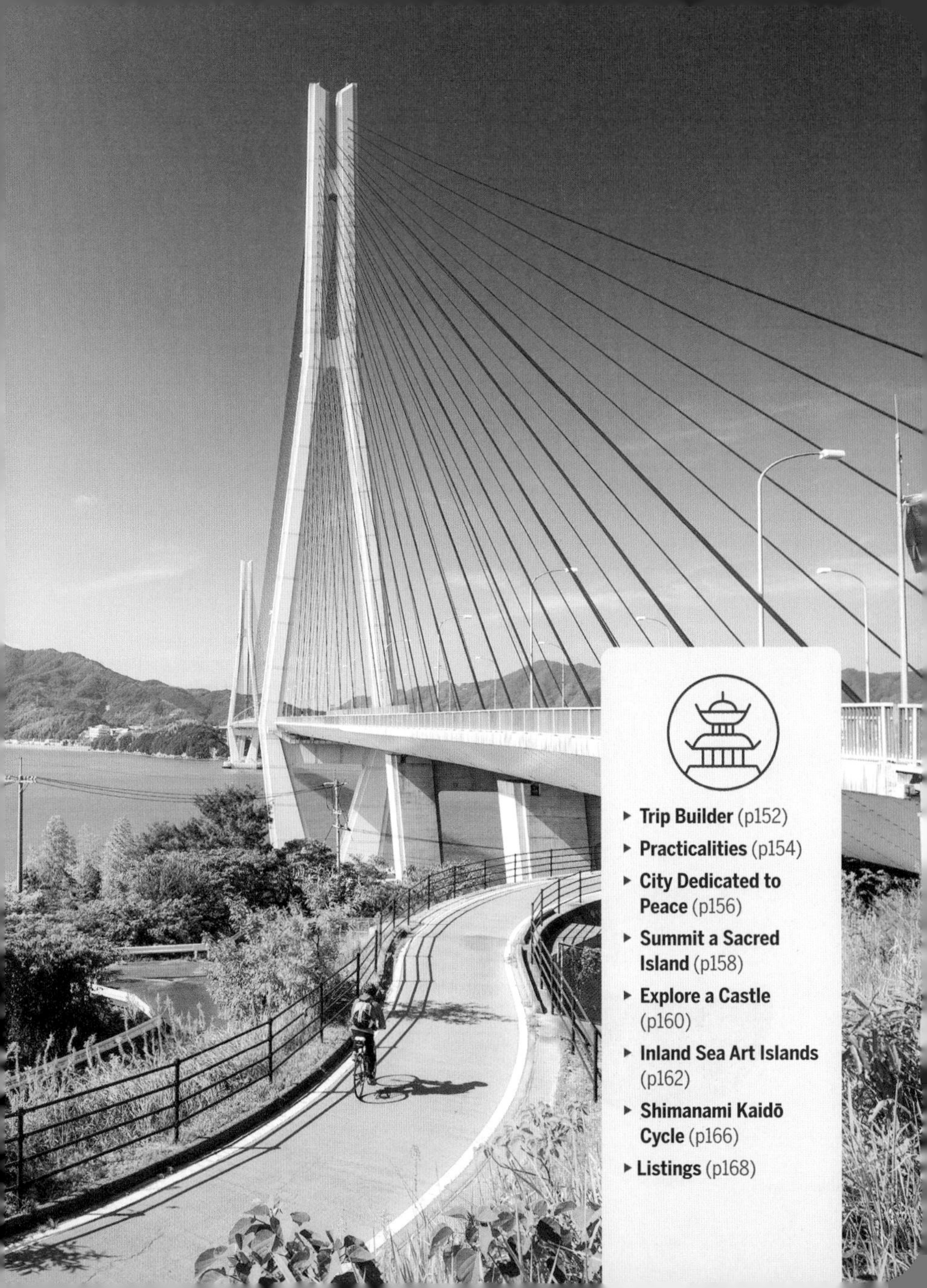

HIROSHIMA & WESTERN HONSHŪ

Trip Builder

Because of its WWII history, Hiroshima draws the crowds, but it's just one of many fine reasons for exploring Western Honshū. Ancient shrines, well-preserved Edo-era castles, unique gardens and serene islands sprinkled with art all await your discovery.

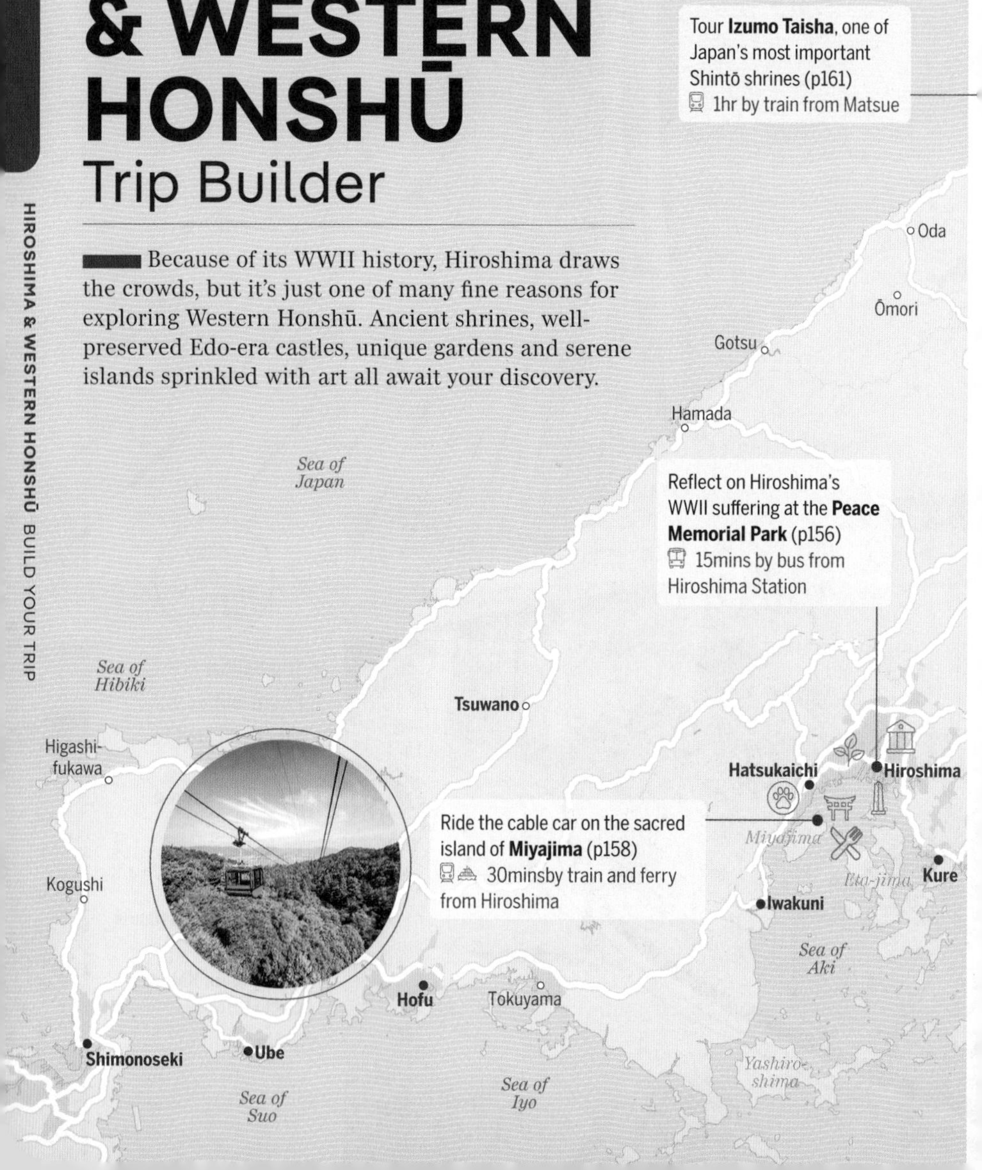
Tour **Izumo Taisha**, one of Japan's most important Shintō shrines (p161)
1hr by train from Matsue
Oda
Ōmori
Gotsu
Hamada
Sea of Japan
Reflect on Hiroshima's WWII suffering at the **Peace Memorial Park** (p156)
15mins by bus from Hiroshima Station
Sea of Hibiki
Tsuwano
Higashi-fukawa
Hatsukaichi
Hiroshima
Ride the cable car on the sacred island of **Miyajima** (p158)
30minsby train and ferry from Hiroshima
Miyajima
Kogushi
Eta-jima
Kure
Iwakuni
Sea of Aki
Hofu
Tokuyama
Shimonoseki
Ube
Yashiro-shima
Sea of Iyo
Sea of Suo

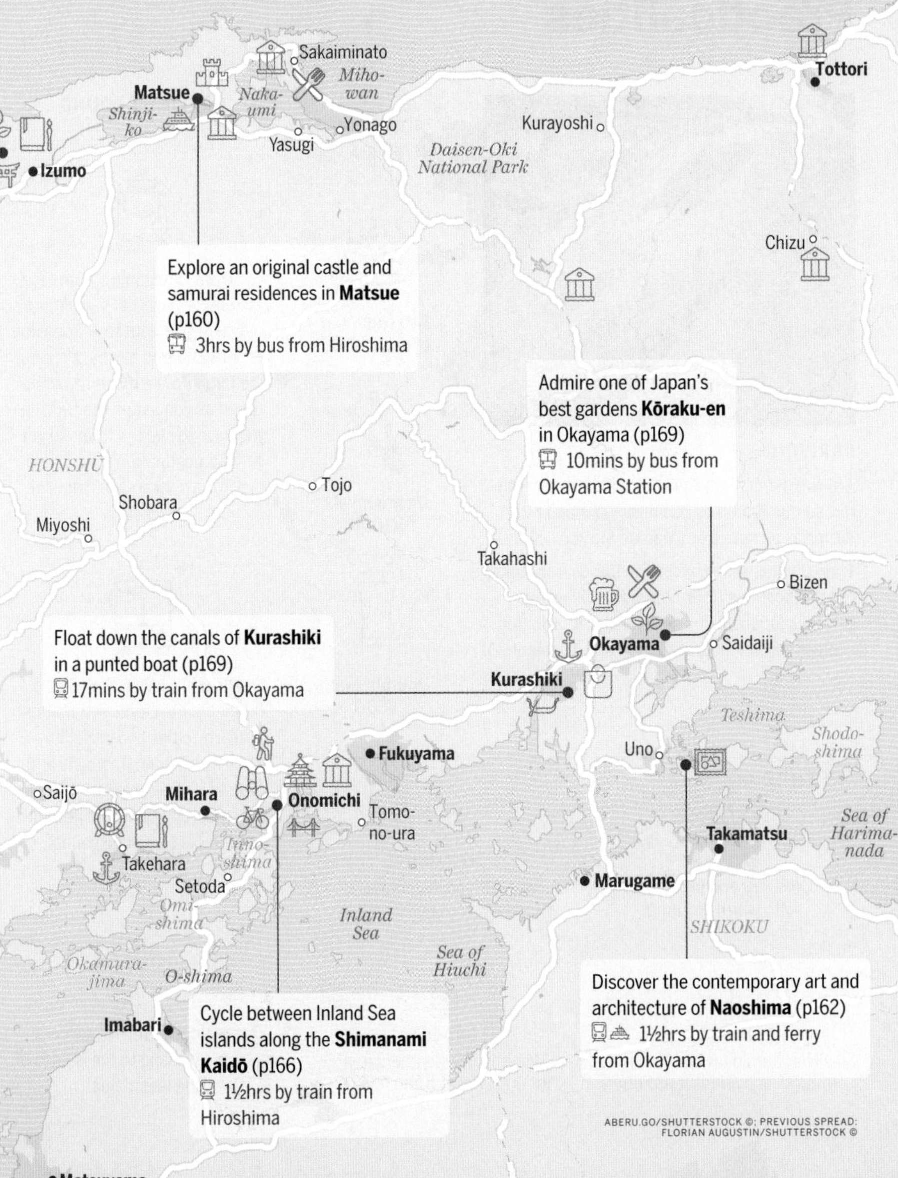

0 50 km
0 25 miles
Sakaiminato
Tottori
Matsue
Miho-wan
Naka-umi
Shinji-ko
Yonago
Yasugi
Kurayoshi
Daisen-Oki National Park
Izumo
Chizu
Explore an original castle and samurai residences in **Matsue** (p160)
3hrs by bus from Hiroshima
Admire one of Japan's best gardens **Kōraku-en** in Okayama (p169)
10mins by bus from Okayama Station
HONSHŪ
Tojo
Shobara
Miyoshi
Takahashi
Bizen
Float down the canals of **Kurashiki** in a punted boat (p169)
17mins by train from Okayama
Okayama
Saidaiji
Kurashiki
Teshima
Shodo-shima
Uno
Fukuyama
Saijō
Mihara
Onomichi
Tomo-no-ura
Sea of Harima-nada
Takamatsu
Inno-shima
Takehara
Setoda
Marugame
Omi-shima
Inland Sea
SHIKOKU
Sea of Hiuchi
Okamura-jima
O-shima
Discover the contemporary art and architecture of **Naoshima** (p162)
1½hrs by train and ferry from Okayama
Imabari
Cycle between Inland Sea islands along the **Shimanami Kaidō** (p166)
1½hrs by train from Hiroshima
Matsuyama

Practicalities

EQROY/SHUTTERSTOCK ©

ARRIVING

Air Hiroshima Airport is about 50 minutes from Hiroshima Station by bus or taxi. Yonago Kitaro Airport is an hour from Matsue Station by bus.

Train Shinkansen services (pictured) from Tokyo run to Hiroshima (four hours) and Okayama (3½ hours), where you can transfer to a limited express train to Matsue (two hours, 40 minutes).

HOW MUCH FOR A

Two fresh raw oysters ¥500

***Okonomiyaki* ¥1000**

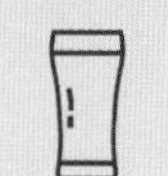

Draught beer ¥500

WHEN TO GO

JAN–MAR
Cold, dry and clear; fine with warm clothing.

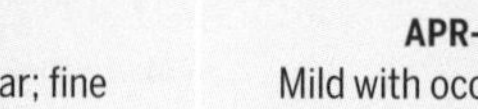

APR–JUN
Mild with occasional rain; increasingly rainy from June.

JUL–SEP
Hot, humid and rainy, but improving by mid-September.

OCT–DEC
Mild and dry weather, great for enjoying autumn foliage.

GETTING AROUND

Tram Hiroshima's trams (streetcars) will get you almost anywhere you want to go for a flat fare of ¥220. You pay by dropping the fare into the machine by the driver as you get off the tram. If you have to change trams to get to your destination, you should ask for a *norikae-ken* (transfer ticket).

Hiroshima Bus Terminal Connects the city to attractions in nearby cities and prefectures, such as Iwakuni, Onomichi and Matsue. Buses are comfortable and reasonably priced, often with valuable tourist discounts.

Ferry Regular ferries connect mainland Honshū to the islands of the Inland Sea.

TOP: LUNAPICS/SHUTTERSTOCK ©
BOTTOM: NICEPIX/SHUTTERSTOCK ©

EATING & DRINKING

Delicious fresh seafood is a constant of the region's cuisine. Hiroshima is famous for oysters and its version of *okonomiyaki* (savoury pancakes made with batter and cabbage, with vegetables and seafood or meat, cooked on a griddle; pictured), and has a wide range of international options and cafes – as do Okayama and Matsue. In Iwakuni try *Iwakuni-zushi* (pictured) a local style of preserved sushi served like a slice of cake. Also look out for locally produced sake.

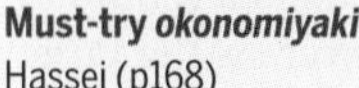

Must-try *okonomiyaki*
Hassei (p168)

Best sake town
Saijō (p169)

CONNECT & FIND YOUR WAY

Wi-fi Japan wi-fi is a free service available nationwide. Download the app to connect automatically when you are near hot spots. For a faster connection with wider coverage, rent a pocket wi-fi from Japan Wireless (japan-wireless.com).

Navigation You will need navigation apps to find locations and figure out how to get there.

WHERE TO STAY

Hiroshima is a good base, but reasonable midrange hotels are available throughout Western Honshū so you can city-hop without breaking your budget.

Place	Pros/Cons
Hiroshima	Large number of midrange hotels downtown and around Hiroshima Station.
Miyajima	Great for ryokans (traditional inns) and guesthouses. No nightlife.
Matsue	Good base for north coast of Western Honshū. Hotels and ryokan around Matsue Station and north of the Ōhashi-gawa.
Naoshima	Guesthouses and a couple of luxury hotels, concentrated in the ports of Miyanoura and Honmura.
Shimanami Kaido	Hotels, guesthouses and hostels in every town along the route. Some places have rooms that allow bicycle storage.

VISIT HIROSHIMA TOURIST PASS

Purchase the Visit Hiroshima Tourist Pass for one, two or three days for unlimited use of trams, many buses and ferries to Miyajima, plus local business discounts.

MONEY

Cash is king, but invest in a PASPY transit card to make it easier to ride trains and buses. Breaking ¥10,000 bills at convenience stores is not a problem, even for small items.

25 City Dedicated TO PEACE

HISTORY | ARCHITECTURE | NATURE

An attractive delta city of bridges and rivers, Hiroshima offers a rebuilt castle, delicious food and great nightlife. It's most famous, however, as the target of the world's first atomic-bomb attack by the US. The Peace Memorial Park and museum commemorate and record that fateful day, drawing millions of visitors from all over the world as latter-day witnesses to the horrors of war.

SEAN PAVONE/SHUTTERSTOCK ©

How to

Getting there Ride a tram from JR Hiroshima Station to either the Genbaku-domu-mae or Chuden-mae stops.

When to go On 6 August, the anniversary of the atomic bombing, thousands of paper lanterns are floated down the river from in front of the Atomic Bomb Dome.

Photo op The cenotaph frames the Flame of Peace, while on the same axis, away across the river, is the World Heritage–listed Atomic Bomb Dome.

LUCIANO MORTULA - LGM/SHUTTERSTOCK ©

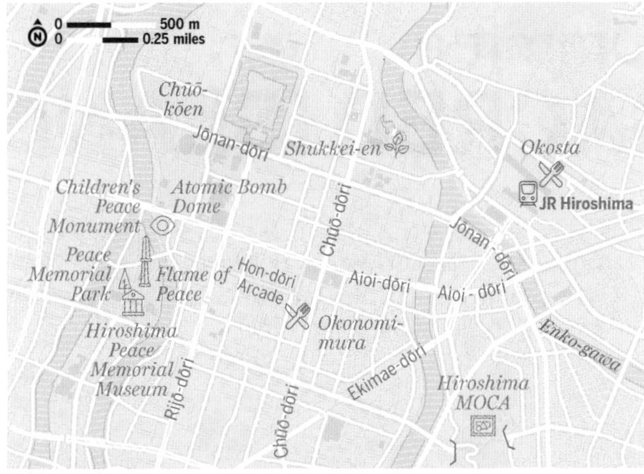

Above left Peace Memorial Park
Below left Atomic Bomb Dome

Hiroshima Peace Memorial Museum

Begin to grasp the impact of 6 August 1945 from the graphic and upsetting images and items exhibited in this must-see **museum** (pcf.city.hiroshima.jp). Before and after photographs of the city sit alongside salvaged items – ragged clothes, a child's melted lunchbox, a watch stopped at 8.15am. Exhibits also cover the history of Hiroshima, why it was the target of the American A-bomb, and all about nuclear weapons. Listen to first-hand accounts from those who lived through the bombing.

Peace Memorial Park

Bordered by rivers and dotted with memorials, this leafy park provides tranquil spaces for reflection. Designed by award-winning architect Kenzō Tange, the park's central features are the **Pond of Peace** leading to the **cenotaph**, a curved concrete monument holding the names of all the known victims of the bomb. The cenotaph frames the **Flame of Peace**, set to burn on until all the world's nuclear weapons are destroyed.

Also look out for the **Children's Peace Monument** festooned with origami cranes, a symbol of the city.

Atomic Bomb Dome

Built in 1915, this World Heritage-listed ruin was originally a Western-style exhibition hall. It stands just 160m from the hypocentre of the blast. Rubble remains scattered around the hollowed-out shell, and scorch marks are visible on the ruins, which were preserved in 1966. Wander past in the evening when it's quieter and the steel and concrete skeleton is floodlit.

DIY Okonomiyaki

Okonomiyaki, Hiroshima's food speciality, is served right across the city. At the touristy but fun **Okonomi-mura** (okonomimura.jp) there are 25 stalls spread over three floors, each serving up hearty variations of the savoury pancake.

Learn how to cook the dish yourself at **Okosta**, an *okonomiyaki* cooking studio next to JR Hiroshima Station. There are three 1½ hour sessions you can book throughout the day, with vegetarian and Muslim-friendly options available, the latter including a halal sauce.

26 Summit a SACRED ISLAND

RELIGION | NATURE | HIKING

The small island of Miyajima is a UNESCO World Heritage Site and one of Japan's most visited tourist spots. Its star attraction is the vermilion *torii* (shrine gate) of Itsukushima-jinja, which appears to float on the waves at high tide.

FRENTAN/SHUTTERSTOCK ©

How to

Getting here Miyajima is around 30 minutes by train or tram, then a ferry from Hiroshima.

When to go Spring and autumn for beautiful foliage. Avoid the crowded holiday periods.

Top tips Stay overnight at a traditional inn to enjoy the evening quiet once the day trippers have departed. The island's tame deer are cute, but will eat right out of your pocket if you're not careful.

The Floating Shrine

With origins as far back as the late 6th century, Itsukushima-jinja's present form dates from 1168. On one side of the shrine is a stage, built by local lord Asano Tsunanaga in 1680 and still used for *nō* (stylised dance-drama) performances in April as part of the **Toka-sai Festival**.

Hiroshima-wan

Omotesando

01 At low tide it's possible to walk across the muddy beach to the red-lacquered *torii* of **Itsukushima-jinja**.

02 The huge pavilion **Senjō-kaku**, built in 1587, has massive wooden pillars and beams and a ceiling hung with paintings. It looks out onto a 28m-tall, five-storey pagoda.

03 Surrounded by forest, **Daishō-in**, Miyajima's oldest Buddhist temple, includes a pathway lined with 500 tiny statues of red-capped monks, and a lantern-bedecked cave.

Miyajima Ropeway Momiji-dani Station

04 Avoid most of the uphill climb of 530m Misen by taking the two-stage **ropeway**; from the upper station it's a 30-minute hike to the summit.

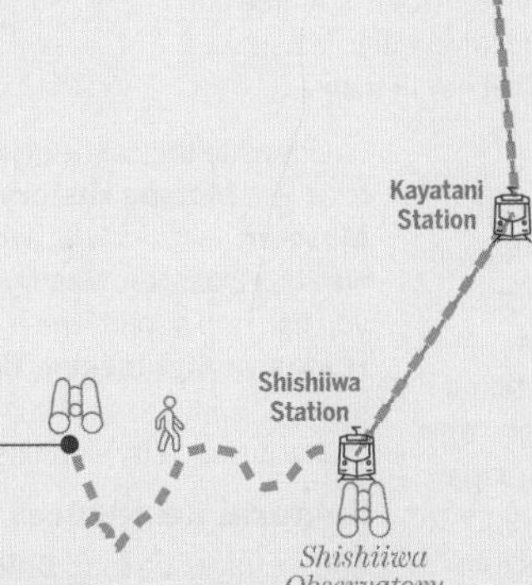

05 At the **Misen Summit Observatory**, kick off your shoes and laze on wooden platforms while enjoying 360-degree views over the Inland Sea.

VLADZUBKOV/SHUTTERSTOCK ©

27 Explore a CASTLE

CASTLE | SAMURAI | SUNSETS

Known as the City of Water, Matsue straddles the Ōhashi-gawa, which connects Shinji-ko (Lake Shinji) and Nakaumi lagoon. Threaded with canals, it's an appealing, slow-paced city with an original castle, a well-preserved samurai quarter and sublime sunsets. The celebrated Greek-Irish writer Lafcadio Hearn lived here in 1890 and is still very fondly remembered.

How to

When to go The **Matsue Suitōro**, a festival during which the castle grounds are illuminated by hand-painted lanterns, is held in late September and early October.

Getting here The nearest airport is Yonago. Alternatively, take the shinkansen (bullet train) to Okayama where you can transfer to a limited express train to Matsue.

Top tip The En-Musubi Perfect Ticket is a three-day pass that covers unlimited travel within Matsue, Izumo and Sakaiminato (but not JR trains).

Original Keep

Matsue's castle, **Matsue-jō** (matsue-castle.jp), is also known as Chidori-jō (Plover Castle) for the graceful bird-like shape of its gable ornaments. Completed in 1611, it's one of only 12 original keeps in Japan. Climb to the keep's top floor to admire its wooden structure and for 360-degree views.

Opposite the castle is the excellent **Matsue History Museum** (matsu-reki.jp), which also has a garden. Nearby you can hop aboard the **Horikawa Sightseeing Boat** (matsue-horikawameguri.jp) for a cruise around city's canals.

Samurai Residences

The picturesque road **Shiomi Nawate** is lined with the

Above right Matsue-jō
Right Izumo Taisha

Shintō Gods' Gathering Place

Izumo Taisha, 1¼ hours by train west of Matsue, is one of Japan's most important shrines. Its founding predates written history, but the shrine's impressive buildings are reconstructed using traditional methods every 60 to 70 years.

Only the head priest is allowed into the inner shrine, most of which is hidden behind huge wooden fences. Also notable is the mammoth *shimenawa* (twisted-straw rope) that hangs in front of the modern hall on the shrine's west side.

homes of former feudal retainers and samurai. **Buke Yashiki** (matsue-bukeyashiki.jp) provides insight into how samurai families lived during the Edo period. Further along is the **Lafcadio Hearn Memorial Museum** (hearn-museum-matsue.jp), which has excellent English information panels.

Sunset Park

Matsue's spectacular sunsets are justly famous. The prime viewing spot is from the aptly named **Sunset Park**, next to the **Shimane Prefectural Art Museum** (shimane-art-museum.jp). The museum displays rotating exhibits from its collection of around 3000 *ukiyo-e* (woodblock prints), most by the master Hokusai.

MTAIRA/SHUTTERSTOCK ©

HUGO TREMOLIERE/500PX ©

28 Inland Sea ART ISLANDS

ART | NATURE | CYCLING

The 3000-plus islands dotted across the Inland Sea provide one of the most scenic vistas in Japan. Art lovers should not miss Naoshima. Its emblem, one of Yayoi Kusama's *Pumpkin* sculptures, is just the yellow polka-dotted tip of a collection of contemporary art and architecture in a gorgeous natural setting.

CHATCHAWAT PRASERTSOM/SHUTTERSTOCK ©

How to

When to Go Any time of year. Winter is the quietest; weekends and holidays the busiest.

Getting there Hop on ferries at the main ports of Takamatsu and Uno.

Top tip Lather up in Naoshima Public Bath 'I Love Yu', a *sentō* (public bath) in Miyanoura on Naoshima. The building is a huge artwork by the artist Ōtake Shinrō and includes a full-scale elephant statue in the bathing hall.

JAMES TALALAY/ALAMY STOCK PHOTO ©

Action Plan

Naoshima, Teshima and Inujima together comprise the Benesse Art Site. A few key locations can be toured in a day, but to fully do the islands justice set aside a couple of days. Bicycles are the way to get around Naoshima and Teshima. E-bicycle are available. But for Teshima renting a moped helps as this island is bigger and hillier – bring an international driving licence, if you plan to do this. Inujima is so small it's easy to walk around.

Museum Buried Underground

Book online for your timed slot to visit the **Chichū Art Museum** (benesse-artsite.jp/en/art/chichu.html) on Naoshima before you arrive. This extraordinary building, designed by the Benesse Art Site's favourite architect Tadao Ando, is a series of concrete-walled galleries fitted into the hillside. Natural light filters into

BISUAL PHOTO/SHUTTERSTOCK ©

Setouchi Trienniale

Every three years the Setouchi Trienniale (setouchi-art fest.jp) sees many new art projects unveiled on Naoshima and its surrounds. The website lists where the artworks are located. It's a highly popular event so be sure to book accommodation well ahead or be prepared to commute from either Okayaka or Takamatsu.

Above left Teshima Art Museum (p165)
Left Chichū Art Museum
Above Naoshima Public Bath

these cool caverns to illuminate, most spectacularly, five of Monet's water-lily paintings. Also here on display are three light installations by James Turrell and an enigmatic, monumental set of sculptures by Walter De Maria.

Benesse House Museum

Hilltop Benesse House Museum (benesse-artsite.jp/en) was one of Ando's first projects on Naoshima. This combined museum and hotel offers both interior and exterior artworks; hotel guests also get to see some of the collection in their rooms. The beach here is the location of Kusama's iconic *Pumpkin*. Also nearby is Kusama's *Narcissus Garden,* an installation of 1700 stainless-steel spheres in the **Valley Gallery**, an indoor-outdoor space designed by Ando in 2022.

Honmura's Art Houses

In Honmura, on the east side of Naoshima, Benesse has converted a handful of the fishing village's empty properties (plus a shrine) into seven Art Houses. Get a ticket to explore

Copper Refinery Reimagined

Inujima once had a copper refinery, but that closed in 1919. A new chapter in the tiny island's history began when Benesse commissioned architect Sambuchi Hiroshi and artist Yanagi Yukinori to create a museum out of the refinery's ruined brick buildings. Their fascinating **Inujima Seirensho Art Museum** is an example of recycling and upcycling on a grand scale. It houses Yanagi's multi-part installation *Hero Dry Cell,* which combines island materials with the parts of a Tokyo house where the writer Yukio Mishima once lived. Inujima has several other art sites included in the museum ticket price, as well as cute cafes.

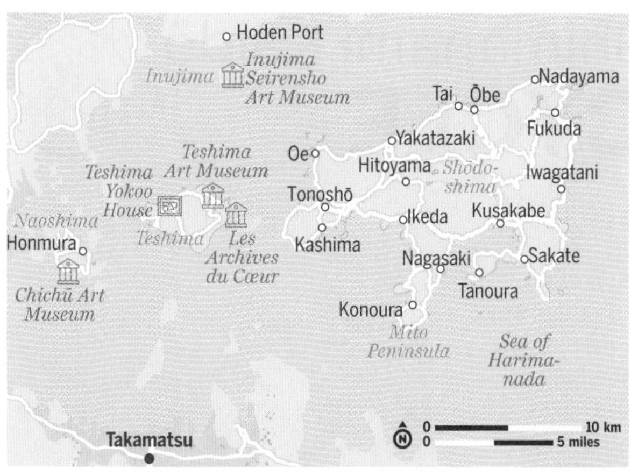

Left Inujima Seirensho Art Museum
Below Haisha

them all from the **Honmura Lounge & Archive** near the harbour. You'll be given a timed ticket for **Minamidera**, a modern building designed by Ando to accommodate an ingenious experiment with light by American artist James Turrell.

Also look out for Ōtake Shinrō's **Haisha**. The former home and office of a dentist has been transformed with painting, scrapbook collages and sculptures, including a giant Statue of Liberty.

Slow Down on Teshima

With a population of around 1000, Teshima has a laid-back, rural vibe. On a hill surrounded by terraced rice fields, **Teshima Art Museum** (benesse-artsite.jp/en/art/teshima-artmuseum.html) is a mesmerising, meditative collaboration between the architect Ryue Nishizawa and artist Rei Naito. An installation rather than a traditional museum, the domed building's concrete shell has large holes open to the elements. On the floor, watch tiny holes pump out drops of water that collide, merge and trickle in perpetual motion.

Other Teshima artworks include **Les Archives du Cœur** (benesse-artsite.jp/en/art/boltanski.html), an audio library of heartbeat recordings from around the world by French sound artist Christian Boltanski; and **Teshima Yokoo House** (benesse-artsite.jp/en/art/teshima-yokoohouse.html), a house converted into a gallery for the surreal art of Tadanori Yokoo.

29 Shimanami Kaidō CYCLE

CYCLING | VISTAS | SHRINES

Since the construction of six road bridges that island-hop their way to Shikoku, Onomichi has become the Western Honshū hub for the hugely popular Shimanami Kaidō. This 70km-long cycling or walking route across the Inland Sea is one of Japan's best two-wheel road trips. It's easily customisable in length and difficulty, with gorgeous scenery around practically every curve.

How to

Getting there By train Onomichi is one to 1½ hours east of Hiroshima and a similar time west of Okayama.

When to go Cycle year-round; there's a greater likelihood of heavy rain or typhoons from mid-June to mid-September.

Take your time The route can be cycled in a day, but you'll enjoy it more if you allow at least two days.

How much E-bikes can be rented from ¥3000 per day.

Follow the Blue Line

The Shimanami Kaidō has plenty of English signage. When in doubt, follow the blue line painted on the road with directions and mileage to each end point.

Bicycle rentals abound in Onomichi and on the islands. E-bikes are a good option for taking the strain out of the inclines leading to each of the bridges. There are a dozen drop-off points along the route, which are useful if you decide to take a bus or ferry back. However, if you do drop off your bike at a different place from where you rented, you'll forgo your deposit.

Above right Shimanami Kaidō route **Right** Kōsan-ji

FLORIAN AUGUSTIN/SHUTTERSTOCK ©

Good Luck Shrine

Ōyamazumi-jinja, in Miyaura on Ōmi-shima, is one of Japan's oldest shrines. In the grounds stands a 2600-year-old camphor tree – locals believe that if you walk three times around its stout trunk, its spirit will grant you a wish. Famous warriors used to visit the shrine to pray for victory and to donate their weapons and armour – which explains the important historical collection in the shrine's treasure hall.

Contemporary reasons for visiting Miyaura include the **Omishima Brewery** and the **Omishima Wine Bar** where you can sample very quaffable locally produced beers and wines.

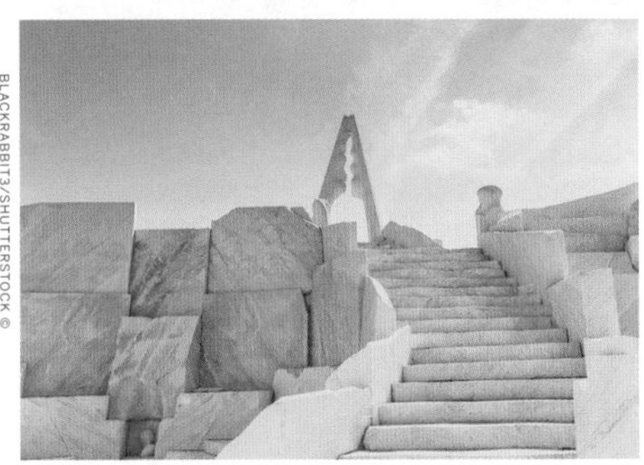

BLACKRABBIT3/SHUTTERSTOCK ©

Day Trip to Ikuchi-jima

A great day trip from Onomichi is to pedal to Ikuchi-jima (about 30km) and return on the ferry. The main town **Setoda** is famous for its kitsch temple complex **Kōsan-ji** (kousanji.or.jp), which also features a creepy 1000 Buddhas Cave and the Hill of Hope, an acropolis of 2700 tonnes of Carrara marble with panoramic views over the island. There are also lovely places to stay in Setoda such as **Yubune**, an upmarket, bike-friendly hotel and public bath with fab mosaic murals.

Listings

BEST OF THE REST

Locally Famous Cuisine

Hassei ¥

Hiroshima hole-in-the-wall joint famous for its tasty, generous layers of cabbage, noodles and other ingredients in *okonomiyaki* pancakes. They can do half-orders, if you're not so hungry.

Kisetsu Ryōri Nakashima ¥¥¥

Book well ahead for superb *kaiseki ryōri* (fine-dining set menu) at this elegant Hiroshima restaurant. Dishes are served on exquisite antique lacquerware and ceramics.

Kakiya ¥¥

Sophisticated dining bar on Miyajima serving delicious local oysters freshly barbecued in their shells. Good wine list.

Hirasei ¥

Venerable restaurant in Iwakuni with views of the town's famous wooden bridge. A good spot at which to sample *iwakuni-zushi* (sushi made in large square moulds).

Unique Museums

Mizuki Shigeru Museum

Manga artist Mizuki Shigeru, creator of famous cartoons about the supernatural world of *yōkai* (mythical ghosts, goblins and monsters; p94), is honoured at this museum in his hometown of Sakaiminato.

Adachi Museum of Art

Displaying a selection of mostly 20th-century Japanese art, this museum's windows frame the living art of the surrounding Japanese gardens. It's an easy day trip from Matsue.

Hiroshima MOCA

In a building designed by leading Metabolist architect Kishō Kurokawa, MOCA specialises in contemporary art, mainly by Japanese artists. Sculptures surround the museum.

Shinshōji Zen Museum & Gardens

This serene complex, a 30-minute drive east of Onomichi, is devoted to Zen Buddhism, which is reflected in its architecture and beautifully designed gardens.

Sand Museum

Tottori's dunes are impressive, but you'll be even more blown away by the huge, amazingly detailed sand sculptures on a geographical theme at this museum. It's 1½ hours north-east of Matsue by train.

The Scenic Inland Sea

Tomo-no-ura

A picture-perfect historic fishing port in eastern Hiroshima Prefecture. The charming architecture inspired the Studio Ghibli–animated film *Ponyo*.

Onomichi Temple Walk

The starting point of the Shimanami Kaidō has a walking route connecting 25 of the port's temples. The path winds through the backstreets, with scenic views from the hillside along the way.

Art Base Momoshima

An abandoned school, cinema and other buildings are part this contemporary art project spearheaded by conceptual artist Yukinori Yanagi. It's on an island 25 minutes by ferry from Onomichi.

Tobishima Kaidō

Cycle this 46km route over a chain of seven bridges connecting the Aki Nada Islands. It starts on Shimo-kamagari and ends on Okamura-jima.

Shōdo-shima

This mountainous, forested island features olive groves, sandy beaches, soy sauce factories, an 88-temple pilgrimage and a super-fun Yōkai Museum celebrating Japan's pantheon of ghosts and monsters.

 Architectural Marvels

Kintai-kyō

For over 350 years people have been admiring this wood and stone bridge in Iwakuni. A marvel of traditional carpentry, it looks like a scene from an old wood-block print brought to life.

Ishitani Residence

The peaceful streets of Chizu, an old post town south of Tottori, are lined with old wooden houses and sake breweries. This grand complex has over 40 rooms, seven storehouses, a beautiful garden and the backdrop of a cedar forest.

Simose Art Garden Villa

Pritzker Prize–winning architect Shigeru Ban designed this luxury hotel and art museum that includes eight movable galleries sheathed in candy-coloured glass that appear to float on water.

 Beautiful Gardens

Kōraku-en

One of Japan's top gardens, built to entertain feudal lords and officials visiting Okayama. It's beautifully illuminated on summer nights, when visitors can picnic on the vast lawn.

Sesshuteien

At Yamaguchi's Jōei-ji, this garden is a National Site of Scenic Beauty. It was built as a strolling garden to be admired from many viewpoints, and can be enjoyed differently in all seasons.

Yūshien

On an island in Nakaumi lagoon near Matsue, this is a beautifully landscaped garden where some 250 species of peonies bloom in a hothouse year-round or in the garden itself mid-spring.

Shukkei-en

This serene Hiroshima garden's name means 'shrunken view garden', as it recreates grand vistas in miniature based on West Lake in Hangzhou, China. Walking paths meander around a central pond.

 Characterful Towns & Villages

Hagi

On Western Honshū's northwest coast, Hagi has a lovely seaside location, beautifully preserved Edo-era streetscapes, a collection of World Heritage Sites and fine local ceramics.

Kurashiki

Go for a punt down the historic canal of this merchant city, with its preserved Edo-period Bikan quarter packed with interesting shops, cafes and restaurants.

Tsuwano

In this delightful town in the far west of Shimane Prefecture enjoy strolling beside old samurai houses, sake breweries and water channels teeming with carp.

Ōmori

One of Japan's most picturesque traditional villages is the gateway to the World Heritage–listed silver mines of Iwami Ginzan. Check out artisan clothing business Gungendō.

Saijō

Seven sake breweries in historic buildings are clustered within easy walking distance of the station. Saijō has been producing sake for around 300 years – most offer free tastings of their liquors.

30 Escape to SHIKOKU

MOUNTAINS | LEGENDS | MYSTERY

A trip to Shikoku is about connection: to nature, to the past and to the people. You could spend weeks exploring this intriguing island, but if you only have a few days, get some wheels and drive to these spots.

DAVID MADISON/GETTY IMAGES ©

How to

Getting there To get to Takamatsu, either fly direct, take a ferry via the 'art island' of Naoshima (p162), or train or drive over the Seto-ōhashi bridge from Okayama on Honshū.

Getting around To make the most of your visit, pick up a rental car in Takamatsu, or Honshū before arrival.

Top tip Give yourself as much time as you can; Shikoku is perfect for exploring as an independent traveller.

KONSTANTIN PETRUSHA/SHUTTERSTOCK ©

Despite its proximity to Osaka and Kyoto, Shikoku has always been considered remote, isolated and mysterious – the realm of Buddhist pilgrims seeking enlightenment and vanquished warriors who famously disappeared into its rugged mountainous interior.

88 Sacred Temples Pilgrimage

SANGA PARK/SHUTTERSTOCK ©

This epic 1400km journey around 88 temples has been walked for 1200 years. Pilgrims follow in the footsteps of the great saint Kōbō Daishi, the founder of Shingon Buddhism, the only major sect that believes that enlightenment can be achieved in this lifetime. It's said that Kōbō Daishi achieved enlightenment on Shikoku and modern-day pilgrims are hoping for the same result. There are still walkers, but these days many more head out on bicycles or mopeds, or in cars, taxis or buses on their

Japan's Oldest Onsen

According to legend, **Dōgo Onsen** was discovered during the age of the gods when a white heron was found healing itself in the spring. Nowadays, it's one of Japan's best known onsen destinations, only a tram ride away from the centre of Shikoku's largest city, Matsuyama.

Above left Ryuku-ji (Temple 41), 88 Sacred Temples Pilgrimage
Left Ishite-ji, 88 Sacred Temples Pilgrimage
Above Dōgo Onsen

search for enlightenment. Allow 40 to 60 days if walking, or a week to 10 days if travelling by car.

If you only have time to visit one of the 88, head to **Unpen-ji (Temple 66)** (88shikokuhenro.jp/kagawa/66unpenji), the 'Temple in the Clouds'. At over 900m, it is the highest of the temples, accessed by cable car from the north (a one-hour drive from Takamatsu) or by road from the south (not far from the entrance to the Iya Valley). At the temple, you'll be further transported by the incredible 500 life-sized stone Arhat statues of Buddha's disciples, atmospherically stationed among the pole-straight cedar trees. They convey the depth of just about every human emotion in their etched faces and evocative poses. Search among them for your lookalike; according to legend everyone has one.

In the words of Kōbō Daishi, 'do not just walk in the footsteps of the men of old, seek what they sought'.

Udon-ken

Chances are you've arrived on Shikoku in Takamatsu by ferry from Naoshima (p162) or by train from Okayama. The capital of Kagawa, the smallest of Japan's 47 prefectures, Takamatsu is a bustling, buoyant port city of 420,000. Don't leave town without trying the local culinary speciality, known Japan-wide as *Sanuki-udon* (Sanuki was the old name for Kagawa Prefecture). You'll find a *Sanuki-udon* shop on just about every corner in Takamatsu, and the prefecture's udon noodle dish is so well known that Kagawa's nickname is Udon-ken (Udon Prefecture). Don't feel self-conscious about slurping your noodles – in fact, it's encouraged.

Left *Sanuki-udon* **Below** Oku-Iya Ni-jū Kazura-bashi bridge

The Hidden Iya Valley

Once the notorious hideout of vanquished warriors and bandits, the remote Iya Valley, deep in the mountains of central Shikoku, boasts some unforgettable highlights plus exciting driving on a narrow, winding road high above the Iya River.

You'll want to head up-valley to **Oku-Iya (Deep Iya)**, where you'll find the atmospheric **Oku-Iya Ni-jū Kazura-bashi**, a pair of vine bridges over the river that were designed to be chopped down once traversed, to prevent escapees from being followed.

A little further east, tiny **Nagoro** is the original 'scarecrow village', where local resident Ayano Tsukimi, becoming lonely as the population of her village declined to next to nothing, made life-size dolls to memorialise former friends and neighbours. Those 'people' – waiting at the bus stop, gossiping on a porch, toiling in the fields – are actually straw dolls.

At the head of the Iya Valley, climb **Tsurugi-san** (1955m), the second-highest mountain in Shikoku, which is easily summited in 45 minutes from the top of a small chairlift. For a fascinating Shikoku experience, stay at the peak at **Tsurugi-san Chōjō Hutte** (tsurugisan-hutte.com) (book direct online in English).

KYŪSHŪ

ONSEN | ISLANDS | FOOD

Unzen Onsen (p181)

KYŪSHŪ
Trip Builder

Smouldering volcanoes, mystical islands, steaming onsen and mouth-watering food – you'll find it all here in Kyūshū.

Korea Strait

Hirado-shima

Hirado

Imari

Sasebo

Saikai

Ōmura

Nishisonogi Peninsula

Gotō Islands

Fukue

Tomie

Sea of Sumo

Nagasaki

Nomo-zaki

Sea of Amakusa

Ushibuka

Koshiki Islands

Dine on pufferfish, a possibly toxic delicacy in **Fukuoka** (p185)
5min walk from Tenjin

Walk through a steaming, sulfurous 'hell' in **Unzen** (p181)
3hr bus from Nagasaki

Marvel at the ash eruptions of impressive **Sakurajima** (p189)
30min ferry from Kagoshima

Take a hot sand bath at **Ibusuki Onsen** (p181)
1hr train from Kagoshima

Hike **Mt Miyanoura** in Yakushima, the tallest mountain in Kyūshū (p187)
1hr flight from Kagoshima

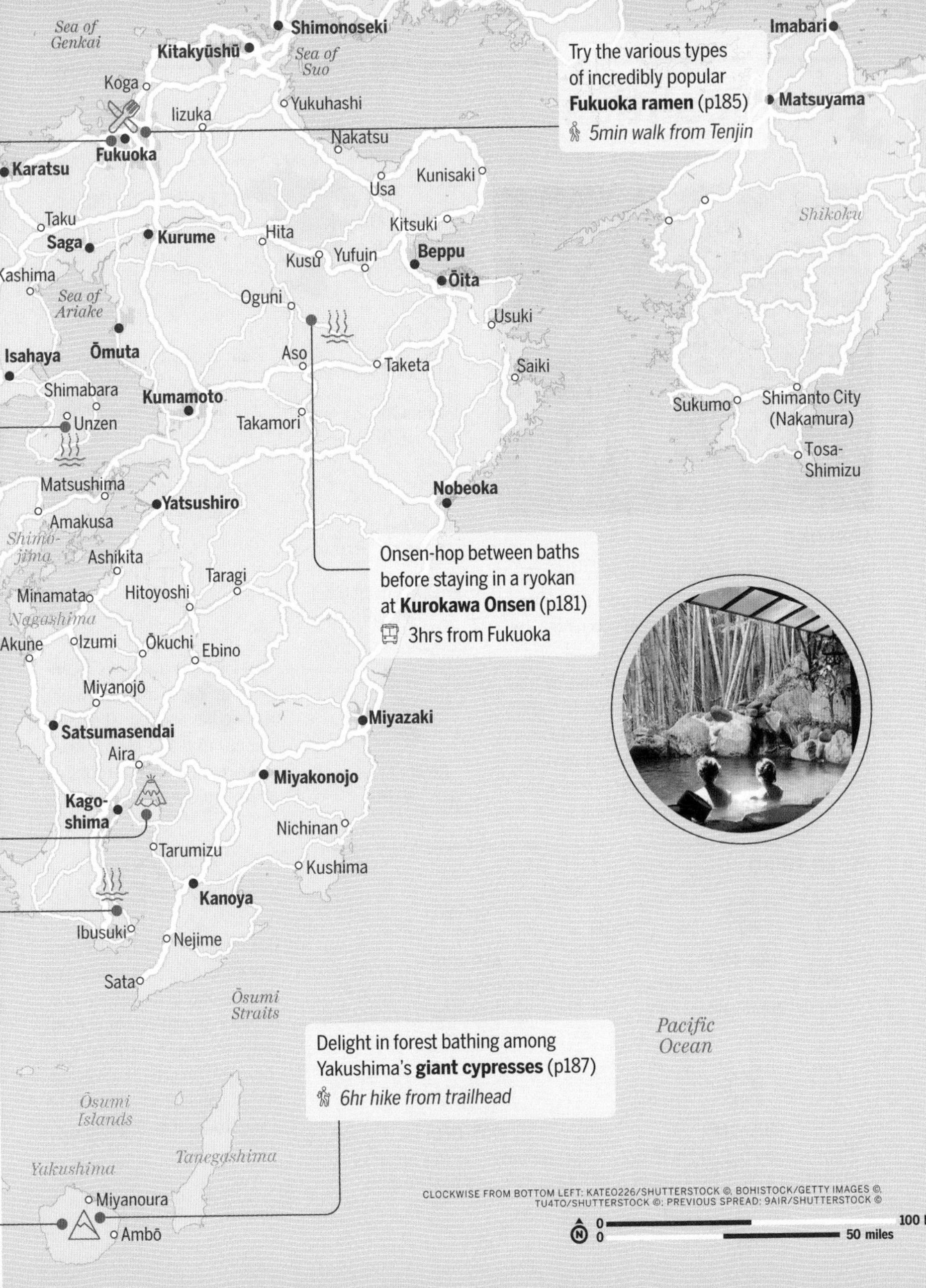

Sea of Genkai
Shimonoseki
Kitakyūshū
Sea of Suo
Imabari
Try the various types of incredibly popular **Fukuoka ramen** (p185)
5min walk from Tenjin
Matsuyama
Koga
Yukuhashi
Iizuka
Nakatsu
Fukuoka
Karatsu
Kunisaki
Usa
Shikoku
Taku
Kitsuki
Saga
Kurume
Hita
Beppu
Kusu
Yufuin
Ōita
Kashima
Sea of Ariake
Oguni
Usuki
Isahaya
Ōmuta
Aso
Taketa
Saiki
Shimabara
Kumamoto
Sukumo
Shimanto City (Nakamura)
Unzen
Takamori
Tosa-Shimizu
Matsushima
Yatsushiro
Nobeoka
Amakusa
Shimo-jima
Ashikita
Onsen-hop between baths before staying in a ryokan at **Kurokawa Onsen** (p181)
3hrs from Fukuoka
Taragi
Minamata
Hitoyoshi
Nagashima
Akune
Izumi
Ōkuchi
Ebino
Miyanojō
Miyazaki
Satsumasendai
Aira
Miyakonojo
Kago-shima
Nichinan
Tarumizu
Kushima
Kanoya
Ibusuki
Nejime
Sata
Ōsumi Straits
Pacific Ocean
Delight in forest bathing among Yakushima's **giant cypresses** (p187)
6hr hike from trailhead
Ōsumi Islands
Tanegashima
Yakushima
Miyanoura
Ambō
0 100 km
0 50 miles

Practicalities

ARRIVING

Train Shinkansen (bullet train) service from Tokyo Station takes five to seven hours to Hakata, Fukuoka (¥22,750; pictured) and seven hours to Kagoshima (¥31,090).

Air Fukuoka Airport is just a few minutes by train to Hakata Station and central Fukuoka (¥260). Kumamoto, Nagasaki, Kagoshima and Ōita all have major airports that are fairly far from the city. Renting a car from the airport is advisable when exploring these parts of Kyūshū.

HOW MUCH FOR A

Handmade tea cup
¥1500

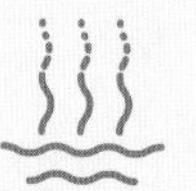

Private onsen (1hr)
¥1800

Bowl of ramen
¥700

GETTING AROUND

Train The Kyūshū shinkansen line connects Fukuoka, Kumamoto and Kagoshima with the rest of the nation. Other major cities can be reached by local train lines, but not always conveniently.

Bus Highway buses are a convenient way to travel between major cities and tourist destinations in Kyūshū. Major cities and airports have bus terminals where you can purchase tickets.

Car By far the most convenient way around Kyūshū, unless you plan to stay in the area of one or two major cities. Major highways are easy to drive on, but beware of shortcuts involving mountainous roads that can be narrower than expected.

WHEN TO GO

JAN–MAR
Crisp, clear and sometimes windy; bundle up warmly.

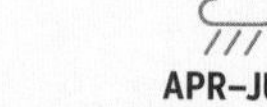

APR–JUN
Mild with some rain, a lot in June; more rain in southern Kyūshū.

JUL–SEP
Oppressively hot and humid; improving a bit in September.

OCT–DEC
Milder temperatures and less rain; Kyūshū's best season.

EATING & DRINKING

Yatai The quintessential Kyūshū dining experience is at the *yatai* (hawker stalls; pictured top right) of Fukuoka, open from 6pm every evening. Ramen (pictured bottom right), *yakitori* (skewers) and fried *gyoza* (dumplings) are common, but each stall is unique and some serve dishes you won't find elsewhere. The key is not to fill up too quickly and keep moving to sample different dishes. *Yatai* dining is both a social and gastronomic experience – guests are encouraged to introduce themselves and engage in conversation, so make new friends over great food.

Must-try ramen
Hakata-style ramen

Best for first-timers
Mamichan (p201)

CONNECT & FIND YOUR WAY

Wi-fi Japan Wi-Fi is a free service available nationwide. Download the app to connect you automatically when you are near hot spots. For a faster connection with wider coverage, rent a pocket wi-fi from Japan Wireless (japan-wireless.com).

Navigation Wi-fi is crucial as you'll need navigation apps to find locations and figure out how to get there.

DRIVING

If you plan to drive, bring an International Driving Permit (IDP) or for certain countries without an IDP, an official Japanese translation of your driving licence.

WHERE TO STAY

You can stay in hotels anywhere, so pamper yourself at a Japanese ryokan. On a smaller budget, enjoy friendship and home-cooked meals at a farmstay, or retreat to nature by glamping.

Place	Pros/Cons
Fukuoka	Plenty of hotels and hostels around Hakata Station and Fukuoka Airport; easy access to many local attractions.
Yakushima	A few large chain hotels and smaller ryokans make it easy to stay here. Camping is also possible.
Yufuin	Many midrange to top-end ryokan options, but it can be crowded and pricey during high season.
Beppu	Ryokan and hotels in every price range exist here in onsen heaven; difficult access to the rest of Kyūshū without a car.

MONEY

Carrying lots of cash is surprisingly safe, and may be the best way to pay for things in rural areas. However, if you're short, you no longer need to hunt for the official Japanese Postal ATMs. Most convenience stores now offer international cash withdrawals.

31 Kyūshū's Sublime ONSENS

REFRESH | RELAX | RESTORE

For many visitors, a trip to an onsen (hot spring) is the highlight of their whole time in Japan. There's something magical about the process, not just of soaking in hot mineral water but also carefully washing beforehand, easing yourself into the water, and leaving refreshed and restored. Add a gurgling stream or forest view and it's even more transcendent.

How to

Tattoos If you're tattooed, don't bathe in public. Look for inns that have *kashikiri* (private) baths, where you'll be only by yourself or with your partner.

Onsen passes Ask about *nyūtō tegata,* passes that allow visitors to hop from one onsen to the next. Kurokawa Onsen's *yumeguri* pass allows visitors to enjoy any three onsen for just ¥1500.

BYOT Bring your own towel; otherwise you'll have to rent or buy one at each onsen. Or drip dry.

Kurokawa Onsen (kurokawaonsen.or.jp) A prized collection of 29 onsen including public bathhouses and ryokan await, and the visitor centre can help you find one that suits your needs. The community takes great care to maintain a traditional feel for both facilities and the entire village. It's nestled in a valley, so you'll enjoy views of the forest and the sound of the river as you bathe.

Yunohira Onsen Yunohira Onsen maintains a peaceful atmosphere on a street that seems unchanged in half a century. Visit Yunohira to relax in one of its 21 inns with their own onsen. For a budget onsen day trip, there are five public baths, each costing just ¥200 to use.

Above right Kurokawa Onsen
Right Ibusuki Sunamushi Kaikan Saraku

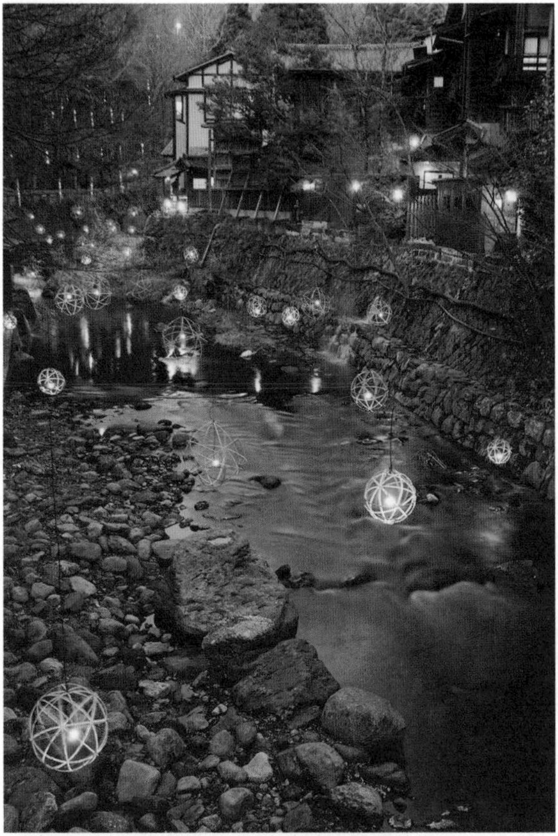

IMAGE NAVI - QXQ IMAGES/ALAMY STOCK PHOTO ©

BRIZE99/SHUTTERSTOCK ©

Types of Onsen

Onsen is a well-regulated industry in Japan, with specific standards to ensure quality and safety. There are 10 different water qualities that are defined, each with certain health benefits. What types of water should you try? Simple alkaline springs are popular as beauty treatments, leaving your skin feeling smooth. Chloride springs are salty and said to be good for improving circulation and dry skin. Acidic springs are purportedly good for treating dermatitis and psoriasis. Give each one a try and stick with the ones that feel the best!

Unzen Onsen (unzenvc.com) Bathe in hot, steamy waters at any of the inns and ryokans, walk the pretty paths through the 'hells', and take a scenic ropeway to some hiking trails, where you'll see some stunning vistas of the Shimabara Peninsula below. It's accessible from the major cities of Fukuoka and Nagasaki by bus, although it's worth the effort to get there.

Ibusuki Onsen (sa-raku.sakura.ne.jp) At Kyūshū's southern tip, Ibusuki Sunamushi Kaikan Saraku offers the island's best sand baths. Don a cotton *yukata* robe and lie down in a trench dug by friendly grandmothers, who then cover you with heavy, hot volcanic sand.

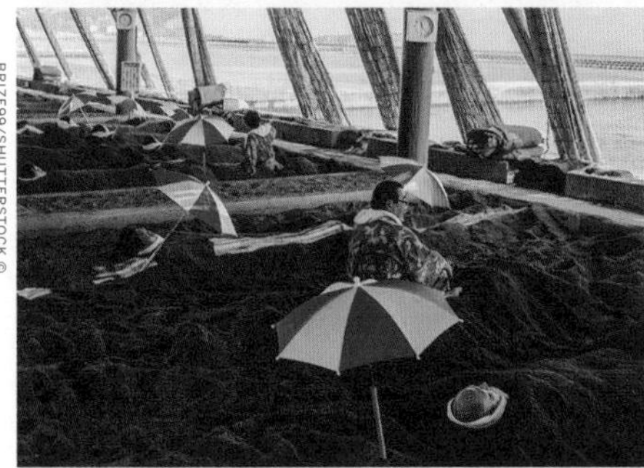

Onsen – Medicine & Relaxation

HISTORY AND ETIQUETTE OF JAPAN'S BATHING CULTURE

Natural hot springs are not unique to Japan, but nobody in the world loves the soothing mineral waters quite like the Japanese. How did onsen become such an important part of Japanese culture as a whole?

Left Plastic bath chairs for washing
Centre Small towel folded on man's head during onsen soak
Right Drying after leaving an onsen

KUREMO/SHUTTERSTOCK ©

The Onsen Culture of Japan

According to legend, onsen – as hot springs are called in Japanese – have been a part of Japanese culture and history as long as 3000 years. They can reliably be traced to the 8th century, when they were mentioned in Japan's oldest text, the Manyōshū. Whatever the case, enjoying a soak in the mineral-enriched waters of more than 25,000 onsen in Japan has long been engrained in the local way of life.

The indigenous religion of Shintō places a high importance on cleanliness, so daily bathing has always been an important part of Japanese lifestyle. Before people understood how the various minerals found in hot-springs water interact with the human body, onsen were believed to have mystical healing powers and were sought out and prized by many, including prominent Buddhist monks. Long before onsen became popular with the masses, people would make lengthy pilgrimages to various hot springs based on ailments they were suffering from. Even the shogun recognised the healing properties of onsen and would send a magistrate to bring barrels of water daily from a chosen hot spring along the Tōkaidō Road between Kyoto and Edo (present-day Tokyo).

It wasn't until the mid-19th century that onsen made the shift from health spas to entertainment. With the advent of printing, several wood-block artists popularised onsen with prints and illustrated books of beautiful people enjoying the soothing waters at luxurious locations, and suddenly everyone wanted to visit onsen not to cure their ailments but for fun and relaxation. Such is the attitude

SMALLDARUMA/SHUTTERSTOCK ©

TAGSTOCK1/GETTY IMAGES ©

that continues today, with onsen-hopping one of the favourite leisure activities for domestic tourists. They are even popular as company-sponsored trips, because socialising in onsen is seen as a way to build camaraderie among co-workers.

A Guide to Onsen Etiquette

Onsen are for relaxation, so familiarise yourself with this basic etiquette so you can spend more time relaxing and less time worrying.

> The indigenous religion of Shintō places a high importance on cleanliness, so daily bathing has always been an important part of Japanese lifestyle.

Wash thoroughly Onsen are for soaking, not for cleansing, so make sure you wash well – head to toe – and rinse off any soap before entering the actual bathwater.

No clothes or towels No clothing of any kind is allowed in the bathwater, and if you're carrying the small towel from the shower area to cover yourself while walking around, leave it outside the bath or fold it up and rest it on top of your head.

Tattoos Generally, tattoos are forbidden in most public onsen facilities, though individual onsen may allow them. Often, small tattoos are permitted to be covered with a bandage. If you have large tattoos, your best bet is to rent a private onsen bath, which costs an average of ¥1500 to ¥2500 per hour.

Just chill The atmosphere of an onsen is peaceful, so remain silent or talk quietly – and definitely, no splashing, swimming or misbehaviour in the bath.

Tips from an Onsen Sommelier

Use your towel to regulate your body temperature. In the winter, a hot towel on your head can keep your body warm, especially when using an outdoor onsen. In the summer, a cool towel on your head can keep you from overheating too quickly.

Unless you have sensitive skin, it's not necessary to rinse off after using an onsen. Leaving the onsen water on your skin enables you to absorb more of the nutrients in the water.

Pat yourself dry to remove the liquid after bathing.

■ **Tips from Tomoko Matsuo**
Certified Onsen Sommelier, Shiga Prefecture

32 Fukuoka's Fantastic FOOD

RAMEN | YATAI | PUFFERFISH

Fukuoka takes the top honours for Kyūshū cuisine. Its famous ramen are as popular as baseball teams, with residents taking sides about which brand makes the best. The fun *yatai* (street-side food carts) offer a wealth of tasty treats, and the truly adventurous will want to try the city's excellent *fugu* (pufferfish).

NIRAD/SHUTTERSTOCK ©

How to

Getting here Fukuoka has an international airport so many people arrive direct.

Transit passes Several cards offer convenient access to subways, buses and trains.

Cherry-blossom viewing Mid-March is the best time to see the famous blossoms blooming, but expect crowds aplenty and book well in advance.

VASSAMON ANANSUKKASEM/SHUTTERSTOCK ©

Above left *Yatai*, Fukuoka
Below left *Fugu*

Fukuoka ramen Mention Fukuoka to any Japanese person and you'll see their eyes start to glaze and perhaps their mouth water. The next word out of their mouth will probably be 'ramen'. Fukuoka's speciality is *tonkotsu,* a type of broth, and popular ramen chains go head to head in a Coke versus Pepsi kind of standoff. To the average uninitiated tourist, you may not notice a difference. Try them both, and who knows, you may leave a firm fan of Team Ippūdo or Team Ichiran.

Food carts As famous as its ramen, Fukuoka's *yatai* (push-carts) are another dining experience worth detouring for. Every night rows of pushcarts appear, often setting up shop along the canal in Tenjin. Customers flock to these carts, each with its own speciality. One might have the city's best grilled chicken *yakitori* (kebabs), while another might serve umami-rich dumplings in delicious broth. A third may grill small river fish that have been salted to perfection, serving them on skewers.

Fantastic *fugu* (pufferfish) What's not to like about a fish that – if prepared incorrectly – will kill you in days, if not minutes? Japanese pufferfish is a delicacy here, the flavour prized despite the (albeit tiny) risk of death that comes with it. Done right the flesh is said to make your mouth tingle. If you notice other symptoms, well, this delicious meal may have been your last. Try it for yourself at **Hakata Izumi**, a classy *fugu* spot with traditional sunken footrests (so you don't have to sit with your knees falling asleep!)

Quick Eats

Many tourists (and even some Japanese out-of-towners) expect to sit down at a food stall and have a leisurely chat the way they might in a pub or restaurant, but if you're going to try a food cart, make sure it's a targeted attack and then move on. The cart owners don't want to waste precious seat real estate on people who are talking when a line of hungry customers might be wanting to order. Get your food, eat, pay and move on – perhaps to the next cart...then the next...and so on. Just don't linger at any one spot too long.

33 An Island **ESCAPE**

HIKING | NATURE | BEACH ONSEN

It may seem paradoxical to be on an island (ie the island of Kyūshū) and still to want to get away from it all, but there are many delightful islands to visit, some of them so spectacular they're unmissable parts of a trip to this region of Japan. Yakushima is a prime example, a stunning spot with pristine forests and ancient cypress trees.

RITSU MIYAMOTO/SHUTTERSTOCK ©

How to

Getting here Arrive by plane or ferry. The ferry is beautiful and less expensive; a plane is quick and pricey.

Rainfall Plan on getting wet: Yakushimans joke the island gets 13 months of rain a year.

Look for tree sprites The forests are rumoured to be the home of tree sprites, so keep your eyes peeled.

LACHOUETTEPHOTO/ALAMY STOCK PHOTO ©

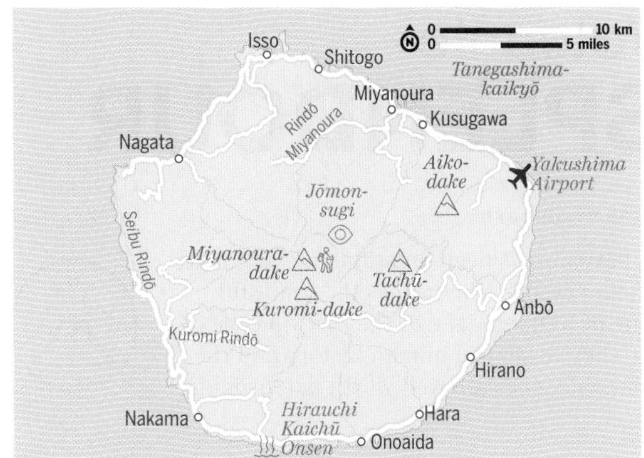

Mt Miyanoura This massive mountain is the tallest peak in all of Kyūshū, and hiking it is one of many trekkers' prime goals. Taking you from coral reefs and tropical climes at the base all the way to chilly subalpine fields above the tree line, the Miyanoura-dake hike takes about 10 to 12 hours, and only the luckiest of hikers manage to go up and down without a bit of rainfall.

Jōmon Sugi In the depths of Yakushima's dense, verdant forest lies a massive cypress tree, one of only a few survivors still standing after logging cleared most of the old growth. It's a solemn reminder of how spectacular nature can be. The walkways and trails through the moss- and lichen-covered woods are beautiful at every turn. The tree is estimated to be over 3000 years old.

Onsen bliss If you don't mind a bit of nudity among strangers, oceanside **Hirauchi Kaichū Onsen** is a delight, and as basic as it gets: just a hot pool next to the ocean's waves. You may be the only one here, or you may need to squeeze in next to other bathers. As you look out at the marvellous view you may find that mud-skippers join you, hopping out onto the rocks with their leg-like fins.

Above left Mt Miyanoura hike
Below left Hirauchi Kaichū Onsen

Yakushima's Creatures

Whether you see the mythical forest sprites or not, you may spot some other Yakushima creatures. Monkeys and deer are common sights here, and both are subspecies that are different from their cousins on the mainland. Be attentive if you're camping, as bands of monkeys are quick to take advantage of not only food that's left around, but also books, phones and glasses. Yakushima's deer are small and known for frequently raiding farmers' gardens. The region has a number of rare and endangered birds and insects, while loggerhead turtles use Yakushima's pristine beaches to lay their eggs.

34 Volcanic SPLENDOUR

AWESOME | EXTREME NATURE | POWERFUL

Kyūshū's volcanoes have always been breathtaking, and hold a special power in the human psyche. Whether it's the beautiful geometry of the cinder cone of Kaimon-dake or the raw violence of an eruption of Sakurajima, they've shaped human history and the planet. Kyūshū's spectacular volcanoes are well worth detouring for.

CHIARA SALVADORI/GETTY IMAGES ©

How to

Warning signs Obey posted warnings – that selfie can wait. Stepping over marked boundaries or disregarding signs can be painful or fatal.

Take care with electronics Exposure of electronics to sulphuric acid and ash can damage drones, cameras and mobile (cell) phones.

Cover up Downwind of Sakurajima you'll find that the ash – essentially tiny pieces of airborne glass – can be painful to your eyes. Bringing a bandanna to cover your face is a good idea.

TRAVELINA/SHUTTERSTOCK ©

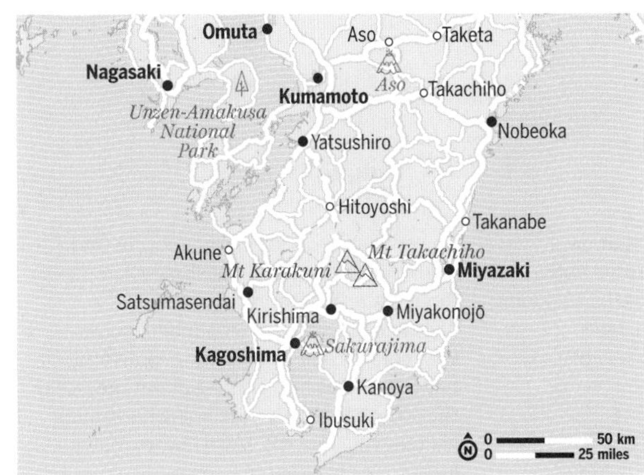

Unzen (unzenvc.com) One of Japan's first designated national parks, Unzen (and its associated onsen; p181) is a wonderful place to experience volcanic action up close. You can meander on walkways through what the Japanese call a 'hell': a steaming, bubbling, boiling natural cauldron. There are baths to dip in and (yum!) eggs that are boiled to perfection in the hot, sulphuric waters.

Aso (asomuse.jp) This fickle monster, the king of one of the world's largest calderas, is only viewable when conditions are right. It's bested most efforts to turn it into a tourist attraction, laying waste to a ropeway that used to dangle viewers above it, and routinely spewing noxious gas that closes roads and cuts off access. If you're lucky, you can park near the crater rim and walk a short way and stare down into its hissing maw. If the wind shifts you may be coughing, choking and dashing back to your car. Check at the **Aso Volcano Museum** for details.

Sakurajima (sakurajima.gr.jp/svc) This Kagoshima Prefecture gem regularly belches ash clouds that reach thousands of feet into the sky, so routinely the ash is often visible in Google Map images. You can't climb it, but you can tour the peninsula by bus and visit a buried shrine gate and other oddities that attest to this being a fickle mountain to live near. The **Sakurajima Visitors Centre** can help you plan a visit.

Above left Sakurajima and Kagoshima **Below left** Crater lake, Mt Karakuni

Hiking the Dormant Ones

Even a dormant volcano can hold a lot of 'wow' for the traveller. In Kagoshima, you can hike a number of dormant peaks, including **Mt Takachiho**, featured as the villain's lair in the James Bond movie *You Only Live Twice*. The highest peak in the region, it's a great day hike and perfect if the weather's clear. Nearby, **Mt Karakuni** offers a chance to peer at a perfect azure crater lake. Both hikes are doable in under five hours, and don't require special gear, though sturdy shoes are a must. The volcanic cinder is sharp, so be careful!

Listings

BEST OF THE REST

Private Onsen

Hyōtan Onsen

This Michelin-starred onsen in Kannawa, Beppu has 14 private coin-operated baths, and numerous unusual public baths, including a sand bath. On-site facilities include restaurants, so you can make a day of it.

Yuka

Nine private onsen hidden away in the forest of Kumamoto's Waita Onsen. The seven standard-quality baths are large enough for a family of four and available 24/7. The two luxurious premium baths include both an indoor and outdoor bath and can be rented from 8am to 10pm.

Yamaga Onsen Seiryūsō

A luxurious ryokan of northern Kumamoto perfect for couples. Some rooms have a beautiful private bath large enough for two. There's also spacious hybrid Japanese-Western-style rooms.

Lamune Onsen

The novelty of this onsen in Ōita Prefecture is its naturally carbonated water, though the facility's playful architecture adds to the fun. Three private baths are available on a first-come, first-served basis.

Sansō Tensui Ryokan

An upmarket onsen experience in secluded environs of Ōita, Sakuradaki (the waterfall that's a muse of Japanese artists) is steps away and can be seen from the *rotemburo* (outdoor bath). There are two open-air baths, two indoor baths and five reservable private baths.

Unique Stays

Nishinokubo ¥

The couple who run Nishinokubo, in Ōita, are experienced with English-speaking foreign guests. Accommodation is in a separate building from the main house, with comfortable beds, sitting room and bathroom. Besides learning about the work they do on their farm, including harvesting shiitake mushrooms, learn how to make local specialities in the kitchen.

Ojika Kōminka ¥¥¥

The little Ojika-jima in Nagasaki Prefecture hosts six fully renovated *kōminka* (Japanese folk houses) spread around the island that are simultaneously historical and luxurious. Cypress bathtubs, private Japanese gardens and views of the harbour are all possibilities depending on your choice of *kōminka*.

Breathtaking Views

Daikanbō Aso Caldera Viewpoint

Best panoramic view of the enormous volcanic caldera and active Aso-san, in Kumamoto Prefecture. On a lucky day,

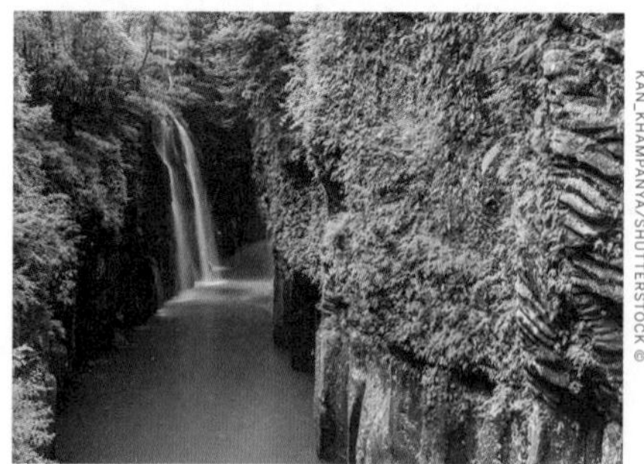

KAN_KHAMPANYA/SHUTTERSTOCK ©

Takachiho Gorge

witness the 'Sea of Clouds' filling the caldera with the mountain rising from the centre. Hike from the car park to the overlook near the edge of the caldera for a different perspective.

Kokonoe Yume Suspension Bridge

This pedestrian suspension bridge in Ōita offers a perfect view of two of Japan's most beautiful waterfalls – especially in autumn, when the foliage turns brilliant dappled shades of red, orange and yellow throughout the valley. At 173m above the valley floor, it's not for the squeamish.

Yunohira Observatory

The closest public viewpoint to Sakurajima, Japan's most active volcano. In the opposite direction, enjoy a sweeping view of Kagoshima on the other side of the bay.

Must-See Historic Sites

Takachiho Gorge

A narrow gorge of otherworldly beauty in Miyazaki Prefecture. The *kagura*, a lively sacred dance telling the legendary story of Shintō sun goddess Amaterasu, is performed nightly in an abbreviated form at Takachiho-jinja, the ancient shrine near the gorge. The falls is considered among the most beautiful in all of Japan.

Uenohara Jōmon no Mori

In the early 1990s excavators planning an industrial park stumbled onto an incredible find: Jōmon-era settlements on the top of a bluff known as Uenohara. Come here to learn about the tools and techniques of one of Japan's earliest known civilisations. The museum is excellent.

Okubungo Course, Kyūshū OLLE

This section of the Kyūshū OLLE is a 12km walk that takes you through the heart of beautiful and historic Ōita Prefecture. Starting from Asaji Station, pass through

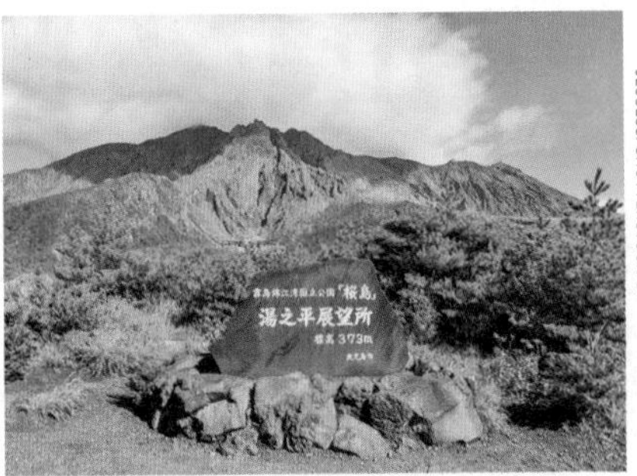

JESSE33/SHUTTERSTOCK ©

Yunohira Observatory

the ruins of Oka-jō, near towering Buddhist images carved into cliff faces, and through the samurai town of Taketa before arriving at Bungo-Taketa Station.

Arita, Ōkawachiyama & Imari

These adjacent towns of Saga Prefecture were responsible for the manufacture and export of Japan's first porcelain ceramics. Browse the shops and museums of these well-preserved towns, which include the Kyūshū Ceramic Museum and Arita Porcelain Park.

Made in Kyūshū

Mamichan ¥

One of the most popular of Fukuoka's *yatai*, the famous street-food stalls that come to life around the Naka-gawa every evening. It's a great introduction to *yatai* with a variety of fantastic dishes.

Itoshima Oyster Huts ¥

From roughly October to March, the port town of Itoshima has several dozen oyster-hut pop-up restaurants run by local fisher folk, who serve freshly harvested oysters and other seafood you grill yourself at your own table.

HOKKAIDŌ

OUTDOORS | NATURE | ADVENTURE

Daisetsuzan National Park (p205)

HOKKAIDŌ
Trip Builder

Japan's second-largest and most northerly island, Hokkaidō almost feels like another country, a place where nature and adventure abound. Discover wide open spaces, untouched wilderness, a fascinating indigenous culture and some of the best powder snow in the world.

Marvel at the ice sculptures of **Sapporo Snow Festival** (p199)
In Sapporo city

Hit the slopes of the world-class ski resorts in **Niseko** (p199)
2hrs from Sapporo

Learn about Hokkaidō's indigenous culture at the **Upopoy: National Ainu Museum & Park** (p201)
2hrs from Sapporo

Soak in the rejuvenating waters of **Noboribetsu Onsen** (p207)
2hrs from Sapporo

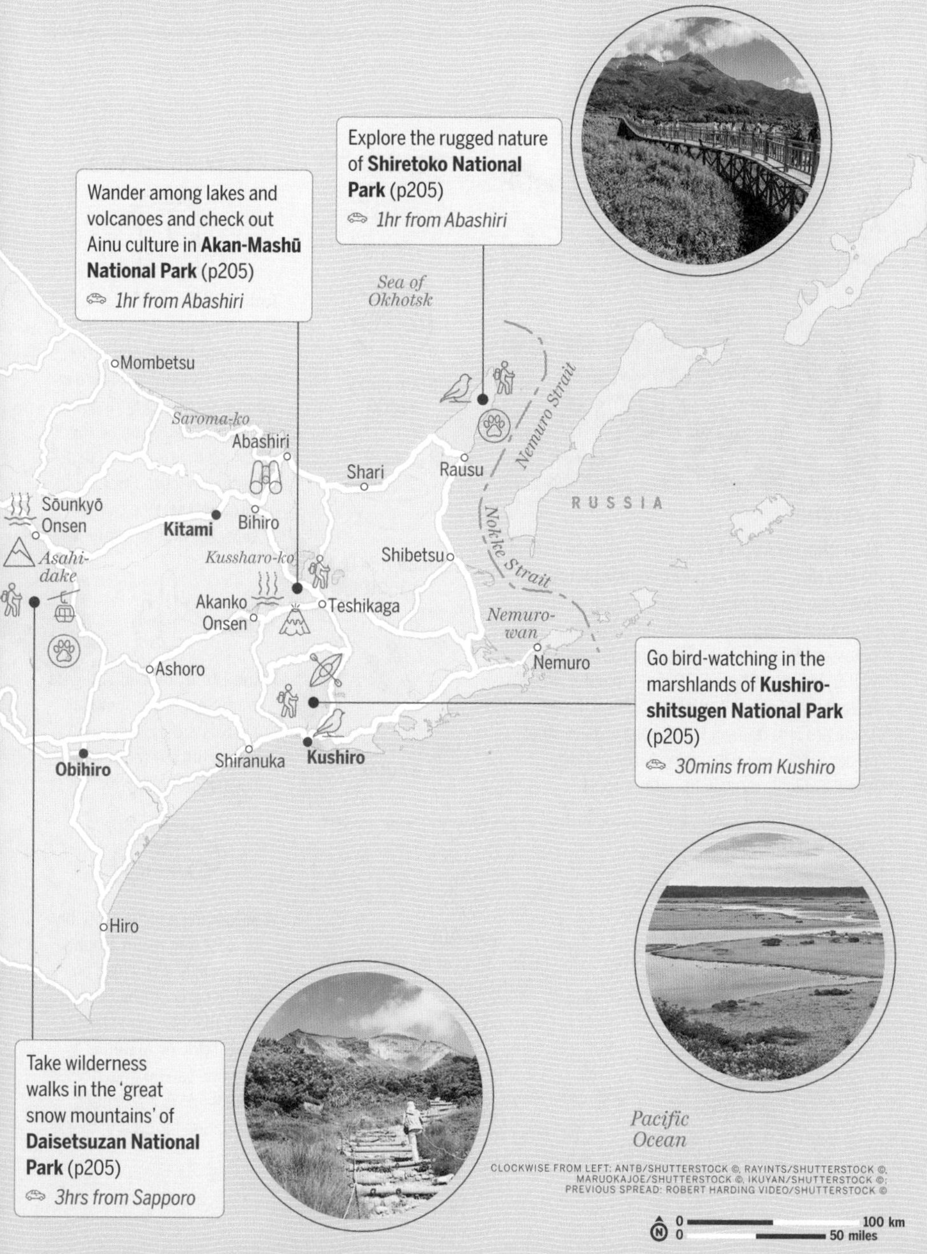
Explore the rugged nature of **Shiretoko National Park** (p205)
1hr from Abashiri
Wander among lakes and volcanoes and check out Ainu culture in **Akan-Mashū National Park** (p205)
1hr from Abashiri
Sea of Okhotsk
Mombetsu
Saroma-ko
Abashiri
Shari
Rausu
Nemuro Strait
RUSSIA
Sōunkyō Onsen
Kitami
Bihiro
Asahi-dake
Kussharo-ko
Shibetsu
Nokke Strait
Akanko Onsen
Teshikaga
Nemuro-wan
Nemuro
Ashoro
Go bird-watching in the marshlands of **Kushiro-shitsugen National Park** (p205)
30mins from Kushiro
Obihiro
Shiranuka
Kushiro
Hiro
Take wilderness walks in the 'great snow mountains' of **Daisetsuzan National Park** (p205)
3hrs from Sapporo
Pacific Ocean
0 100 km
0 50 miles

Practicalities

CHAIYIANYIAN/SHUTTERSTOCK ©

ARRIVING

New Chitose Airport The vast majority of visitors fly into New Chitose Airport (pictured), which is Hokkaidō's main airport, located about 50km southeast of Sapporo. Trains run frequently between the airport and Sapporo (35 minutes, ¥1150) as well as buses (70 to 90 minutes, ¥1100) to various locations and hotels around the city. There are also train and direct bus links to other places in the region including Niseko, and car rental available directly from the airport.

HOW MUCH FOR

Soup curry ¥1200

Seafood rice bowl ¥1500

Jingisukan dinner ¥3000

WHEN TO GO

MAR–MAY
Snowy until April; spring blossoms not until the end of the month.

JUN–AUG
Can be hot, but cooler and less humid than most of Japan.

SEP–NOV
Getting cooler; first snow as early as mid-October.

DEC–FEB
Very cold and often deep snow; February peak for winter activities.

GETTING AROUND

Train and bus Hokkaidō has a more limited public transport network than many other regions of Japan, but there are good train and long-distance bus links between all the island's major cities. Local buses connect to rural spots, although service may be seasonal and infrequent.

Plane There are regular flights from Sapporo to regional airports around Hokkaidō, but flights are sometimes cancelled in bad weather.

Car Renting a car is probably the best way to get around, especially if you plan on visiting fairly off-the-beaten-track places; take extreme care if driving in winter as conditions can be treacherous. Hokkaidō is also a good destination for cycling tours.

EATING & DRINKING

Local speciality Hokkaidō is renowned for its fresh produce, dairy products and excellent seafood. The most famous regional dish is *jingisukan* (pictured top right) – lamb or mutton (rarely eaten in other parts of Japan) barbecued with plenty of vegetables.

Seafood Hokkaidō is said to have the best seafood in the country; be sure to try *kani* (crab), *ikura* (salmon roe) and the exquisite *uni* (sea urchin).

Winter warmers In the cold winter months a bowl of soup curry is a local favourite, along with ramen (especially rich and creamy butter ramen) – both go well with Sapporo beer.

Must-try ramen
Menya Saimi (p209)

Best seafood rice bowl
Takinami Shokudō (p209)

CONNECT & FIND YOUR WAY

Wi-fi Hokkaidō has few free wi-fi spots compared to other areas of Japan (although it is available in many train stations and at New Chitose Airport), so it is best to rent pocket wi-fi (japan-wireless.com) to stay connected.

Tourist information The excellent Hokkaidō Tourist Information Centre (sapporo.travel/en/info/about/tourist-information-center) in central Sapporo can help you with any queries you might have.

TRAVEL PASS

There are a number of Hokkaidō-specific travel passes; the Hokkaidō Rail Pass allows unlimited trips on all JR trains (excluding the shinkansen; jrhokkaido.co.jp/global/) and JR buses.

WHERE TO STAY

There's a wide choice of accommodation in the cities, and plentiful ryokan in rural hot-spring towns. In summer there are campsites, plus super-basic (but cheap) rider houses for bikers and cyclists.

Place	Pros/Cons
Sapporo	Hokkaidō's biggest city. Central Sapporo is a transport hub; Susukino is the lively main nightlife district.
Niseko	Plenty of options, but book early during peak ski season. Summer is quiet.
Asahikawa	Second-largest city in Hokkaidō; plentiful accommodation.
Hakodate	Gateway to Hokkaidō by rail from the mainland and a good stop-off for awesome seafood, views and onsen.
Abashiri	Small city in eastern Hokkaidō; a good base for exploring Shiretoko and Akan-Mashū national parks.
Biei & Furano	Apartments near ski resorts; decent hotel and budget options.

MONEY

Be sure to carry cash at all times, especially if heading out into the wilds – while credit cards are widely accepted in larger cities, in rural areas cash is king.

35 Hokkaidō's Winter WONDERS

SNOW | SKIING | WINTER ACTIVITIES

Hokkaidō is a winter lover's dream – every season freezing Siberian weather fronts bury almost the entire island under a thick blanket of snow, which remains for months on end. As a result, Hokkaidō is home to some of Asia's top ski resorts and famous snow festivals, and is the best place in Japan to experience a whole host of exciting winter activities.

WILLIAM CHU/GETTY IMAGES ©

How to

Getting around Trains, flights and buses operate throughout the winter, although expect delays after heavy snow storms. If driving, take extreme care and avoid the roads during snow storms and at night.

When to go Winter lasts from December until late March, with February the best month for most activities.

Top tip Buy your ski pass in advance online (niseko.ne.jp). Also check snowjapan.com for up-to-date info on winter sports and snow conditions across Japan.

BONSTOCK/SHUTTERSTOCK ©

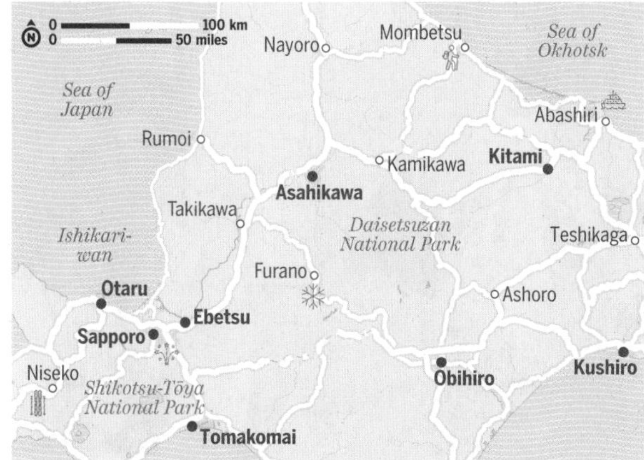

Super skiing Hokkaidō's top winter sports destination, **Niseko** is renowned for its incredible powder snow, world-class slopes and remote back-country possibilities. With good access from Sapporo and the airport, the four main resorts of Hanazono, Grand Hirafu, Niseko Village and Annupuri fall under the moniker of Niseko United and encompass 30 lifts and around 60 runs in total, with an all-mountain pass and free shuttle buses providing unlimited access. English-speaking guides and foreign-run businesses give the area a vibrant, international feel.

Snow festivals Held for one week in early February, the **Sapporo Snow Festival** (Sapporo Yuki Matsuri) is a spectacular celebration featuring giant snow and ice sculptures, concerts and other events. Most of the action takes place at centrally located Ōdōri Park where sculptures are lit up until late, with more attractions dotted around town. Check out the winter festivals at Asahikawa and other places in Hokkaidō around the same time too.

Winter fun (furanotourism.com) If skiing and snowboarding don't float your boat then head to **Furano** and join a guided snow-shoeing tour. Alternatively, ride a snow mobile through the woods or try your hand at dog sledding.

Walking on ice In February, drift ice from Siberia floats down to the shores of **Mombetsu** and **Abashiri** in eastern Hokkaidō, creating an amazing frozen seascape. Don a drysuit and go for an **ice floe walk** (en.visit-eastern-Hokkaido.jp) or take an **icebreaker cruise** (ms-aurora.com) to witness this unique phenomenon.

Above left Icebreaker, Abashiri
Below left Dog sled, Furano

Hokkaidō Winter Tips

To comfortably enjoy the beauty of a Hokkaidō winter, smart clothing choices for staying warm are a must.

Whether you're wandering around the Sapporo snow festival, snow-shoeing or skiing the side-country, layering is key. Think full thermal underwear, underlayer, mid-layer, thick outer layer with hood, high ankle warm boots, thick gloves and a woolly hat.

I also never head out without spare batteries for my smartphone, camera and other electronics. The cold will sap the juice fast.

Convenience stores everywhere have free boiling water on tap, so bring an insulated bottle to keep topped up with your own hot beverages.

By Rob Thomson ■ *Rob lives in Sapporo and is the founder of HokkaidōWilds.org, @Hokkaidōwilds*

36 The Ways of THE AINU

INDIGENOUS CULTURE | HISTORY | TRADITIONS

Hokkaidō has long been the home of its native people, the Ainu, and was only fully colonised by the Japanese from the late 1860s. The Ainu were once persecuted and marginalised to the fringes of society, but moves are now afoot to preserve their traditions and language.

PHOTO BY AHMET FURKAN MERCAN/ANADOLU AGENCY VIA GETTY IMAGES ©

How to

Getting around The Upopoy museum complex is easily reached by train; Akan Mashū National Park can be accessed by rail, but to explore eastern Hokkaidō, it would be best to have some rental wheels.

When to go Upopoy is open year-round; head to eastern Hokkaidō in warmer seasons.

In Sapporo? Visit the Hokkaidō Museum, the Hokkaidō Ainu Center in the central city, or Sapporo Ainu Culture Promotion Centre (Sapporo Pirka Kotan), south of the city.

TKYSZK/SHUTTERSTOCK ©

National Museum

Upopoy: National Ainu Museum & Park is a wonderful complex in Shiraoi that opened in 2020. A centre for the revival and development of Ainu culture, it was opened following the 2019 passing of an act in the Diet, the national legislature, that finally legally recognised the Ainu to be an indigenous people of Japan. After more than a century of forced assimilation and discrimination that saw Ainu culture and language almost disappear, there is now growing enthusiasm for an Ainu renaissance.

The flagship at Upopoy is the **National Ainu Museum**, charged with establishing an accurate understanding of Ainu history and culture. Staffed by local Ainu, its exhibition hall is fascinating, focusing on themes such as Ainu history, beliefs, language and daily

KHANUT888/SHUTTERSTOCK ©

IRANKARAPTE! HELLO!

After almost dying out and being classified as a 'critically endangered language' by UNESCO, Ainu is hopefully now on an upswing. Upopoy offers Ainu language programmes daily. You can also pick up a set of Ainu language playing cards here; each card has a different word on it to help with your study.

Above left Upopoy: National Ainu Museum & Park **Left** Dried fish **Above** Upopoy: National Ainu Museum & Park life. Outside, the park sprawls around Lake Poroto, with a *kotan* (village) of traditional Ainu buildings, where visitors can try on Ainu clothing, watch traditional performances and learn to play the *mukkuri* (mouth harp). There are also craft studios and workshops with daily programs. At the entrance to the park, there are a number of restaurants specialising in Ainu cuisine and shops selling Ainu handicrafts. The entrance is a 10-minute walk from JR Shiraoi Station.

Ainu Culture in Akanko Onsen

The resort town of Akanko Onsen in Akan Mashū National Park (p204) in eastern Hokkaidō is home to an **Ainu Kotan**, a collection of shops and households that is your best opportunity to get a decent look at modern-day Ainu culture in a community setting. The residents make a living promoting their culture, singing and dancing daily on the stage at the theatre **Ikor** (akanainu.jp), cooking *pochie* (fermented potato dumplings) in restaurants,

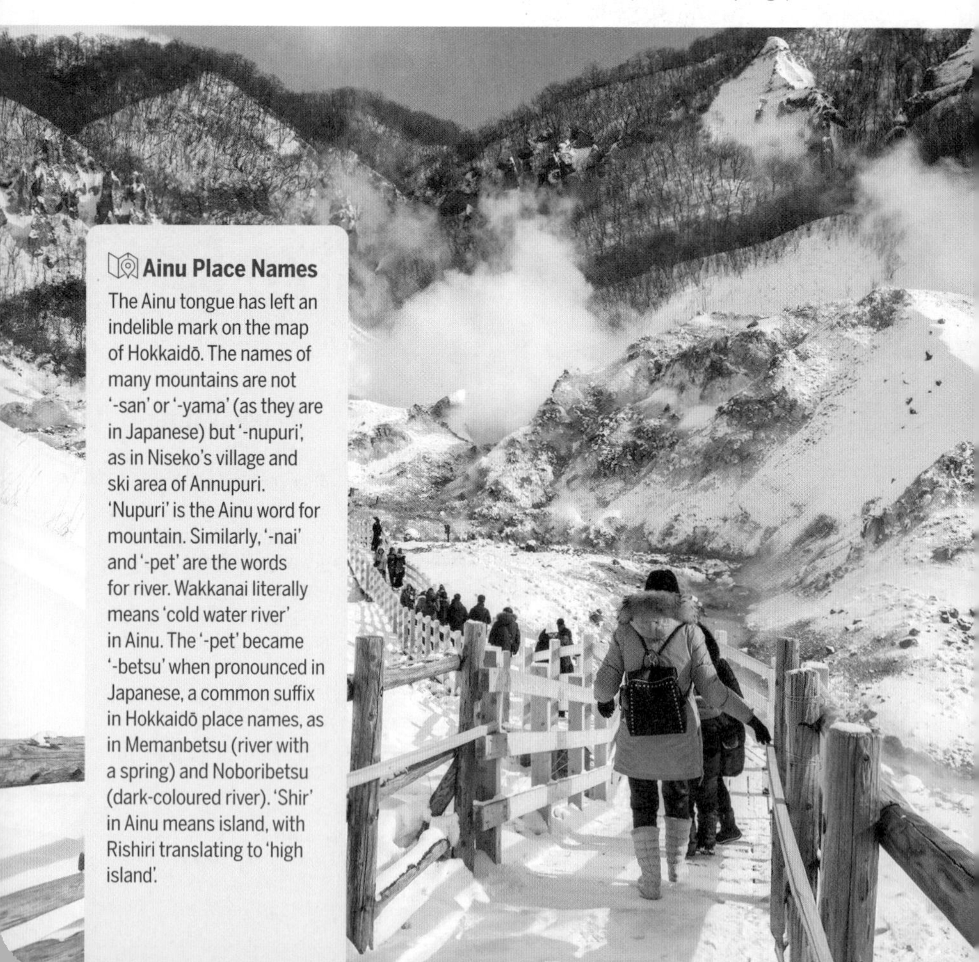

Ainu Place Names

The Ainu tongue has left an indelible mark on the map of Hokkaidō. The names of many mountains are not '-san' or '-yama' (as they are in Japanese) but '-nupuri', as in Niseko's village and ski area of Annupuri. 'Nupuri' is the Ainu word for mountain. Similarly, '-nai' and '-pet' are the words for river. Wakkanai literally means 'cold water river' in Ainu. The '-pet' became '-betsu' when pronounced in Japanese, a common suffix in Hokkaidō place names, as in Memanbetsu (river with a spring) and Noboribetsu (dark-coloured river). 'Shir' in Ainu means island, with Rishiri translating to 'high island'.

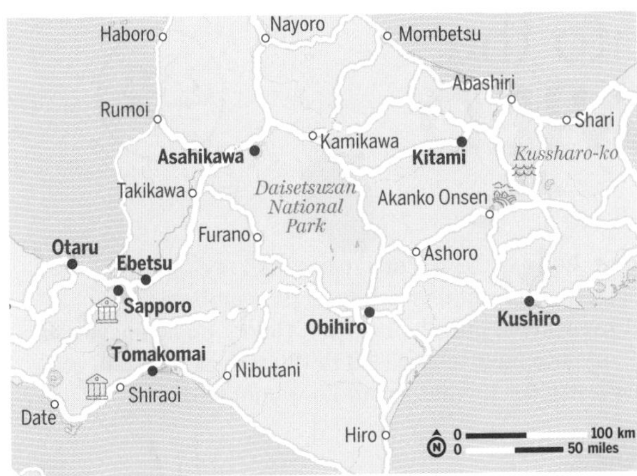

Left Path to Noboribetsu
Below Shop, Ainu Kotan

and selling wood and leather crafts, made with traditional motifs. Lovingly run, tiny **Poronno** (poronno.com) will have you admiring both Ainu handicraft and culinary skills. The **Ainu Folklore Museum** (akanainu.jp) has changing exhibitions of contemporary Ainu artisanal work and some traditional dwellings.

Filmed in Akanko Onsen, with a cast of local actors, the award-winning movie *Ainu Mosir* (2020) provides excellent insights into Ainu culture, both modern and old.

A Real Ainu Treat

The small Ainu *kotan* at the southern end of **Kussharo-ko** in Akan Mashū National Park boasts a couple of highlights. **Kotan-yu** *rotemburo* (outdoor bath) is a superb lakeside, free-to-use, open-air hot-springs bath that is maintained by local volunteers for the benefit of the community. A short walk away, **Marukibune** (marukibune.jimdo.com) is an atmospheric restaurant with tasty Ainu dishes on the menu, such as sashimi of *parimomo* (a local river fish). The restaurant doubles as a venue in the evenings, with impromptu Ainu music sessions. Upstairs there is some lovely visitor accommodation, including an onsen and a luxurious Ainu-style twin room that resembles an art museum. Check it out online in English and stay if you can!

37 Into the WILD

MOUNTAINS | HIKING | WILDLIFE

It's a different world up here, with 20% of Japan's land area but only 5% of its population. With spectacular mountains, wild rivers, remote hot springs and arrow-straight roads disappearing into the horizon, Hokkaidō is a haven for outdoors enthusiasts. Cool, dry summers, compared to the rest of Japan, draw hikers, cyclists and campers north for the nature and national parks.

NARONGSAK NAGADHANA/SHUTTERSTOCK ©

How to

Getting around Most popular trailheads can be accessed by bus, but they're few and far between. To really get into the wild, you'll want your own wheels; pick up a rental car.

When to go Summer and autumn (start of July to early October) are best as hiking trails will be snow-free.

Top tip Be like a Japanese hiker and take *onigiri* (rice balls) on your walk. ¥150 each.

CHEN FANGXIANG/SHUTTERSTOCK ©

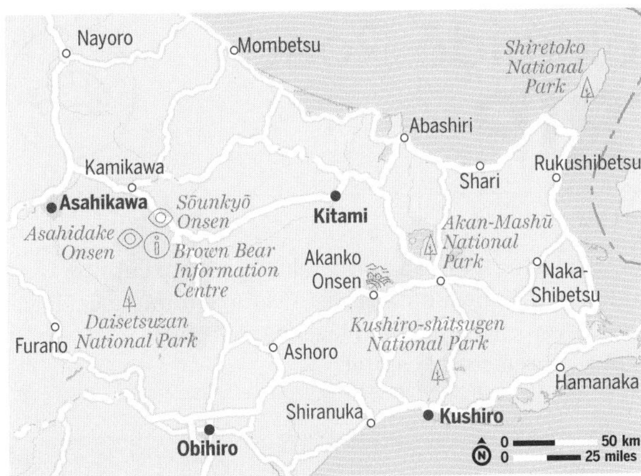

Above left Kuro-dake ropeway
Below left Mashū-k

Keen hikers will want to head to **Daisetsuzan National Park**, known as the rooftop of Hokkaidō, in the centre of the island. It's a vast and untouched wilderness of spectacular mountains, alpine flower meadows and steaming volcanic landscapes. Hiking trails offer day and multiday options, with the chance of encountering wildlife such as red foxes and brown bears. Abundant hot-spring baths provide a spot of relaxation post-hike.

Eastern Hokkaidō boasts three suberb parks. A true wilderness and a World Heritage Site, **Shiretoko National Park** is a 70km-long peninsula packed with waterfalls and ancient forests, with a mountainous interior for hardy hikers to explore. Boat cruises along the coast offer the chance of spotting brown bears, along with other wildlife such as whales, dolphins and sea eagles. The beautiful **Shiretoko Goko** (five lakes) area has gentle nature walks.

Stunning **Akan-Mashū National Park** is an area of steaming volcanic peaks and serene lakes; **Mashū-ko** is said to have the clearest water of any lake in the world! The lakeside hot-spring resort of **Akanko Onsen** lies between the volcanic summits of **O-Akan-dake** and **Me-Akan-dake**, both offering splendid hiking.

Home to the Japanese red-crowned crane and other rare flora and fauna, **Kushiro-shitsugen National Park** is Japan's largest wetland. There are observatories and trails throughout the park, and year-round kayak tours offer unique views of the marshlands and wildlife.

Day Hikes in Daisetsuzan NP

You can climb Hokkaidō's highest peak, **Asahi-dake** (2290m), with relative ease thanks to a ropeway that will lift you up to 1600m from the park's northwestern access village, **Asahidake Onsen**. Alternatively, head to **Sōunkyō Onsen** in the northeast of the park, where a ropeway and chairlift combination whisks hikers up to 1520m to climb **Kuro-dake** (1984m).

Want to meet a *higuma* (brown bear)? Head to extremely remote **Daisetsu Kōgen Onsen** in the east of the park, attend a lecture at the **Brown Bear Information Centre**, then walk the four- to five-hour **Kōgen-numa Meguri** hiking course.

38 Hokkaidō Road TRIP

EXPLORE | ADVENTURE | FREEDOM

Enjoy a few days away exploring from Sapporo, taking in Ainu culture, immerse yourself in Hokkaidō's best-known hot springs, cycling around a caldera lake, visiting Niseko resort and even checking out a legendary Japanese whisky distillery on your way back to the prefectural capital.

GRAFFITI MAIDORG/SHUTTERSTOCK ©

How to

Getting around Pick up a rental car in Sapporo or at New Chitose Airport.

When to go May to October, after the snow has melted away.

Where to stay Overnight in Noboribetsu Onsen, Tōya-ko and Niseko. All have good options that can be prebooked online using search engines.

Top tip Avoid expressways by taking smaller roads through the mountains of Shikotsu-Tōya National Park for a fascinating road trip.

Sculpture Hunt on Two Wheels

Cycling the 36km circumference of the caldera lake, **Tōya-ko**, is more than just a bike ride. The **Tōya Gurutto Sculpture Park** features 58 statues around the lake; information on each can be found in English on the Tōya-ko website (laketoya.com). Rent a bike opposite the **Tourist Information Center (TIC)**.

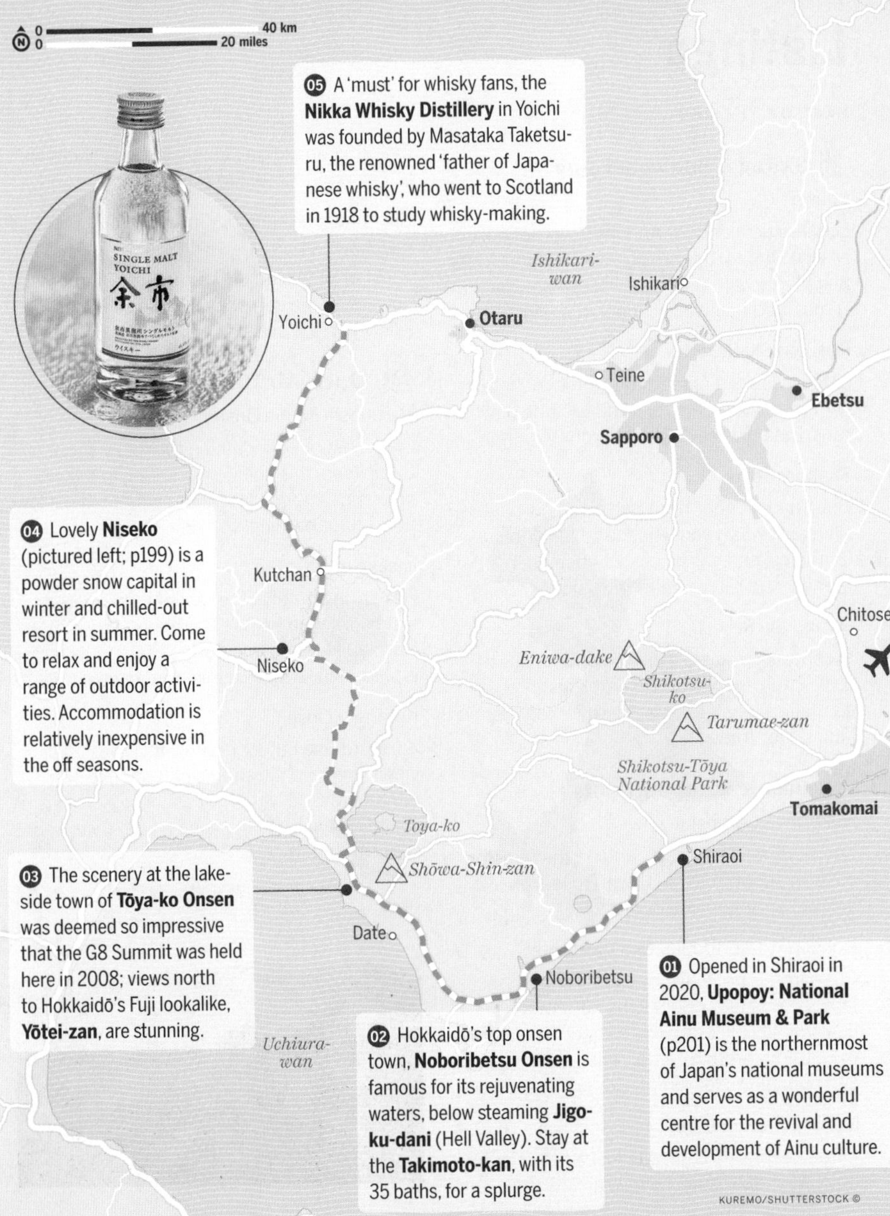

0 40 km
0 20 miles
N
05 A 'must' for whisky fans, the **Nikka Whisky Distillery** in Yoichi was founded by Masataka Taketsuru, the renowned 'father of Japanese whisky', who went to Scotland in 1918 to study whisky-making.
SINGLE MALT
YOICHI
余市
Ishikari-wan
Ishikari
Yoichi
Otaru
Teine
Ebetsu
Sapporo
04 Lovely **Niseko** (pictured left; p199) is a powder snow capital in winter and chilled-out resort in summer. Come to relax and enjoy a range of outdoor activities. Accommodation is relatively inexpensive in the off seasons.
Kutchan
Niseko
Chitose
Eniwa-dake
Shikotsu-ko
Tarumae-zan
Shikotsu-Tōya National Park
Tomakomai
Toya-ko
Shōwa-Shin-zan
Shiraoi
03 The scenery at the lakeside town of **Tōya-ko Onsen** was deemed so impressive that the G8 Summit was held here in 2008; views north to Hokkaidō's Fuji lookalike, **Yōtei-zan**, are stunning.
Date
Noboribetsu
01 Opened in Shiraoi in 2020, **Upopoy: National Ainu Museum & Park** (p201) is the northernmost of Japan's national museums and serves as a wonderful centre for the revival and development of Ainu culture.
Uchiura-wan
02 Hokkaidō's top onsen town, **Noboribetsu Onsen** is famous for its rejuvenating waters, below steaming **Jigoku-dani** (Hell Valley). Stay at the **Takimoto-kan**, with its 35 baths, for a splurge.

Listings

BEST OF THE REST

 Skiing & Snowboarding

Moiwa

Located next door to Annupuri but not part of Niseko United, this small resort has three lifts and plenty of that famous Niseko powder, but is much quieter than its popular neighbours.

Rusutsu Ski Resort

Large ski resort spread over three mountains, with long, groomed trails and exciting powder runs. East of Niseko, not far from Tōya-ko.

Sapporo Teine

Less than an hour from Sapporo, this popular ski resort was a venue in the 1972 Winter Olympics, and has a choice of beginner-friendly and more challenging slopes.

Furano Ski Resort

In central Hokkaidō, Furano has a choice of easy, intermediate and expert runs through its magical birch forests. Great for families as kids ski for free!

Scenic Camping Spots

Naka-Tōya Campsite ¥

Scenic lakeside campground on the forested eastern shore of Tōya-ko, with toilets on site and hot springs close by.

Hoshi-ni-te-no-todoku Oka Campsite ¥

Open from April to October, this charming farm campsite overlooks the patchwork flower fields of Furano, with sheep sometimes wandering through camp. Tents, sleeping gear and bungalows for rent.

Nozuka Campground ¥

A free beachside campsite just a few minutes' drive west of Nozuka on the rugged and beautiful Shakotan Peninsula. Basic facilities but wonderful seaside sunsets.

Kushukohan Camping Ground ¥

Situated on Rebun, a small island off the north coast of Hokkaidō famous for its summer wild flowers. Large campsite with showers, next to a lake and the sea.

 Open-Air Hot Springs

Mizunashi Kaihin Onsen

Lying east of Hakodate on the rocky shore of Cape Esan, this unique hot spring in the sea only appears for a few hours either side of low tide. Mixed bathing, so bring a swimsuit.

Niseko Iroha

Hot-spring hotel at the foot of the Annupuri ski resort, with baths set among snowy Narnia-like woodland during winter. The water is said to have special beautifying qualities.

Kotan-yu Onsen

A free-to-use outdoor bath with amazing lake views, right on the shores of Kussharo-ko in Akan-Mashū National Park. A large rock (barely) separates the genders, so swimwear is permitted.

Kotan-yu Onsen

Kamuiwakka Hot Falls

In the wilds of Shiretoko National Park, bathe beneath a waterfall heated by hot springs seeping into the river above. Bookings a must (goshiretoko.com/kamuywakka/).

Beautiful Views

Hakodate-yama

This 334m-high mountain looms over Hakodate, a city built on a narrow isthmus in southwest Hokkaidō. A ropeway to the summit leads to one of Japan's 'three best night views'.

Shirogane Blue Pond

A popular photo spot, this strikingly turquoise-coloured pond was formed accidentally after aluminium seeped into the water. It's a 20-minute drive from JR Biei Station.

Cape Kamui

Situated at the tip of the windy Shakotan Peninsula, a two-hour drive from Sapporo. Viewpoint with dramatic vistas of the cliffs and the famous 'Shakotan blue' waters below.

Mt Annupuri

Skiers know all about the jaw-dropping panorama of Yōtei-zan, Niseko's Mt Fuji lookalike, and from the top of the Hirafu Summer Gondola there are equally fantastic green views.

Lake Mashū Observatory No 1

Viewpoint on the southwest side of Mashū-ko with outstanding views of the lake and the volcanic caldera of Mt Kamui. Especially breathtaking on a clear winter day.

Farm Tomita

The rolling flower meadows and lavender fields of Furano are a gorgeous sight in summer, and at this farm near Naka-Furano visitors can take photos while feasting on lavender ice cream.

Shirogane Blue Pond

Regional Dishes & Specialities

Menya Saimi ¥

Sapporo ramen shop regarded as one of the best in the city, not far from Misono Station. Excellent miso ramen, but expect a wait.

Soup Curry Garaku ¥¥

Restaurant in Sapporo's Susukino district serving soup curry, a Hokkaidō speciality. Various tasty bowls packed with fresh vegetables and your choice of spice levels, plus an English menu.

Takinami Shokudō ¥¥

Located in Otaru's Sankaku Market; try the *kaisendon* (seafood rice bowl), a cheap and satisfying way to sample an array of Hokkaidō's fabulous fresh seafood in one sitting.

Jingisukan Daikokuya ¥¥

Popular restaurant in central Asahikawa specialising in one of Hokkaidō's most famous dishes, *jingisukan* – succulent grilled lamb that you cook yourself along with an assortment of vegetables.

OKINAWA & THE SOUTHWEST ISLANDS

BEACHES | RYŪKYŪAN CULTURE | COLOURS

Furuzamami Beach (p221)

OKINAWA & THE SOUTHWEST ISLANDS

Trip Builder

Surf, swim and trek through the tropical paradise that is the southern islands. But don't forget to set aside time to learn about the culture, legends and legacy of this diverse corner of Japan.

Amami Islands
Koniya
Naze
Kikai-jima
Kakeroma-jima
Amami-Ōshima
Tokunoshima
Kametsu
Okinoerabu-jima
Wadomari
Iheya-jima
Izena-jima
Ie-jima
Nago
Okinawa City
Kume-jima
Kerama Islands
Naha
Okinawa-hontō
Miyako Islands
Hirara
Miyako-jima
Ishigaki-jima
Kubura
Ohara
Ishigaki
Yaeyama Islands

Drive to **Hedō-misaki** at the northern tip of Okinawa-hontō (p215)

2hrs by car from Naha

Spend a morning browsing the excellent food selection at Naha's **Makishi market** (p215)

In Naha

Explore Iriomote-jima's lush forests and mangroves on an **Urauchi-gawa cruise** (p223)

50mins by boat from Ishigaki-jima

Snorkel in the 'Kerama blue' waters at **Zamami-jima** in Kerama Shotō National Park (p220)

50mins by boat from Naha

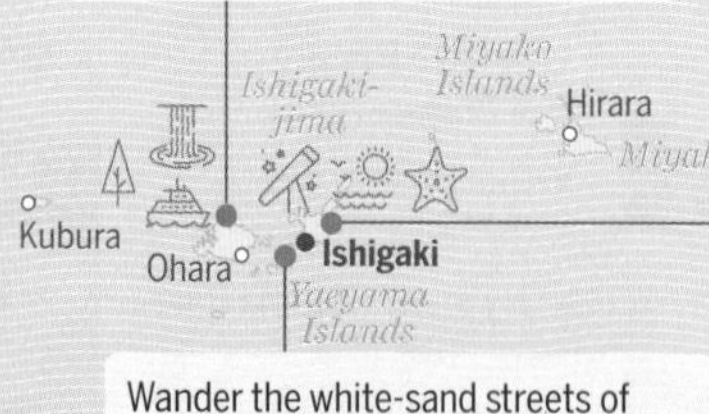

Go snorkelling on **Yonehara Beach** and watch Ishigaki-jima's colourful marine life (p223)

30mins by bus from Ishigaki city

Wander the white-sand streets of Taketomi-jima's **traditional village** (p222)

15mins by boat from Ishigaki-jima

Practicalities

ARRIVING

Naha Airport 5km from central Naha, it handles domestic and some international flights. The Yui Rail monorail offers direct access from the airport to many of Naha's attractions; a one-day pass costs ¥800.

CONNECT

Okinawa has Be.Okinawa Free Wi-Fi, a free wi-fi service available throughout the prefecture. It's easy to connect; just look out for the sign.

MONEY

Bring cash, as many of the region's smaller shops and restaurants don't take cards. Services like PayPay are generally accepted.

WHERE TO STAY

Places	Pros/Cons
Naha	Central, with plenty of bars, nightlife and attractions.
Taketomi-jima	A traditional village on this tiny island in the Yaeyama group.
Ishigaki city	Options near the port in the Yaeyama group's hub.

GETTING AROUND

Car A good way to get around all of the islands.

Scooter A fun option for those who want to travel like a local; avoid the rainy season.

Public transport Even small islands have a bus system. For island escapes, opt for a bicycle.

TOP: KENGO/SHUTTERSTOCK © BOTTOM: DAMADA/SHUTTERSTOCK ©

EATING & DRINKING

Okinawa soba Okinawa's take on the Japanese noodles staple is a ramen-udon-soba hybrid (pictured top left).

Orion beer The prefecture's most ubiquitous beer – light, crisp and refreshing.

Rafute Rich and juicy pork belly, loved by locals.

Must-try snack
Umi budō (sea grapes; pictured bottom left)

Best for browsing
Makishi public market (p215)

DEC–FEB
Mild temperatures, clear skies and less crowds.

MAR–MAY
Great sunny beach weather; busiest season.

JUN–AUG
Hot and humid; peak rainy season.

SEP–NOV
Occasional rain; ideal beach temperatures.

39 Vibrant Naha & OKINAWA

EXCITING | TROPICAL | CULTURE

Okinawa's prefectural capital, Naha is a thriving place with splashes of leafy green, tropical flowers, rows of palm trees and glimpses of azure waters between an expanding skyline of modern high-rise buildings. Here and around Okinawa's main island (Okinawa-hontō), you'll find a mix of young Japanese holidaymakers, retirees from mainland Japan and a growing number of foreign tourists.

How to

Getting there Naha is Okinawa's transport hub; the airport receives international flights from Asia and direct flights from major Japanese cities. You can also come by ferry from mainland Japan.

Getting around The unique elevated monorail, Yui Rail, makes moving around Naha a breeze; ferries head out to nearby islands.

Top tip While you won't want a rental car in busy Naha, it's the best way to explore the rest of Okinawa's main island.

Kokusai-dōri Naha's main drag is a 2km-long riot of neon, noise, souvenir shops, bustling restaurants, enticing bars and Japanese young things out strutting their stuff. It's a festival of Okinawan American fusion and good fun if you're in the mood. Naha is by far the biggest and rowdiest city in the Southwest Islands and most of its nightlife centres on Kokusai-dōri, plus the streets and lanes either side of Wakasa Ōdori. Don't miss exploring the small side streets.

Covered shopping arcades Three covered shopping arcades run south off

Above right Kokusai-dōri
Below right Dragon boat, Naha Hari

TUNGCHEUNG/SHUTTERSTOCK ©

KALAPANGHA/SHUTTERSTOCK ©

Festivals

Naha Ōzuna-hiki This massive three-day event in October features large teams competing in the world's biggest tug-of-war, using a gigantic 200m-long, 1m-thick rice-straw rope weighing 43 tonnes.

Naha Hari Okinawa's dragon-boat races are held across the prefecture, but the biggest is in Naha (3 to 5 May). The festival is to pray for the safety of fishermen and for bountiful catches.

Kokusai-dōri: Ichibahon-dōri, Mutsumibashi-dōri and Heiwa-dōri. Here you'll find a huge array of small shops and the enthralling **Makishi Public Market**. There's a colourful variety of produce on offer, plus everyday cheap Okinawan eats on the 2nd floor, up the escalators.

Further afield **Shuri-jō** is easy to get to by Yui Rail, but to explore further afield on Okinawa-hontō, you'll want a rental vehicle. Okinawa's most important WWII memorials, including the **Peace Memorial Park**, are clustered in the south of the island. If you're after some quiet, small-town Okinawa and virtually untouched greenery, drive to **Hedō-misaki** at the island's northernmost tip. From here, on a good day, you can spot **Yoron-tō**, only 23km away.

Ryūkyū History & Culture

INFLUENCES REMAIN FROM THE RYŪKYŪ DYNASTY

Collectively known as the Southwest Islands, the Nansei-shotō comprises a long archipelago of semitropical, coral-fringed isles, far removed from the concerns of mainland Japanese life. Here, the slow pace and unique cultural heritage of the former Ryūkyū kingdom endures. It's a vibrant contrast to Japan's focus on modernity and technology.

Left Cycle path, Kudaka-jima
Centre Nakagusuku-jō
Right *Awamori* clay pots

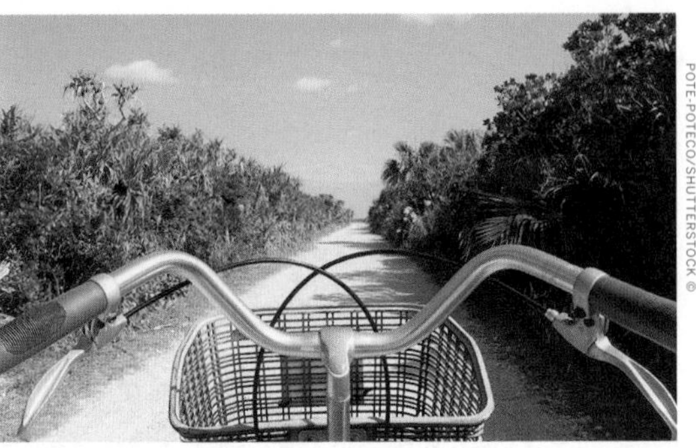

POTE-POTECO/SHUTTERSTOCK ©

Ryūkyū History

After centuries ruled by *aji* (local chieftains), in 1429 the islands were united by Sho Hashi of the Chūzan kingdom, which led to the establishment of the Ryūkyū dynasty. During this period, Sho Hashi increased contact with China, which contributed to the flourishing of Okinawan music, dance, literature and ceramics. In this 'Golden Era' weapons were prohibited, and the islands were rewarded with peace and tranquillity.

Consequently, the Ryūkyū kingdom was not prepared for war when the Shimazu clan of Satsuma (modern-day Kagoshima) invaded in 1609. The Shimazu conquered the kingdom easily and established severe controls. With the restoration of the Meiji emperor, the Ryūkyū islands were annexed by Japan as Okinawa Prefecture in 1879. Life hardly changed for the islanders. They were treated as foreign subjects by the Japanese government, which supressed local culture.

In the closing days of WWII, the Japanese military used the islands of Okinawa as a shield against Allied forces. This cost the islanders dearly: more than 100,000 Okinawan civilians lost their lives in the Battle of Okinawa. Following the war, the occupation of the Japanese mainland ended in 1952, but Okinawa remained under US control until 1972. Its return was contingent upon Japan agreeing to allow the US to maintain bases on the islands, and a large US military presence remains.

Language

Although the Ryūkyū Islands used to have their own distinctive languages, by and large these have disappeared. Standard Japanese is spoken by most islanders, though perhaps

KENDO NICE/SHUTTERSTOCK ©

YANGXIONG/SHUTTERSTOCK ©

with some strong regional dialects, especially among the elderly on remote islands. You might also hear some Okinawan phrases, such as *mensōre* (welcome) or *nifei dēbiru* (thank you).

Visible Remains

Formerly the seat of power of the Ryūkyū dynasty, Okinawa-hontō is the largest island in the Nansei-shotō and its capital, Naha, the busiest city. Most visible traces of Ryūkyū culture were obliterated in WWII, but in spite of this, the Ryūkyū influence remains strong and is evident in Okinawa's unique culinary, artistic and musical traditions.

> Most visible traces of Ryūkyū culture were obliterated in WWII, but in spite of this, the Ryūkyū influence remains strong.

The symbol of Ryūkyūan culture is **Shuri-jō**, east of central Naha. Originally built in the late 1300s, this castle was the former capital, administrative centre and royal residence of the Ryūkyū kingdom. Its uniquely Chinese-influenced design separates it from Japan's other castles.

Nakagusuku-jō is the most iconic of many castles built across Okinawa during the Ryūkyū dynasty. While today only stone wall ruins remain, the castle's sections can still be quite clearly recognised, and the views are spectacular.

Tiny **Kudaka-jima** is known as 'the island of the gods' because, according to Ryūkyū legend, this is where the goddess Amamikyū first descended, making it the birthplace of the kingdom. It's only 15 minutes by high-speed ferry from Okinawa-hontō and a perfect place to experience practically untouched Ryūkyūan culture.

Awamori

Don't leave Okinawa without trying the local liquor. During the Ryūkyū era, *awamori* was served to Chinese envoys and sent as tribute to Japan's shōgun. Its main ingredient is Thai Indica rice, a legacy of the Ryūkyū kingdom's trade with Siam (present-day Thailand). The entire batch of rice is inoculated with black *kōji* (a strain of mould responsible for ferments including miso and sake), then brewed with water and yeast into a mash that's single-distilled in a pot still, and diluted to 30% to 40% alcohol. Traditionally, *awamori* is aged in clay pots for six months to a year before bottling.

Okinawan **ICONS**

01 Sanshin

The soul of Okinawan folk music, this beautiful, long, three-stringed instrument's body is usually covered in snakeskin.

02 Awamori

The oldest distilled alcoholic drink in Japan, *awamori* is the local firewater, made from rice and traditionally stored in clay pots.

03 Kariyushi Shirt

The Okinawan version of the Aloha shirt; it has become the summertime 'uniform' for most businesses and for dress occasions.

04 Ryūkyū Glass

Bright and bubbly glassware taking inspiration from the colours of Okinawa's beautiful sea, sky and flowers.

05 Karate

A martial art developed in Okinawa that has proudly been exported around the world; it involves blocking, punching and kicking.

06 Ryūkyū Bingata

A traditional Okinawan textile in which colourful designs are stencilled onto cotton or linen fabric, more recently with modern motifs.

07 Orion Beer

The popular local brew representing the spirit of Okinawa'a regional identity: 'If you love Orion, you love Okinawa'.

08 Goya

This bitter superfood resembles a prickly cucumber; it's served sliced in *gōya champurū*, a stir-fry dish with *gōyā* (bitter melon), tofu, egg and pork belly.

09 Okinawan Pottery

Yachimun (to the locals) boasts distinct colours and textures; head to Yachimun-dōri in the Tsuboya district of Naha to find it.

10 Shisa

Lion dog statues displayed to ward off evil spirits and bad luck; often spotted in pairs at entrance doors or on the roofs of houses.

11 Beniimo Tart

A startlingly bright dessert tart made from purple sweet potato; a popular souvenir of Okinawa.

40 Try Some KERAMA BLUE

BEACH TIME | SNORKELLING | RELAX

Experience some of the best snorkelling around in Kerama Shotō National Park, where the water is so clear and brilliant its colour has its own name: Kerama blue. Zamami-jima is the best of the islands to visit on a day trip from Naha, with a lively port town and gorgeous Furuzamami beach, plus sea turtles, whales and tropical fish.

D3_PLUS/SHUTTERSTOCK ©

How to

Getting there The direct high-speed *Queen Zamami* takes 50 to 60 minutes one way from Naha's Tomari Port; the slower *Zamami Ferry* takes two hours, via Aka-jima.

Getting around Take the local bus, or consider renting an e-bike, scooter or car to explore the island.

Top tip First stop should be Ao no Yukuru-kan Visitor Centre at the port for advice, tide times and everything from bus tickets to coffee and coin lockers.

SHUTTERBUG78/SHUTTERSTOCK ©

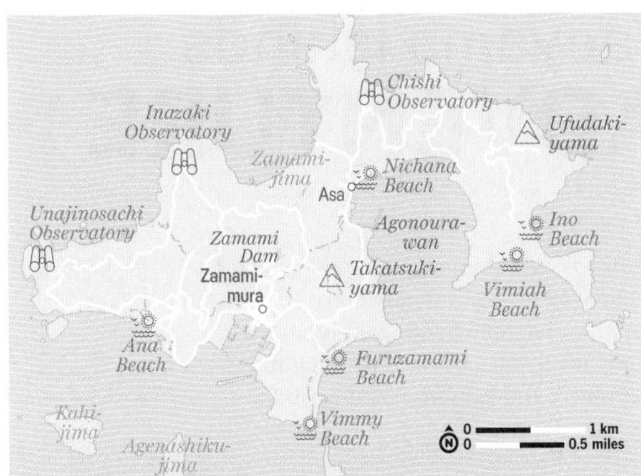

Beach time Want to just lounge on the beach or swim? Head to the white-sand beauty that is **Furuzamami Beach**, up and over the hill east of the port. It's a 20-minute walk or catch the local bus. Here you can dip in the 'Kerama blue' even at low tide. There's a snack shack, and you can rent snorkels, floaties and beach chairs.

Sea turtles A 20-minute walk west of the port, head to **Ama Beach** to spot to sea turtles; you can only swim and snorkel at high tide. Signage near the beach has photos and names of the turtles that hang out here, and the common-sense rules for respecting them. The turtles are used to people, and will likely just go about grazing on seagrass as you observe them.

Tours While most will be satisfied with snorkelling from Furuzamami Beach, seasoned snorkellers and divers may want to get out to an alternative universe on a boat tour with a local guide. Stand-up paddleboard (SUP) and sea kayak tours are also available. Whale-watching tours depart between January and March when humpbacks whale breed and raise their young around the Kerama Islands.

Exploring Zamami-jima You need to love hills (or rent an e-bike, scooter or car) to ride around Zamami, but it's worth it for the scenery. The island has six purpose-built observation decks offering stunning views in all directions. Pick up a map at the visitor centre and allow two to three hours if you've got some motorised wheels.

Above left Sea turtle, Ama Beach
Below left Furuzamami Beach

Island Escape

If **Zamami-jima** sounds all too idyllic and you're thinking of staying on the island, the news is good. For those on a budget, there's a campground at Ama Beach, while near Zamami port, there are a number of family-run *minshuku*, guesthouses and small resorts; see visit-zamami.com. While you can't go wrong by planning ahead and bringing supplies with you from from Naha, there are also small restaurants, bars and a couple of grocery outlets – though don't expect to find a large supermarket. This is a 'get away from it all' island escape – but book ahead if you're turning up in Japanese holiday periods.

41 Yaeyama Islands ADVENTURE

CULTURE | WATER SPORTS | EXPLORE

Venture southwest from Okinawa's main island and you'll find an archipelago reaching all the way to Taiwan's doorstep. The Yaeyama Islands are the pick of this impressive bunch; Ishigaki-jima is the transport hub and boasts some lovely beaches and snorkelling. Use it as a base to experience Taketomi-jima and explore Iriomote-jima.

LEUNGCHOPAN/SHUTTERSTOCK ©

How to

Getting there There are no ferries southwest from Naha. Fly to Ishigaki-jima from either Naha or direct from big cities on the mainland.

Getting around Rent an electric moped on Ishigaki-jima or use the public bus; it's just a 15-minute ferry ride to Taketomi-jima and 50 minutes to Iriomote-jima.

Top tip Stay around Ishigaki Terminal, the ferry port, for easy access to shopping, dining, nightlife and public transport.

TAKASHI IMAGES/SHUTTERSTOCK ©

Above left Kabira Bay, Ishigaki Island
Below left Iriomote Island

Ishigaki-jima This island is known for its beaches and pristine waters. **Kabira Bay** is home to popular glass-bottom boat tours, diving and manta ray spotting from April to October. Neighbouring **Yonehara Beach** is equally gorgeous and a little less busy, making it great for snorkelling. **Sukuji Beach**, west of Kabira Bay, is a haven for SUP and families looking for fun in shallower waters.

Taketomi-jima Take the ferry from Ishigaki Terminal to this small island with its remarkably well-preserved village, which resembles a living museum. The streets are of white sand, while the houses are gorgeous, with traditional red roof tiles, and are surrounded by coral walls punctuated with tropical flowers. Most visitors come for a day trip, but the real charm of Taketomi-jima shows itself after the last ferry leaves and a quiet calm falls over the village. Accommodation is limited, so book well in advance. There's no supermarket or convenience store; arrange dinner at your accommodation.

Iriomote-jima World Heritage Site–listed Iriomote-jima is known for its mangroves and waterfalls. Hop on a jungle cruise on the **Urauchi-gawa**, Okinawa's largest river, or paddle into the interior by SUP or kayak. The island even boasts its own threatened native species, the Iriomote *yamaneko,* a nocturnal wildcat. Homages to the *yamaneko,* considered the island's 'spirit animal', are found islandwide, across everything from T-shirts to cars.

Dark-Sky Stargazing

Iriomote-Ishigaki National Park was designated as Japan's first official International Dark Sky Park in 2018, part of an initiative to reduce light pollution and preserve dark skies. It's an amateur astronomer's paradise! Just about anywhere on the islands, you can step out on a clear night and see stars, but the further you get from the lights of Ishigaki city, the better they are. There are observatories on Ishigaki-jima with big telescopes, and a handful of operators offer stargazing tours, where they'll take you to a dark outdoor spot for admiring far-away galaxies and identifying planets and constellations.

Listings

BEST OF THE REST

Spiritual Landmarks

Seifa Utaki

Okinawa's most sacred destination; according to legend, this corner of the Chinen Peninsula is where goddess Amamikyū came to populate the islands. Stroll the lush forest path and soak up the energy of this power spot.

Shuri Akagi

Near the cobblestone streets of Naha's Shuri Kinjō sits a cluster of six *akagi* trees, more than 200 years old. Lumpy and full of character, they survived the devastation of WWII and are said to be divine, as almost all of their siblings fell victim to the fires of war.

Daisekirinzan

Located in the northern part of Okinawa-hontō, this jungle is known in Ryūkyū mythology as an area overflowing with natural power.

Gangara Valley

These limestone caves in Nanjō are where people come to pray to find true love and admire a 20m-high banyan tree.

Crafts & Culture

Ishigaki Pottery Studio

'Ishigaki Blue' is the term for this local variation of ceramics. By combining glass and pottery, artisans replicate the shades, depth of colour and rhythm of Ishigaki-jima's surrounding waters.

Shiisa Park

Bright, bold and a little bombastic (in a good way), this public, mountain-backdropped garden near Yonehara Beach features a family of multicoloured, monster-sized *shiisa* (mythological Okinawan creatures). It's perfect for a photo opportunity and a short stroll on a sunny day.

Ishigaki Yaima Village

An amusement park and open-air museum hybrid on Ishigaki-jima where local grannies teach traditional dance, relocated century-old homes built in Okinawan style stand proud, and fresh tropical fruit is in abundance.

Yaeyama Minsa

Learn all about Iriomote-jima's unique and fiercely protected *minsa* (weaving) style with a workshop visit. Historians estimate the fabric made its way to Okinawa from Afghanistan via China.

Relax & Recharge

Halekulani ¥¥¥

A combination of Okinawan flair and Hawaiian influence, this resort on Okinawa-hontō is the epitome of the luxurious beach lifestyle. But there's more than just lounging around: guests can join a Halekulani Okinawa Escapes programme to learn about the island's culture.

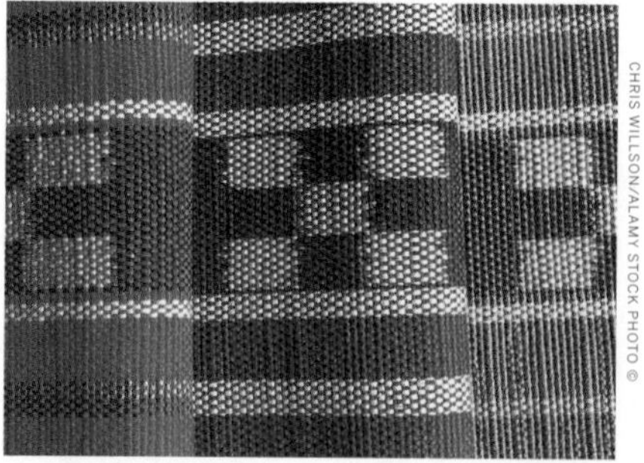

Yaeyama *minsa*

Ryūkyū Onsen Ryūjin-no-yu

Embrace the onsen life surrounded by sand, not snow, with a soak in these natural hot springs near Naha Airport. With open-air baths allowing the soothing rhythm of the sea to wash over you, it's complete relaxation.

Awamori Icons

Awamorikan ¥

Try then buy the local liquor at this place in Shuri, where they feature over 1000 types of *awamori* representing 200 brands from all 48 breweries in Okinawa.

Bar Daisy ¥¥

It looks like a moodily lit, jazz-loving cocktail bar. But pay closer attention to the bottles in the bartender's hands and you'll notice they're switching out vodka and gin for *awamori* to craft artful cocktails. It's the perfect place in Naha to sample the south's signature spirit.

Hikes & Trails

Jawbone Ridge Loop

Looping around the mountains located near Kunigami on Okinawa-hontō, this moderately challenging trail makes you work for its gifts – and it has plenty of them. Incredible views, excellent bird-watching and mysterious landmarks (keep an eye out for the abandoned hotel).

Hiji Ōtaki

An easy, almost 3km walk through the backtrails with waterfalls along the way near Kunigami, this hike offers two options: a river route or a forested trail. Entry comes with a fee, and the trail shuts at 4pm (3pm in winter), but it's a well-maintained and worthy mid-morning hike.

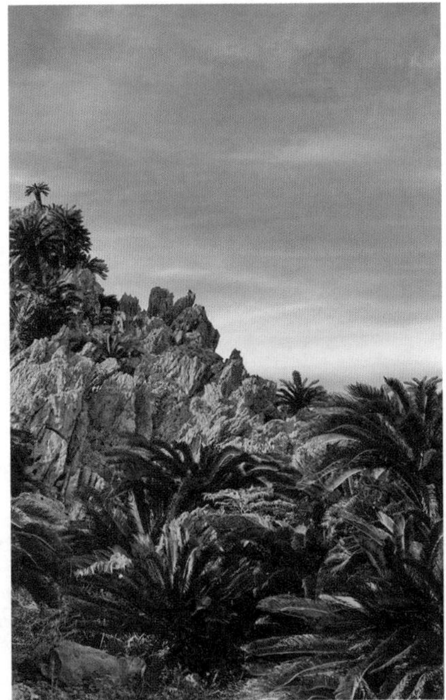

JORDAN TAN/SHUTTERSTOCK ©

Daisekirinzan

Indy Jones Mile

At just under 1.5km, this unforgettably named trail, located near Nanjō, is moderate in terms of challenge level and extreme in terms of beauty. With sweeping views, deep caves and the odd rope for climbing obstacles, Mr Jones would be proud to have his name attached to such a great adventure.

Practicalities

Right Train journey near Mt Fuji

EASY STEPS FROM THE AIRPORT TO THE CITY CENTRE

Most travellers to Japan arrive at Narita Airport, located about 60km from Tokyo's city centre. There are three terminals – international flights are divided between Terminals 1 and 2. The airport is well equipped with restaurants, shops, wi-fi rental kiosks, ATMs and luggage drop-off areas.

AT THE AIRPORT

SIM CARDS Buy SIM cards at the airport, where you'll find a lot more variety than in the city. Vending machines are also available. Pocket wi-fi is a popular choice and flexible plans are available at Japan Wireless (japan-wireless.com) and NINJA WiFi (ninjawifi.com).

CURRENCY EXCHANGE Available at bank counters at the airport upon arrival, or at automatic machines. Good rates for highly traded currencies like the US dollar. Visitors from countries in Southeast Asia will find more competitive rates back home.

NATTASAK BURANASRI/SHUTTERSTOCK ©

WI-FI Connect for free anywhere within the airport using FreeWiFi-NARITA. No sign-up or personal information required.

ATMS Withdraw money at the airport with your foreign bank card using SevenBank ATMs. Also available country-wide at 7-Eleven stores.

CHARGING STATIONS Available at select locations (mostly departure halls and near terminals) and free to use. Japan uses a type A plug.

CUSTOMS DECLARATION FORMS All travellers must fill one out. Forms are available at the baggage-claim area and are to be submitted to a customs officer before leaving. If you have unaccompanied mailed baggage, fill out two copies.

DUTY-FREE Limits include three bottles (up to 2280mL) of alcohol, 200 cigarettes and 60mL of perfume.

GETTING TO THE CITY CENTRE

EXPRESS TRAINS The quickest way to get to the city (40 minutes). Choose between the Narita Express or Keisei Skyliner. Some walking or taxi to your final destination required.

AIRPORT LIMOUSINE BUSES Slower (1½ to two hours, depending on traffic), but often service major hotels in the city so there's no transfer required. Guaranteed seat and luggage space.

LOCAL TRAINS The cheapest option, these are shared with regular commuters and can get crowded – best avoided when travelling with large baggage.

HOW MUCH FOR A...

Express train
¥3000
40min

Bus
¥3500
1½–2hr

Local train
¥1200
1½–2hr

COMMUTER PASSES (SUICA, PASMO, ICOCA) The quickest way to board public transport and slightly cheaper than buying a ticket each time. Buy the pass at ticket-vending machines at any train station by putting down a ¥500 deposit that will be refunded upon return of the pass.

PRICE AND VALIDITY PERIOD
Top up any amount starting from ¥500, whenever you please. The amount is good for 10 years from last use date.

HOW TO USE
Beep it at all station turnstiles. It can also be used to pay for goods at many shops, and when riding buses and taxis.

OTHER POINTS OF ENTRY

Haneda Airport is 30km from Tokyo's city centre, mostly for domestic flights and international flights to neighbouring countries. Take the express train to Shinagawa Station (¥300 to ¥500, 15 minutes) for easy transfer.

Kansai International Airport is 50km from Osaka's city centre. Take the train to Osaka Station (¥2400, 65 minutes) or to Kyoto (¥2850, 75 minutes). Buses are also available to either city.

Chūbu Centrair International Airport is 50km from Nagoya's city centre. The Sky Limited Express goes to Meitetsu Nagoya Station (¥1230, 28 minutes). Ideal for exploring the central Honshū region.

Fukuoka Airport gives easy access to all of Kyūshū, Okinawa and the Southwest Islands. Take the subway to downtown Hakata (¥260, 10 minutes). Okinawa is a two-hour flight from here.

New Chitose Airport is Hokkaidō's main airport, 50km from the city centre of Sapporo. Get to Sapporo Station by train (¥1150, 35 minutes) or bus (¥1100, 1½ hours depending on traffic).

TRANSPORT TIPS TO HELP YOU GET AROUND

You can explore a lot of Japan using public transport alone, but a rental car will unlock some otherwise inaccessible destinations while giving you more flexibility. Travel across prefectures quickly and (relatively) cheaply by shinkansen (bullet trains) or express trains, then hop on a bus or hire a car locally to explore at your own pace.

CAR HIRE
Major car-rental companies like Nissan and Toyota have offices in most towns; all offer similar rates. Smaller companies like Niconico (niconicorentacar.jp) can offer cheaper prices with older cars, but may not be as widely available in rural areas.

AUTOMOBILE ASSOCIATIONS
The Japan Automobile Federation (english.jaf.or.jp) has helpful resources for driving in Japan, such as information on traffic rules and emergency numbers. Breakdown assistance is available to FIA or AIT members. Have a valid membership card on hand.

CAR RENTAL

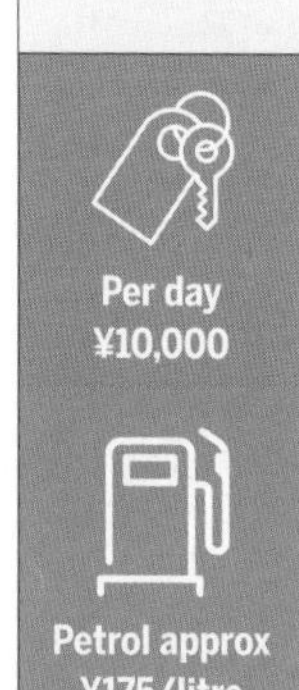

Per day ¥10,000

Petrol approx ¥175/litre

Insurance ¥1800/day

Japan is well connected by railway networks, and it is by far the cheapest and easiest way to get around. Train travel is reliable, but while trains are frequent in the city, they can be incredibly sparse in rural areas. It's therefore imperative to check train schedules well ahead of time and to arrive at the station with time to spare. If you have purchased a JR Pass, note that not all trains are covered, so plan accordingly.

JR PASS A one-week JR Pass, valid for travel across Japan and only available to those on a tourist visa, now starts at ¥50,000: buying individual tickets may work out cheaper. Alternatively, look into the cheaper regional train passes.

INSURANCE Car insurance is mandatory and can be applied for with the rental-car company when you make your booking or collect the vehicle. Plans come in a range of prices and can vary depending on the car; a basic plan is usually under ¥2000 per vehicle.

DRIVING ESSENTIALS

Drive on the left; the steering wheel is on the right.

Tolls can be quite expensive. For cashless payment, rent an ETC device and card along with the car.

Speed limit is 100km/h to 120km/h on highways, 60km/h in other areas.

All cars are equipped with easy-to-use GPS.

Always slow down and stop for pedestrians at crossings.

TRAINS Japan's trains are famously punctual, but there are some exceptions. Trains can be delayed by rough weather conditions such as strong winds and heavy snow, which can lead to extreme crowding at stations in Tokyo. Unforeseen circumstances like accidents can sometimes stop train lines entirely. While issues are usually resolved quickly, consider other options like taking a bus or taxi when these situations arise.

AIR Flying domestically can often be cheaper than taking the shinkansen. Most people fly to Hokkaidō, Kyūshū and Okinawa. You'll need more time travelling to and from airports, but it's a good option to save a bit of money.

COMMUTER PASSES Different regions have their own versions of commuter passes – Kansai primarily uses ICOCA, while Tokyo has Suica and Pasmo. If you already have one, there's no need to buy a separate regional one – they're all valid across Japan.

KNOW YOUR CARBON FOOTPRINT

A domestic flight from Tokyo to Fukuoka emits about 350kg of carbon dioxide per passenger. A train emits about 66kg, while a bus emits 120 tonnes for the same distance.

There are a number of carbon calculators online. We use Resurgence (resurgence.org/resources/carbon-calculator.html).

SAFE TRAVEL

Low crime rates make Japan one of the safest countries in the world, but it's no excuse to let your guard down. Natural disasters are frequent, and it helps to stay vigilant and aware of emergency protocols.

TYPHOONS Typhoon season is July to October. Okinawa and the southern islands are more prone to them, while the main islands experience about three to four each year. A typical typhoon doesn't pose much risk, but severe cases can cause train lines in the city to delay or shut down, and lead to landslides and floods, prompting evacuation. Check the Japan Meteorological Agency (jma.go.jp) for warnings.

EARTHQUAKES & TSUNAMI Earthquakes are frequent, and visitors to coastal areas should be aware of tsunami warnings. If a high-magnitude earthquake or tsunami is expected, an advance warning will be automatically sent to mobile phones in the area. If a strong earthquake occurs, stay indoors and shelter under furniture unless instructed to evacuate.

VOLCANOES Many popular hiking destinations in the country are in fact active volcanoes – even Mt Fuji. Always be cautious when approaching one, and never venture into prohibited areas. Check the Japan Meteorological Agency for warnings before you go.

Bears are common in Japan's wilderness, particularly in Hokkaidō. Stay alert when trekking at national parks, and watch out for bear warning signs. Carry bear repellent spray and travel in groups.

IMAGINGL/SHUTTERSTOCK ©

SMARTPHONE APP Get updated information on weather forecasts, disaster warnings and other helpful information on the app Safety Tips. It also includes a handy search for medical institutions in case of emergency.

STREET TOUTS
Do not follow a tout into any bars or *izakaya*, particularly in large entertainment districts like Shinjuku, in Tokyo. These establishments tend to tack on shady charges to your final bill, and some may target tourists specifically.

INSURANCE
Clinics and hospitals don't take foreign health insurance, so you'll have to pay upfront. All pharmacies sell a wide variety of over-the-counter medicine for common ailments, though dosage is lower compared to what's found in other countries.

QUICK TIPS TO HELP YOU MANAGE YOUR MONEY

CREDIT CARDS Accepted in many shops in cities, but this isn't the case across the board. Many ramen shops, bars and small businesses are cash-only. Visa payWave is available, but not commonly used. Visa and MasterCard are the most widely accepted; Diners Club and American Express cards less so. Many cashier counters in the city will have a sign showing the kinds of cards and payment options accepted.

CASH
Carry cash everywhere you go in Japan. Also have a coin pouch handy, because you'll inevitably end up with too many coins.

CASHLESS OPTION
Travellers can use their commuter-pass balance to pay for goods. All convenience stores and many chain restaurants accept them.

CURRENCY

Yen (¥)

HOW MUCH FOR A

Coffee ¥450

***Onigiri* (rice-ball snack) ¥120**

Dinner for two ¥4000

PAYING AT THE TILL

When paying, always set your credit card or cash on a tray placed in front of you. The cashier will also usually put your change back on the tray. When dining at a restaurant, a cash register at the front of the restaurant means you pay there after your meal.

TAX The consumption tax is 8% on takeaway food and drink, and 10% for dining in and everything else. Tourists get a tax exemption on certain products exceeding ¥5000 in a single receipt.

ATMS
Local Japanese bank ATMs don't accept foreign cards. Instead, look for SevenBank ATMs, found at almost every 7-Eleven and available 24/7. ATMs are unavailable from 9pm to midnight on Sundays and public holidays.

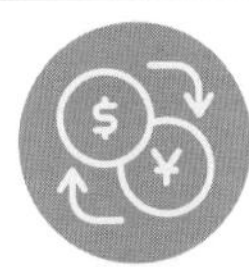

CURRENCY EXCHANGE
The best way to exchange currency is at your home country or at the airport. Hotels, bank branches and department stores will exchange currency too, albeit at less favourable rates.

TIPPING Not required in Japan. Even if you insist, locals might refuse.

RESTAURANTS Pay only the amount printed on your bill. Fancier restaurants will tack on a 10% service charge or a table charge. *Izakaya* (Japanese pub-eateries) may serve an obligatory appetiser and charge around ¥500.

Taxis Taxi drivers will always give your change back.

Guides Local guides don't expect tips, but may occasionally accept. When tipping, never hand money directly to them – instead, put the money in an envelope.

RESPONSIBLE TRAVEL

Tips to leave a lighter footprint, support local and have a positive impact on local communities.

ON THE ROAD

Calculate your carbon footprint Try an online carbon calculator (resurgence.org/resources/carbon-calculator.html).

Choose an EV EVs are slightly cheaper to rent than a standard vehicle. Online booking available in English (nissan-rentacar.jp).

Rest stops are spaced along the highway and will have toilets and bins to throw out your rubbish.

Reusable bags and cutlery Decline bags and cutlery by saying *'Sono mama de daijoubu desu'* (It's fine as it is).

Public bins These are scarce, so leave some room in your bag to stash your rubbish until you find somewhere to dispose of it.

Carry a water bottle Tap water in Japan is safe to drink, but many Muji stores (muji.com) around the country have free filtered water refill stations.

Public transport systems These are well established across the country, and discount passes make them easier on your wallet too.

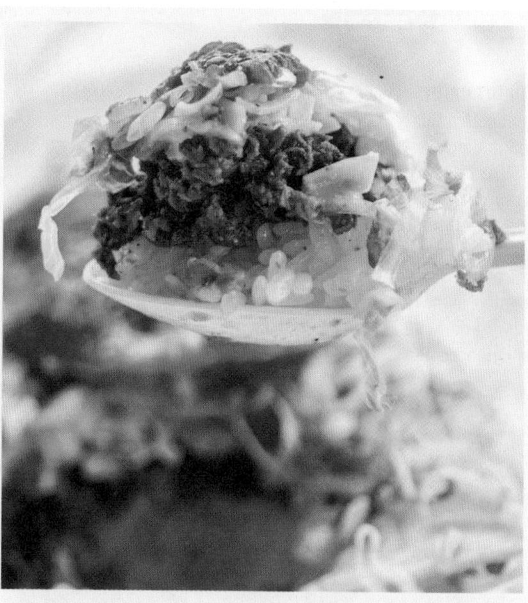

OKIMO/SHUTTERSTOCK©

GIVE BACK

Try some taco rice and help kids in need Taco Rice Lovers (tacorice-lovers.okinawa) partners with local restaurants to feed children who go without a meal. When you eat taco rice (pictured) at a participating restaurant in Okinawa, purchase a Mirai Ticket along with your meal. A child can then use the ticket to get a free taco rice meal.

Help clean up Tokyo's rivers Join group volunteer efforts and make some friends along the way. Tokyo River Friends (tokyoriverfriends.org) hosts multiple clean-up events each month.

Support wildlife Make a donation to wildlife conservation and animal welfare in Japan by donating to the Japan Wildlife Conservation Society (jwcs.org) or Animal Refuge Kansai (arkbark.net).

DOS & DON'TS

Do take your shoes off when entering some temple halls.

Don't take anyone's photograph without asking permission and always respect locals' privacy. This not only applies to geisha, *maiko,* priests and shrine maidens, but also everywhere in public.

Do keep voices low when on public transport.

LEAVE A SMALL FOOTPRINT

Low impact transport See more of the city and discover lesser travelled areas on a bike. Docomo Cycle (docomo-cycle.jp) bikes are red and can be found in major cities across the country. Download the app to locate and rent bikes.

Go rural The most beautiful parts of Japan are often rural – experience ecofriendly farmstays, see the sights, then meet some locals and support small businesses too.

Try WWOOFing Make lasting connections while getting your hands dirty with the locals. You'll also be directly supporting local agriculture via WWOOF (wwoofjapan.com).

Eco-friendly cutlery Pick up a pair of *bentō* chopsticks or cutlery (usually in cute designs and a small case) as a fun away to avoid using disposables.

PIXHOUND/SHUTTERSTOCK ©

SUPPORT LOCAL

Stop for tea or buy snacks from small businesses to support local economies.

Sustainable fashion When choosing a souvenir, consider buying old kimonos from secondhand shops. In Tokyo, they can be found in neighbourhoods like Nakano and Kōenji.

Local crafts Make unique gifts to take home and also support local artists when you buy directly from their shops or sign up for a workshop.

CLIMATE CHANGE & TRAVEL

It's impossible to ignore the impact we have when travelling, and the importance of making changes where we can. Lonely Planet urges all travellers to engage with their travel carbon footprint. There are many carbon calculators online that allow travellers to estimate the carbon emissions generated by their journey; try resurgence.org/resources/carbon-calculator.html. Many airlines and booking sites offer travellers the option of offsetting the impact of greenhouse gas emissions by contributing to climate-friendly initiatives around the world.

RESOURCES

wwoofjapan.com
zenbird.media
japanfs.org
ecotourism.gr.jp

UNIQUE & LOCAL WAYS TO STAY

Hotels and ryokan aren't just places to stay – they're where Japan's spirit of hospitality,* omotenashi*, comes to life. A night at a ryokan and soak in an onsen after dinner is an experience every traveller must have at least once. Get to know the locals when you book a farmstay; for a taste of the unique and futuristic, try bunking at a capsule hotel.

HOW MUCH FOR A

Capsule hotel ¥4000/night

Ryokan from ¥10,000/night

Farmstay from ¥8000/night

MR. JAMES KELLEY/SHUTTERSTOCK ©

FARMSTAYS This is the way to go if you're looking for a place to rest as well as to experience the local way of life. There are farmstays sprinkled across the country – by the coast, at the foot of mountains, near hot springs and even at tea farms. You'll be staying with a local family in their home and dining with them too, so it's the opportunity to make lasting connections. Not all hosts are fluent in English, but if they're used to hosting tourists, they might be.

From ¥8000 to ¥10,000 per night/per adult.

CAPSULE HOTELS
Hallways lined with pods designed to house a bed, a single person and very little else – the capsule hotel certainly isn't for the claustrophobic. The upside is that you'll get plenty of privacy, and they're often in central city locations. Amenities are provided, and facilities are good, clean and well maintained.

Around ¥4000 per night/per adult.

GLAMPING The 'glamorous camping' trend has become quite popular in Japan in recent years. Guests can book high-end tents with hotel-like facilities; campgrounds sometimes have a bathhouse too. While it's not cheap, stepping out of your cosy bed and being greeted by fresh mountain air and expansive views is well worth the price.

From ¥25,000 per night/per adult.

LIGHTRECORDS/SHUTTERSTOCK ©

RYOKAN

On a trip anywhere in the country, a stay at a ryokan (traditional Japanese inn) is something many locals look forward to. They're easy to find, but are especially ubiquitous in hot-spring towns. These days, ryokan come in different forms: some are decades- or even centuries-old traditional establishments, while others are modern hotel-like buildings that retain the atmosphere and service of lodging at a traditional inn.

From ¥10,000 per night/per adult.

THE RYOKAN EXPERIENCE

Kaiseki dinner The fee usually includes breakfast and a *kaiseki* (multi-course) dinner, served either in a dining hall with other guests or in the privacy of your own room. Every ryokan has its speciality, usually featuring a premium local ingredient.

Yukata These cotton kimono-like robes can be found in your room. They are for guests to wear when lounging around, and many wear them to dinner in the hall. Don't be afraid to ask for help putting it on; put the left side of the robe over the right – you should be able to insert your right hand between the folds.

Onsen The main bathing facility at a ryokan may be shared between all guests, so you may have to get naked with strangers – no swimsuits allowed. Always wash yourself before going in. If you have large tattoos or want more privacy, some ryokan offer rooms with private baths.

BOOKING

The best way to find and book accommodation is online and through travel organisations or websites. Be aware that some accommodation options, especially in rural areas, may not have foreign-language support.

Book in advance for the following seasons: Lunar New Year (late January to early February), cherry-blossom season (late March to early April), Golden Week holidays (late April to early May), Obon (mid-August), autumn foliage season (late October through November), and in winter (from December) for places like Shirakawa-gō and Hokkaidō.

Japan Ryokan and Hotel Association (ryokan.or.jp) Search hotels and ryokan across the country and compare prices between major booking companies.

Relux (rlx.jp) Find and book luxury hotels and ryokan.

Stay Japan (stayjapan.com) Book farm- and homestays across Japan.

JapaniCan (japanican.com) Easy booking for hotels, ryokan and guesthouses.

Japanese Guest Houses (japaneseguesthouses.com) Book farmstays and ryokan.

PRICING

Because your package typically includes up to two meals, ryokan and farmstay prices are always listed as per person. At an onsen ryokan, a small bathing tax will also be added to your bill (typically ¥150 per person).

ESSENTIAL NUTS-&-BOLTS

TATTOOS

Public baths and spas often don't allow entry if you have large tattoos. If yours is small enough, some places give you a plaster to cover it up.

SMOKING

Many bars and clubs allow smoking. Some restaurants have smoking rooms. In public, only smoke at designated areas and not on the street.

TAXIS

There's no need to open or close taxi doors. Stand clear while the driver operates them.

GOOD TO KNOW

Citizens from 65 countries are automatically issued a tourist visa upon arrival, valid for 15 to 90 days.

Tourist-visa holders enjoy duty-free shopping at some retailers for purchase amounts exceeding ¥5000.

The legal drinking age in Japan is 20.

Never stand side by side on an escalator. Keep to one side; follow the lead of the person in front of you.

Public rubbish bins are rare. Carry your rubbish with you until you find one, and always sort rubbish and recyclables.

ACCESSIBLE TRAVEL

Accessible Japan (accessible-japan.com) is a great resource to help prepare for your trip.

Elevators are found at most city stations. Station staff will help you get on and off the train with a temporary slope.

Some train cars have wider areas meant for wheelchairs. Symbols for these cars are clearly marked on the platform.

Multipurpose toilets are common and can be found at stations, tourist destinations, shopping malls and public spaces.

Bmaps is an app that can help you find accessible dining options, locate bathrooms, and gauge the accessibility of an area before you go.

WATER
Tap water in Japan is completely safe to drink, though bottled water is inexpensive (¥100).

STATION EXITS
Look up the ones closest to your destination. Taking the wrong exit may lead to unwanted detours.

BATHHOUSE RULES
No clothes (including swimwear) are allowed in most onsen. Children up to age seven can accompany either parent, regardless of gender.

TOILETS
In the city are Western-style and have bidet features. Squat toilets are rare, and are indicated by a symbol placed outside the cubicle. In rural areas, squat toilets are more common. Some women's toilets have speakers that play a flushing sound; this is to mask other less favourable noises.

FAMILY TRAVEL

Dining Family restaurants like Royal Host, Denny's and Saizeriya have kids menus and baby chairs.

Toilets and changing areas Most department stores and stations have multipurpose toilets, with a baby seat and nappy (diaper) changing area.

Transport Children 12 and under pay half price for train rides. Up to two children under six years can ride trains for free.

Attractions Children under 12 get ticket discounts, and young children sometimes get in for free.

TIPS TO SAVE MONEY

- Snag discounted food at supermarkets in the evening.
- Visit karaoke boxes on a weekday afternoon.
- Ditch expensive onsen and go to a public bathhouse *(sento)* instead.
- Walk from one train station to the next; in Tokyo, this only takes 15 to 20 minutes.

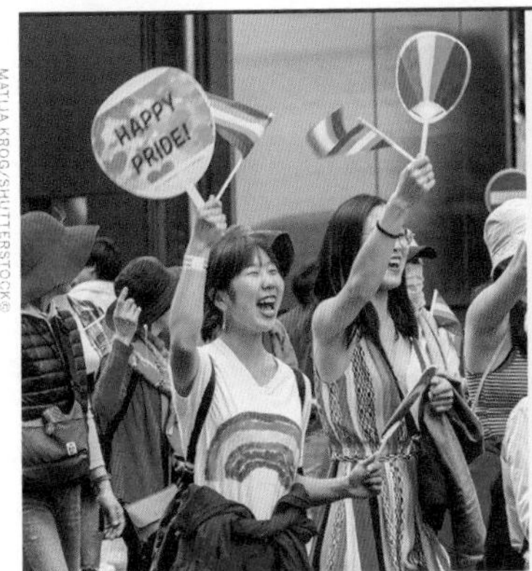

MATIJA KROG/SHUTTERSTOCK©

LGBTIQ+ TRAVELLERS

Discrimination is rare, but society remains conservative when it comes to public displays of affection, regardless of sexual orientation.

Shinjuku Ni-chōme in Tokyo is the largest LGBTIQ+ neighbourhood, with lively bars, clubs and entertainment. Engaging in public displays of affection here is generally fine.

Dōyama-chō in Osaka is another nightlife area similar to Shinjuku Ni-chōme.

Tokyo Rainbow Pride (tokyorainbowpride.com) is the country's largest LGBTIQ+ event and takes place in spring.

Stonewall Japan (stonewalljapan.org) is a good online resource.

LANGUAGE

Japanese pronunciation is easy for English speakers, as most of its sounds are also found in English. Note though that it's important to make the distinction between short and long vowels, as vowel length can change the meaning of a word. The long vowels (**ā**, **ē**, **ī**, **ō**, **ū**) should be held twice as long as the short ones. All syllables in a word are pronounced fairly evenly in Japanese. If you read our pronunciation guides as if they were English, you'll be understood.

To enhance your trip with a phrasebook, visit **shop.lonelyplanet.com**.

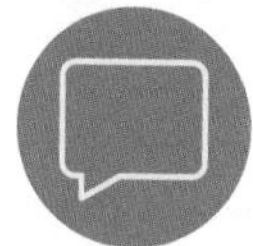

BASICS

Hello.	こんにちは。	*kon·ni·chi·wa*
Goodbye.	さようなら。	*sa·yō·na·ra*
Yes.	はい。	*hai*
No.	いいえ。	*ī·e*
Please.	ください。	*ku·da·sai*
Thank you.	ありがとう。	*a·ri·ga·tō*
Excuse me.	すみません。	*su·mi·ma·sen*
Sorry.	ごめんなさい。	*go·men·na·sai*

What's your name?
お名前は 何ですか? — *o·na·ma·e wa nan desu ka*

My name is ...
私の 名前は…です。 — *wa·ta·shi no na·ma·e wa ... desu*

Do you speak English?
英語が 話せますか? — *ē·go ga ha·na·se·masu ka*

I don't understand.
わかりません。 — *wa·ka·ri·ma·sen*

TIME & NUMBERS

What time is it?	何時ですか?	*nan·ji desu ka*
It's (10) o'clock.	(10)時です。	*(jū)·ji desu*
Half past (10).	(10)時半です。	*(jū)·ji han desu*

morning	朝	*a·sa*
afternoon	午後	*go·go*
evening	夕方	*yū·ga·ta*
yesterday	きのう	*ki·nō*
today	今日	*kyō*
tomorrow	明日	*a·shi·ta*

1	一	*i·chi*	**6**	六	*ro·ku*
2	二	*ni*	**7**	七	*shi·chi/na·na*
3	三	*san*	**8**	八	*ha·chi*
4	四	*shi/yon*	**9**	九	*ku/kyū*
5	五	*go*	**10**	十	*jū*

EMERGENCIES

Help!	たすけて!	*tasu·ke·te*
Go away!	離れろ!	*ha·na·re·ro*
Call the police!	警察を呼んで!	*kē·sa·tsu o yon·de*
Call a doctor!	医者を呼んで!	*i·sha o yon·de*
I'm lost.	迷いました。	*ma·yoi·mashi·ta*

Index

000 Map pages

000 Map pages

U

V

W

Y

Z

000 Map pages

'My favourite experience is taking the time to visit Ibusuki Onsen (pictured left; p181). I love onsen baths in general but there's something intense and magical about the hot sand experience. I come out feeling refreshed, calm, and happy every time.'

RAY BARTLETT

'My favourite experience is spectating the RISE World Series kickboxing tournament in Ota-ku, Tokyo. Sporting matches in Japan have such a vibrant and inclusive atmosphere.'

SAMANTHA LOW

'Catching my breath at the summit of Misen (pictured right; p159), Miyajima's tallest peak, then taking in the panoramic vista of islands in the Inland Sea.'

SIMON RICHMOND

'My favourite experience is riding the ferry from Naha out to Zamami-jima in Kerama Shotō National Park, Okinawa for some quality snorkelling, beach time and Orion beer (p220).'

CRAIG MCLACHLAN

THIS BOOK

Destination editor
James Smart

Production editor
Kathryn Rowan

Cartographer
Mark Griffiths

Book designer
Dermot Hegarty

Assisting editors
Peter Cruttenden, Gabby Innes, Charlotte Orr

Cover researcher
Katherine Marsh

Thanks
Sofie Anderson, Katie Connolly, Karen Henderson, Jenna Myers